BURPEE EXPERT
GARDENER SERIES

Peter Schneider
on Roses

MACMILLAN • USA

Photographer • Paul E. Jerabek

Editorial Consultant • Beverly R. Dobson

To Susan, with love

MACMILLAN
A Prentice Hall Macmillan Company
15 Columbus Circle
New York, NY 10023

All photos by Paul Jerabek except as follows:
Dr. Charles Beutel, pages 7, 53, 59, 90, 96, 97 (lower
right), 101, 157, 163, and 164 (top); Stuart C. Dobson,
pages 49, 71, 92, 95, 108, 113, 119, 120, 122, 124, 125,
131, 133, and 148; Andy Shkolnik, page 60; and
Kim Rupert, page 132.

MACMILLAN is a registered trademark
of Macmillan, Inc.

Burpee is a registered trademark
of W. Atlee Burpee Company.

Library of Congress
Cataloging-in-Publication Data
Schneider, Peter, 1959 Sept. 21
Peter Schneider on roses / photographer, Paul E. Jerabek.
    p. cm.—(Burpee expert gardener series)
Includes bibliographical references and index.
ISBN 0-02-860038-X

    1. Roses. 2. Rose culture. 3. Roses—United States. 4. Rose
culture—United States.   I. Title.   II. Title: Roses.   III. Series:
Burpee expert gardener.
SB411.S36   1995   94-37125
635.9'33372—dc20   CIP

Manufactured in the United States of America

First Edition

10 9 8 7 6 5 4 3 2 1

Cover: *One of the original* Canterbury Tales *roses, 'The
Yeoman' is a blend of warm pink and yellow not found in any of
the later Austin introductions. (Photo by Paul Jerabek.)*

Page i: *A short plant bearing large blooms, 'Tournament of
Roses' is an example of the different kinds of roses that have been
called grandifloras.*

Page iv: *The free-blooming 'Anisley Dickson' has set new
standards for floribunda excellence.*

ACKNOWLEDGMENTS

This book could not have been written without the encouragement and support of Bev Dobson, my mentor in the quest for rose knowlege.

Paul E. Jerabek made several treks to photograph roses in my garden, as well as providing shots of his own roses. If a picture is worth a thousand words, this book is more Paul's than mine. I'm also very grateful to Chuck Beutel, Stu Dobson, Kim Rupert, and Andy Shkolnik for additional photographs.

Thanks to my father, Gustav Schneider, for all of his help and to Thomas Jones of Napa, California, for his many useful suggestions.

At Macmillan, Rebecca Atwater, Rachel Simon, Barbara Berger, Kristin Juba, Jennie McGregor Bernard, and Cathy Felgar have been a pleasure to work with.

And, of course, my deepest thanks to Susan, my wife and partner in rose growing, for all her patience.

CONTENTS

INTRODUCTION

Why do I like roses? Roses change. A rose plant can take a long time to make a bloom, and every day along the way reveals something new: a breaking shoot, the first hint of a bud, flower color finally showing through, and eventually a bloom that may take an hour—or a week—to unfurl. Multiply this process by *x* number of rose plants, and the rose garden is revealed as a stage with a new set every day.

Roses change. Our grandparents grew plants that might prove unwieldy by today's standards, with flowers we might find fragrant but disappointingly short lived, and not find at all after early summer. Our parents were surprisingly indulgent to spindly hybrid teas that made good cut flowers. Today we can expect long-lasting cut flowers from plants that are good for bedding too. There is no longer any good reason to grow geraniums in the front yard while hiding the roses out back.

Roses change and remain the same. Propagated asexually by cuttings or bud grafts, each rose is an identical clone of one original specimen. If you grow 'Peace', you have the same rose Francis Meilland developed before World War II. If you grow 'Apothecary's Rose', you have

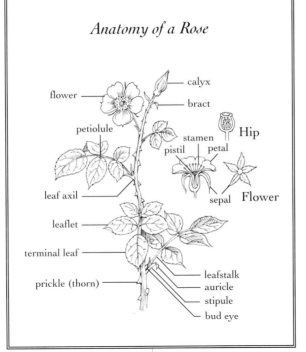

Anatomy of a Rose

flower
calyx
bract
petiolule
stamen
Hip
pistil
petal
leaf axil
sepal
Flower
leaflet
terminal leaf
leafstalk
auricle
prickle (thorn)
stipule
bud eye

a plant that the Romans grew. Grow the roses we know as 'Old Blush' or 'Slater's Crimson China', and you have a living piece of long-lost history, a rose hybrid developed centuries ago in China by an unknown genius.

Today, new roses are bred by rose men and women who plant thousands of seedlings from scores of crosses in hopes of finding a few improved varieties. This is hard and uncertain work, and there is still a generous element of luck involved in one's success. Eventually, serendipity will give way to science, and genetic engineers will provide us with petunia- and delphinium-blue roses, and begonia-rose crosses for the shade and roses mated with fireflies for evening garden enjoyment. However, rose lovers will still be able to grow any rose that has ever been grown before—as long as someone has preserved it. Roses change but remain the same. They have been mankind's favorite flower for thousands of years.

Over the past fifteen years, I have grown over fourteen hundred different rose varieties. In this book, I describe the ones I have enjoyed the most. Some of them have names you will recognize; others might be new. I hope that you will try some of them, and enjoy them too.

Hardy and tough, 'Félicité Parmentier' produces a mass of bloom each spring.

Hybrid Teas

On a rose timeline, stretching from the mists of prehistory to the present day, the hybrid teas are no more than a blip. But they are our blip, the twentieth century's favorite roses, the kind of rose that is grown more than all others combined.

The hybrid tea's high-centered, spiral form has become such an ideal that roses in other categories are praised when they attain it, and often condemned when they don't. Miniature roses, for example, have built much of their present popularity on an ability to mimic the classic shape of a hybrid tea. But no other rose can make the statement the hybrid tea makes in our society: a bouquet of miniature roses, however perfectly formed, simply does not convey the same sentiment as a bouquet of long-stemmed, large-flowered hybrid teas.

And it was the florists who kept the class going, at a time early in this century when hybrid teas could not match the landscape performance of either the old garden roses they followed or the floriferous hybrid polyanthas that threatened to supplant them. A cut rose can be beautiful, even when the bush it comes from is not, and as breeders concentrated on creating new hybrid teas with elegant blooms, the plants that supported them suffered. Compare the lanky, sparse habit of almost any hybrid tea introduced before 'Peace' with the robust, lush growth of today's best varieties and it's easy to wonder if they belong in the same class.

A generation after 'Peace', hybrid teas received a new infusion of vigor through 'Silver Jubilee', a landmark variety bred with a species rose in its ancestry. 'Silver Jubilee' helped produce the healthiest hybrid teas ever, with excellent habits, but has also passed down a tendency for smaller blooms and softer petals. Today, a healthy, large-flowered, high-centered hybrid tea is the most difficult kind of rose to breed, and the number of worthwhile introductions has diminished. However, the market for them has not because, when gardeners think of a rose, they are still most likely to think first of a hybrid tea. This is, after all, the hybrid tea's century.

A hybrid tea rose should grow and bloom well in its first season and reach peak production in its second year. With good culture, a hybrid tea can be expected to remain productive for fifteen to twenty years. All hybrid teas are remontant, meaning that they offer repeat bloom. The speed with which repeat bloom is offered varies with the variety, with many-petaled varieties taking longer to rebloom than those with fewer petals. The typical hybrid tea will recycle its bloom in seven to eight weeks, taking less time in hot weather and more time in cool.

'CRIMSON GLORY'
Kordes, Germany, 1935

This was the greatest red hybrid tea of its time. 'Crimson Glory' remains widely available, and it is still a thrill to get a perfect specimen on a rare, strong stem; most 'Crimson Glory' stems are weak.

Excellent for both bedding and cutting, 'Olympiad' is the best red hybrid tea.

'Crimson Glory' is a dark crimson red, classically formed, with as luxurious a damask fragrance as you will find in a modern rose.

'Crimson Glory' was the first breakthrough rose for the great German rose breeder Wilhelm Kordes. In hybridizing, Kordes noted that fragrance is what he called a "go and come" characteristic. Even seedlings resulting from a cross of two very fragrant parents are often virtually scentless. The fragrance, however, might show up again in the next generation. This was often the case with the many offspring of 'Crimson Glory'.

The ultimate downfall of 'Crimson Glory' was its susceptibility to powdery mildew, a weakness it shares with many other fragrant roses. Indeed, fragrance and a disposition to mildew are intimately connected in the genetic structure of roses. As hybridizers have improved disease resistance, scent has often suffered. Unlike most hybrid teas, 'Crimson Glory' can appear to grow more sideways than upright, a habit that can be corrected easily by pruning to an inside-, rather than outside-, pointing eye.

'DAINTY BESS'
Archer, England, 1925

In the first part of this century, before there was a classification for shrub roses, a lot of single-petaled roses were introduced as hybrid teas. Many of these came from Ireland, with names such as 'Irish Brightness', 'Irish Elegance' and the somewhat less lyrical 'Irish Engineer'. A lovely lemon yellow single-petaled climbing hybrid tea was raised by the noted Beverly Hills yachtsman and rosarian Captain George C. Thomas, Jr., and named 'Captain Thomas' in his memory.

But the most beautiful and enduring single-petaled hybrid tea is 'Dainty Bess', with its

A great red hybrid tea of yesteryear, 'Crimson Glory' boasts a rich damask fragrance.

The vigorous 'Dainty Bess' is the most enduring of the single-petaled hybrid teas.

'Doris Tysterman' brings a cheerful informality into the hybrid teas.

striking purple stamens presiding over wavy, dusky pink petals. Best of all, 'Dainty Bess' is a vigorous plant that grows and blooms well in all climates all season long. If it has a fault, it is that its foliage, while healthy, can appear sparse.

Occasionally, a hybrid tea with very few petals is still introduced. 'Snow Cream', an eleven-petaled hybrid tea from the North Carolina nurseryman Dennis Bridges, appeared as recently as 1986. While 'Snow Cream' is no rival for 'Dainty Bess', it is an example of the lingering appeal of light-petaled hybrid teas.

'DORIS TYSTERMAN'
Wisbech, England, 1975

A fun rose for cutting and garden display, everything about 'Doris Tysterman' is informal. Her loosely shaped buds begin as a bright tangerine orange overlaid with bronze. As the bloom opens and starts to resemble a peony, the bronze glazing becomes more pronounced. The full-blown flower is often a rich, coppery bronze. If you have a bed of the old-style hybrid teas, the ones that look more or less like "blooms on a stick," nothing could do more to fill it out and cheer it up than a few plants of 'Doris Tysterman'.

'DOUBLE DELIGHT'
Swim & Ellis, USA, 1977

Composed of cream blending to red in degrees that correspond to the amount of sunlight it receives, this rose is a glorious sight in the heat of summer. This is a great rose, but in some ways an old kind of hybrid tea. Its strong points are all in the wonderfully fragrant flower instead of in the bush, which has matte green, mildew-prone foliage and

Nothing is more disappointing than a rose without fragrance, and on that count the colorful 'Double Delight' is a hybrid tea that never disappoints.

an uneven habit. Most roses look very good planted in groups of three, but plant three 'Double Delight's and you will very likely get three plants of different heights.

'Double Delight' is a rose that photographs very well, and one dubious midwestern nursery uses a picture of 'Double Delight' to sell 'Shades of Autumn', a hybrid tea that might have been hot stuff upon its introduction in 1943, but is quite passé today.

Every summer I get telephone calls from gardeners who describe black leaves—not the fungus disease blackspot—on their bushes of 'Double Delight'. When I ask if they have been spraying a fungicide containing Daconil, they invariably answer yes. 'Double Delight' and its near relatives (such as 'Granada' and 'Mon Cheri') all exhibit a phytotoxic reaction to this chemical which, although not fatal to the plants, is quite distracting in the garden.

'DUBLIN'
Astor Perry, USA, 1983

In the 1960s, Astor Perry, a peanut specialist with North Carolina State University, read in a book written by an expert rosarian that an amateur could not produce a quality rose seedling. And so he tried. 'Dublin' is just one example of his success, which extends to more than a dozen varieties. All of Perry's creations are hybrid teas bred with the rose exhibitor in mind. As such, they can be counted on for outstanding blooms, but may have

Bred especially for rose exhibitors, the hybrid tea 'Dublin' marked success for an amateur rose breeder.

Vigorous and free-blooming, 'Elina' is the best yellow hybrid tea.

various minor faults that would have prevented their introduction by a major nursery. The dusky red-pink 'Dublin', for example, has leaflets that would usually be considered too tiny in proportion to the flower and stem. For keen rose exhibitors, though, taking small leaves in exchange for perfect blooms is a bargain.

When officials in Ireland wanted a rose to commemorate the 1,000th anniversary of the city of Dublin, they were chagrined to find the name already taken by an American Dublin. Astor Perry named almost all of his roses for towns associated with the peanut industry. This one is for Dublin, Georgia. (Another A. Perry was active in breeding hybrid teas at the same time. Anthony Perry of California, creator of 'Gold Glow', 'Pure Love' and the award-winning 'Broadway', did not name any of his roses after peanut towns.)

'ELINA' (DICJANA, 'PEAUDOUCE')
Dickson, N. Ireland, 1984

The best yellow garden hybrid tea there is, 'Elina' covers itself with a primrose yellow bloom all summer long, out-blooming many floribundas and yet producing huge true hybrid tea blooms. These always arrive one-to-a-stem, with no need for pinching out sidebuds. If you've ever been

Code Names for Roses

You will see code names attached to many of the modern roses described in this book. Rose breeders assign each of their introductions a code name by which their rose is always identified regardless of how many commercial names it accumulates as it travels around the world. This code name is composed of a three-letter designation based on the breeder's name followed by any pronounceable series of two or more letters. The code name for 'Elina' is DICjana, *DIC* standing for the breeder, Patrick Dickson of Northern Ireland. Dickson uses the alphabetical system in assigning his code names, so all of the other roses he raised in the same year as 'Elina' share a *DICj__* designation. All of the roses he raised the next year are code named *DICk__*.

Occasionally, the three-letter code designation represents a nursery (such as *JAC* for Jackson & Perkins) that employs several rose breeders. For this reason, the code designation may not always be similar to the rose hybridizer's name. Some nurseries have fun with their code names. Bees, for example, gave their light pink hybrid tea 'Cleo', named for Cleo Laine, the code name BEEbop. Sanday's pink blend hybrid tea 'Esperanto Jubileo' is code named SANrozo, *rozo* being, of course, Esperanto for rose. (However, this rose has gone the way of the language it commemorates, and almost no one grows it anymore.)

disappointed with the garden performance of yellow hybrid teas, 'Elina' may be a godsend.

'Elina' is beautiful at every stage of bloom—bud, bloom and fully open flower—and can be faulted only for blooms that pick up spots when they are left out in the rain. If you cut buds of 'Elina' before it rains, they will develop very nicely indoors. When cutting buds of any rose variety,

Despite being a very good rose, the hybrid tea 'Evensong' is faced with commercial extinction.

it is essential that the sepals be down, with color showing, for the bloom to open properly. Even if frost is approaching, it is no use to cut rose buds if the sepals are not yet down.

Originally named 'Peaudouce' in the United Kingdom, after a popular brand of disposable diapers, this rose has now gained worldwide acceptance under its American synonym of 'Elina'. Roses often change names as they change countries. In fact, it is rare for a really good modern rose to have only one name. German names are often very difficult for people in English-speaking countries to pronounce and are usually the first to be changed. The rise in commercial sponsorship of rose names is another factor; often the company or

product for which the rose is named is completely unknown in other countries. 'Peaudouce' is a good example of that.

'EVENSONG'
Arnot, Scotland, 1963

Except for 'Evensong', all of the roses in this book are commercially available in the United States, either at your neighborhood garden center or by mail from a specialist rose nursery. I include it as a favorite rose and an example of one of the many roses that must disappear each year so that a new one can take its place in the catalogues. The problem is, while the new ones are new, they are not necessarily any better.

'Evensong' is a strong grower, with good disease resistance and exceptional repeat bloom capability. Its large blooms attain classic hybrid tea form, but because they don't hold their perfect shape, this variety has never been popular with rose exhibitors. Pink blended with salmon, it is not a particularly novel color. Exhibitors will preserve any rose that might win them a trophy, and varieties with unusual colors are also relatively secure. But the ordinary pink 'Evensong' is on the road to extinction.

'FLAMING BEAUTY'
Winchel, USA, 1978

A stunning combination of butter yellow and bright red, this rose produces perfectly shaped blooms on a bush that appreciates coddling. Grown in a pot, my 'Flaming Beauty' is liberally top-dressed with compost and fish meal and stored in an unheated garage over winter.

'Flaming Beauty' was the first commercial success for hybridizer Joe Winchel, whose hybrid teas can be counted on for classic form. His later introductions, such as 'Lynn Anderson' and 'The

'Flaming Beauty' produces remarkably colorful hybrid tea blooms on a plant that appreciates tender loving care.

Temptations', come with improved vigor. I can recommend them highly to southern rosarians. Unfortunately, they are not all winter hardy in the North (Zone 6 and northward).

'FOLKLORE' (KORlore)
Kordes, Germany, 1977

This perfectly formed rose is a favorite of rose exhibitors in the northern United States. Soft orange with a creamy yellow reverse, 'Folklore' blooms late in the spring and takes a long time to cycle into a repeat bloom. One recent book about roses warns that its long, long stems violate the rose show rules of balance and proportion. But because rose show judges do not make house calls, exhibitors can, of course, cut stems as short as they wish to take to the show. Exhibitors, who often have to struggle to get long cutting stems on their favorite varieties, are only too happy to be faced with this problem. A more practical concern is that 'Folklore' produces stems that are crooked, especially in the fall.

'Folklore' grows to eight thorny feet and makes an excellent barrier hedge. It has produced numerous mutations, of which the apricot 'Revival', discovered in Italy, is the most widely distributed.

'GARDEN PARTY'
Swim, USA, 1959

One of the hundreds of children of 'Peace' introduced in the 1950s and 1960s, 'Garden Party' remains a stalwart favorite. Its blooms are ivory shading to palest yellow and tinged with lilac pink. After thirty-five years, this variety is still a strong grower, but may be troubled by powdery mildew.

The elegantly formed hybrid tea 'Folklore' supplies stems as long as you want them.

'Garden Party' remains a favorite hybrid tea more than thirty-five years after its introduction.

'Garden Party' received a gold medal at the rose trials in Bagatelle, France, in 1959 and was an All-America Rose Selection (AARS) for 1960.

'GARDENS OF THE WORLD' (JACCOEUR)
Christensen, USA, 1992

This red and white blend rose is so colorful and often so well formed that one can forgive its rather stumpy-looking plant. 'Gardens of the World', named for the PBS television series hosted by Audrey Hepburn, was denied official registration by the American Rose Society, which prohibits any rose name consisting of more than three words. These rules are not always consistently enforced, and the fact that a new rose called 'Yeller Rose O'Texas' was recently approved makes one wonder if Jackson & Perkins, or PBS, should have tried for 'Gardens o'the World'. In the end, registration under the code name of JACcoeur was granted. (Lack of registration means that a rose cannot be entered in a rose show conducted

Rose Trials

The AARS awards are not true rose trials because winners are decided, in part, on the basis of anticipated commercial sales appeal. The rose receiving the highest score from a panel of independent judges does not necessarily go on to win an award. The final decision is made by a cartel of nurserymen, and there is a sense of "You won last year, it's my turn this year" about the whole operation. But the nurserymen do not want to embarrass themselves, of course, and most AARS roses are good garden performers, especially in the South and West, where the majority of AARS trial grounds are located. Recently, several AARS winners, including the hybrid teas 'Brandy' and 'Perfect Moment', have proven to be disappointingly winter tender in northern gardens.

A gold medal from Bagatelle may mean nothing more than that a rose did well in Bagatelle for one year, or even for one day. Most French rose trials are heavily skewed to favor a rose's performance on the particular day that a "jury"—often composed of government officials and celebrities who may know nothing about roses—is convened. Similarly, Scandinavian rose trials have lost a lot of credibility for allowing schoolchildren to vote for their favorites.

The most stringent rose trials may be in England, Germany and The Netherlands. A Golden Rose of The Hague award is a reliable indicator that a variety will look good planted en masse because that is how they judge them, rather than two or three bushes at a time as in many other venues. Winners of Germany's ADR (*Anerkannte Deutsch Rose*) award can be counted on for winter hardiness and disease resistance. A top award from England's Royal National Rose Society is also an indication of excellent health.

Having one too many words in its name for the rose authorities, the hybrid tea 'Gardens of the World' must officially be known as 'JACcoeur'.

'Jan Guest' is an outstanding garden hybrid tea in moderate climates.

under American Rose Society rules and that its pedigree and other descriptive information will not be recorded in official ARS publications.)

'JAN GUEST'
Guest, England, 1975

Bright cerise pink with a golden reverse, clothed in exceptionally glossy foliage, 'Jan Guest' makes a stunning color impact in the garden. Its growth is vigorous and compact, and on visual inspection one could fault the plant only for having too many thorns. The blooms are at their best in the spring and fall, and this variety will not thrive in areas of unrelenting heat.

Bred by an amateur in England, 'Jan Guest' has achieved success not only at home, but across

---

ARS Rose-Naming Rules

The American Rose Society prohibits rose names over three words long. This rule was a reaction to a number of roses introduced in Europe many years ago, honoring members of some of the more obscure royal families and commemorating their activities. Rose names such as 'Mme. la Princesse de Bessaraba de Brancoven' and 'Les Fiancailles de la Princesse Stéphanie et de l'Archiduc Rodolphe' were not well received in America, and measures were taken to prevent their recurrence. Other rose registration regulations prohibit hyperbolic names or roses named for other flowers

(although 'Daisy Rose' and 'Jonquille' were both approved in 1982).

There is also a ban on naming a rose after any "notorious person." Standards in this regard are strict—some would say old-fashioned—and people who become notorious after a rose has already been named for them can wake up one morning to find their rose name revoked by the introducing nursery. In this manner the rose 'Margaret Trudeau' was renamed 'Sweepstakes', and, after a week in the south of France with her financial advisor, 'Duchess of York' became 'Sunseeker'.

the ocean as well. I once touted 'Jan Guest' when speaking to a garden club about "Roses You May Not Know," only to be confronted afterward by a rather matronly member who curtly informed me that she did not want any roses raised by amateurs in her garden. As Astor Perry demonstrated with 'Dublin', roses do not need to be hybridized by trained professionals. It helps, of course, to have years of experience and tens of thousands of seedlings from which to choose. But such large-scale operations are forced to seek varieties for every niche purpose and to introduce a handful of new roses every year. It is not unreasonable to expect that the dedicated amateur, working single-mindedly for a number of years, might come up with a worthwhile rose. 'Jan Guest' is living proof.

'JULIA'S ROSE'
Wisbech, England, 1980

Most attempts at russet, or brown-shaded, roses come out looking a burnt, rusty orange, or worse. 'Julia's Rose' is a happy exception, flowering in unique and pleasing shades of parchment tan. It is one of the first hybrid teas to bloom each spring, and it blooms on all summer when well fed. In growth it is a lot like an old tea rose and resents being cut back. Even skinny canes will produce good blooms, and so when pruning it is best to remove only obviously dead or diseased wood and to keep the center of the plant cleaned out.

Julia Clements, the doyenne of British flower arrangers, has the rare honor of having three roses

In the hybrid tea 'Julia's Rose' we find the most successful of all the russet-shaded roses.

People are drawn to the fringed, coppery buff blooms of the hybrid tea 'Just Joey'. There is no other rose like it.

named after her, the first two being 'Julia Clements', a red floribunda introduced in 1957, and 'Lady Seton', a light pink hybrid tea introduced in 1966. 'Julia's Rose' is the one that will be remembered.

'JUST JOEY'
Pawsey, England, 1972

There is no other rose like 'Just Joey'. Its fringed, coppery buff blooms appear in wavy profusion on short, rounded plants that can give a flowing effect to the rose landscape. Its mounded habit makes 'Just Joey' a particularly good standard (or tree) rose.

'Just Joey' has no particular disease problems, but will benefit from a soil especially rich in organic material. It has not grown as well in the Deep South as it has in the rest of the United States. It was named for the wife of the raiser; the success of 'Just Joey' has prompted a rash of other "Just" roses, including 'Just Buddy', 'Just Judy', 'Just Lucky' and, unfortunately, 'Justa Little Goofy'.

'LA FRANCE'
Guillot, France, 1867

The putative first hybrid tea—a cross between a hybrid perpetual and a tea—'La France' has

The putative first hybrid tea, 'La France' was introduced in 1867 and is still an attractive garden rose today.

numerous challengers for this honor. But they are like the Norse warriors and the Irish monks who preceded Columbus to the New World: While they may indeed have been first, nothing much came of it.

With the arrival of 'La France', a new classification was promptly made, and the floodgates were opened. The original (if never quite completely realized) ideal of a hybrid tea would have been a rose combining the vigor, hardiness and strong stems of a hybrid perpetual, with the elegant form, relatively restrained habit and repeat bloom of a tea. Soon hybrid teas were being crossed with each other much more frequently than hybrid perpetuals were mated to teas, and perhaps for lack of further exploration some of the potential of this class was lost.

Although its blooms are small by today's standards, 'La France' is still a good grower in the 1990s. Its color is silvery pink with a brighter pink reverse, the overall effect being more eye-catching than gentle. It boasts a superb fragrance.

'Limelight' is one of the rare hybrid teas that appreciates partial shade.

'LIMELIGHT' (KORikon, 'GOLDEN MEDAILLON')
Kordes, Germany, 1985

Although never large by hybrid tea standards, the glowing, soft yellow blooms of 'Limelight' are often perfectly formed. 'Limelight' is the rare hybrid tea that is actually happiest in half-shade. So situated, it will produce plenty of urn-shaped buds on long stems excellent for cutting. In full sun, 'Limelight' becomes so eager to bloom that its production becomes ragged, with even smaller blooms than usual.

'LYNETTE' (KORlyn)
Kordes, Germany, 1985

'Lynette' is cream with a broad, salmon-pink border, the color varying according to the time of season and usually at its best in the heat of summer. In cool and rainy weather 'Lynette' can appear to be almost completely white.

The plant is a strong and healthy grower and sometimes grows so quickly that it doesn't manage to form its leaves properly. Observant rosarians will notice that 'Lynette' occasionally sets bracts instead of leaflets, but this defect has no effect on the quality of the blooms, which remain excellent regardless of what kind of foliage is underneath them.

'MARIJKE KOOPMAN'
Fryer, England, 1979

One bush of 'Marijke Koopman' can supply you with an armload of cut flowers. They begin as elegantly shaped, satin pink buds and will last a good long time in the spring and fall. But 'Marijke Koopman' does not like heat and is not as productive in the southern United States as it is in the North.

Like most good roses, 'Marijke Koopman' will renew itself by producing basal breaks on a regular basis. As these new shoots develop on hybrid

The hybrid tea 'Lynette' thrives in hot weather.

teas, it is a good idea to pinch them off at the top when they are about 12 inches high. This will encourage several lateral stems to spring from the basal shoot, each of which will provide you with an excellent bloom.

Light Requirements of Roses

Few roses actually prefer half shade, but many will do very well in it (see "Roses for Half Shade," page 205). As shade increases, so do leaf size and stem length, as the plant reaches for the sun and tries to absorb as much light as possible. Because blooms take longer to develop in the shade, they are sometimes larger than when grown in full sun. However, shade always greatly reduces the total number of blooms produced. If you cannot give your roses full sun, try to take advantage of morning sun, which is always preferable to afternoon sun because it will prevent fungus spores from germinating in the dew.

'Marijke Koopman' is a great hybrid tea to plant if you want lots of cut flowers.

'MONTRÉAL' (GAUSECA, GAUZECA)
Gaujard, France, 1980

Commissioned as the official rose of the World Garden Exposition held in Montréal in the early 1980s, the many-petaled 'Montréal' has adapted well to the American South. It is also a highlight of midwestern summers, but may be too substantial to open properly in coastal climates, such as the Pacific Northwest.

'Montréal' is a horse of a rose, growing powerfully to 7 feet in Ohio. It is perfectly healthy, and its 6-inch blooms release an excellent fragrance. Rose breeders know that no matter which two colors they cross, pink will be the most likely result. 'Montréal' is a good example of that, being bred from the shining red 'Americana' and the bright orange-red 'Dora'.

'NIGHTINGALE' (HERGALE)
Herholdt, South Africa, 1970

This is a great rose, but for liability to mildew. If you garden in the wide-open spaces where powdery mildew is not a problem or if you are willing to protect 'Nightingale' with regular applications of fungicide, you will be rewarded with outstanding production of big, silvery cerise blooms. These last a long time when cut; rose exhibitors have discovered that 'Nightingale' stops developing after it is removed from the bush.

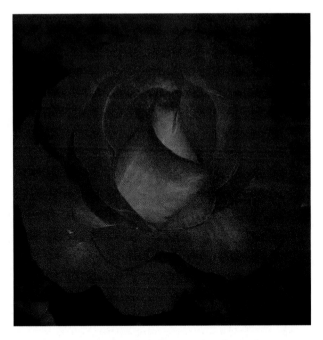

The hybrid tea 'Nightingale' holds its perfect shape when cut.

'OLYMPIAD' (MACAUCK)
McGredy, New Zealand, 1984

This was the official rose of the 1984 Summer Olympics in Los Angeles. *Olympiad* originally meant the four-year period between Olympic games; by that measure, a red rose this good comes along only every four or five Olympiads.

Despite its northern name, the robust hybrid tea 'Montréal' has been especially successful in the American South.

Breeding Climate

Rose breeders understand their climate best, and their roses should be expected to thrive in similar conditions. A great rose is a great rose regardless of where it is bred or grown, and a mediocre rose will not be redeemed by familiar weather. But, in general, roses raised in England are traditionally favorites in the Pacific Northwest, and Midwesterners can look to German roses with confidence. Recently, roses such as 'Nightingale', bred in the heat of South Africa, have proven especially well adapted to the American South.

The ruby-edged 'Paradise' is a more colorful alternative to the usually bland mauve hybrid teas.

'Olympiad' is brilliant clear red, on a healthy bush that grows with vigor to medium height (4 feet in the Midwest). No other red hybrid tea can match it as a bedding rose, and it is also a superior source of cut flowers. If only it were fragrant, this might be the perfect rose.

'PARADISE' (WEzeip; 'BURNING SKY', 'PASSION')
Weeks, USA, 1979

'Paradise', advertised as a "blue" rose, has pale lavender petals enlivened by a striking ruby red border. This is a rose that, despite the best of care, may thrive for only a few years before it needs to be replaced. In my garden, I have found it happiest when grown in a large tub. Most mauve roses have a nice fragrance, and 'Paradise' is no exception.

Blue Roses

Most nurseries sell at least one blue rose, the kind that their customers can plant to amaze their friends and neighbors. None of these roses is actually blue, and unfortunately many are actually rather putrid shades of pale lavender.

The blue pigment, delphinidin, does not yet exist in roses, and all mauve roses raised so far are really pink or red roses with less than the usual quota of pigment. It is, in a sense, color by subtraction. Some of these mauve roses can prove quite useful in flower arrangements, but their pale coloring always disappears in the rose garden. If you must plant mauve roses in any quantity, planting white, cream or lighter yellow roses with them will improve their garden value.

'PASCALI' (LENip, 'BLANCHE PASCA')
Lens, Belgium, 1963

In addition to the saxophone, the waffle and Jean-Claude Van Damme, Belgium has also given us the best white hybrid tea. 'Pascali' grows and blooms so reliably in so many different climates that in 1991 the World Federation of Rose Societies voted it the World's Favorite Rose.

Too many contemporary white roses are so stark that looking at them for too long can hurt your eyes. Many others are so blended with secondary hues that the gardener is left wondering if the rose isn't really a washed-out pink, apricot or yellow. 'Pascali' is a pure creamy white, delicious looking against its healthy, dark leaves. It makes a super cut flower.

'PAUL SHIRVILLE' (HARqueterwife, 'HEART THROB')
Harkness, England, 1981

Very fragrant, perfectly formed, soft coral-pink blooms appear both singly and in clusters. Its superior health record and slightly spreading,

Belgium's gift to the rose world, 'Pascali' is the most dependable white hybrid tea.

The very fragrant 'Paul Shirville' blooms in incredible profusion for a hybrid tea.

bushy habit makes 'Paul Shirville' an excellent choice if you want to plant a large bed of one hybrid tea variety. This rose makes so many basal breaks that one would think it would eventually wear itself out; however, 'Paul Shirville' has gone on as vigorously as it began in my garden, with not a sign of decline after twelve years.

'Paul Shirville' was originally registered as a shrub, and later converted to a hybrid tea. If raised commercially in America, it would undoubtedly have been sold as a grandiflora. Whatever you call it, 'Paul Shirville' is an extraordinary rose. The British timber executive Paul Shirville was expecting a trip to a lumberjacks' convention in Canada for his retirement gift. He must have been surprised when he got a rose named after him instead.

'PEACE' ('GIOIA', 'GLORIA DEI', 'MME. A. MEILLAND')
Meilland, France, 1945

'Peace' is the most famous rose of the century and one of the few modern roses to become entangled in the myth and legend that surrounds so many old garden roses. The story, so often told, is that budwood of 'Peace' was smuggled out of the south of France by a heroic U.S. embassy official in November 1942, just hours before the arrival of the invading German armies. It's a very good story, and one can almost imagine it as a movie featuring Harrison Ford, but the truth, as set down by the creator of 'Peace', Francis Meilland, is that budwood was sent to Germany, Italy and the

The most famous hybrid tea of all, 'Peace' revolutionized the rose world in the mid-twentieth century.

United States via ordinary postal channels in the summer of 1939. Fateful as that summer was, southern France remained very much uninvaded. But what this 1939 despatch lacks in drama, it makes up for in good timing. Receiving a few sticks of propagating material in 1939, the Pennsylvania nursery of Conard-Pyle would be ready to introduce this rose on the day that Berlin fell in 1945 at the San Francisco conference to found the United Nations. If they had received budwood in November 1942 they could not have started budding until 1943, and stock of this rose would never have been built up in time for nation-wide distribution three years later.

Everything about 'Peace' is big. It's a big, husky plant, with thick shoots and oversize foliage. 'Peace' is happiest as a big plant and resents heavy pruning. The flowers, golden yellow edged in rose pink, were seen as gargantuan in the 1940s. That rose blooms 6 inches across are now quite common is a tribute to all the breeding that has been done with 'Peace'—it is very difficult to find a hybrid tea bred since the 1950s that does not have at least a little 'Peace' blood in it. Of the many mutations of 'Peace' introduced over the years, the coppery pink 'Chicago Peace' remains the most popular.

'Pristine' (JACpico)
Warriner, USA, 1978

This is one of the few American-raised roses to achieve widespread distribution around the world in recent years. It even went to England and got fragrance, winning the Royal National Rose Society's Edland Fragrance Medal in 1979, despite giving off very little scent in gardens at home in the United States. Fragrance appears to be an attribute that varies from country to country, just as the appreciation of it varies from nose to nose. David Austin's English rose 'Perdita', winner of the Edland Fragrance Medal in 1984, is another example of a rose considered to be much more fragrant in England than America.

'Pristine' is a very healthy rose and, because it has only about 22 petals, is able to offer repeat

'Pristine' offers unusually speedy repeat bloom for a large-flowered hybrid tea.

bloom very quickly for a hybrid tea. The blooms are large and have outstanding substance. They are white, with a light mauve-pink border. Fanatics have found that the pink color can be intensified by adding zinc, in the form of vitamin supplement tablets, to the soil around where 'Pristine' grows.

A clear white sport—or mutation—of 'Pristine' was discovered by Muriel Humenick in California and named 'Fountain Square'. It is now widely available too.

'Senator Burda' (MEIvestal)
Meilland, France, 1988

Truly an international rose, 'Senator Burda' is known as 'Dreams Come True' in Australia, 'Spirit of Youth' in England and 'Victor Hugo' in France and the rest of continental Europe.

'Senator Burda' produces intensely fragrant, currant red blooms. This rose is beautiful but not long in bud, exploding into an attractive, platter-size, fully open stage. 'Senator Burda' may be a rose for all climates. The bush itself thrives in heat, and the blooms are able to open perfectly in cool

A hybrid tea for all climates, 'Senator Burda' is intensely fragrant.

Varietal Deterioration

Science disputes the notion of varietal deterioration, or "budding down": the idea that a rose variety will over time become weaker, perhaps through the budding of marginal eyes. The best propagating eyes are said to be those that reside behind five-leaflet leaves in the first 12 inches of stem under a superior bloom. The tiny bud-eyes directly under a rose bloom and not attached to proper leaves and the woody ones far down the cane are seen as marginal by amateur propagators, who view with suspicion the budding practices of large nursery operations. Anyway, science tells us that a clone is a clone and that all of the budding eyes on a given plant—large eyes or small, juicy or dried out—will contain identical genetic maps. Nevertheless, if you live near where plants of 'Peace' planted in the 1940s are still thriving— at a well-maintained public garden, around a library, war memorial or church, or at the home of a veteran gardener—compare the blooms on those plants with those on the plant of 'Peace' you will receive from any nursery today. Even if science tells you that it can't be so, you may think that the 'Peace' marketed today is just a pale imitation of its former self.

---

autumn weather when most other hybrid teas blooms stall out and proceed to rot. The foliage can be widely spaced on the bush, giving a sparse appearance that should not be confused with poor health. 'Senator Burda' grows to 4 feet, which is average for a hybrid tea in Ohio.

'THE LADY' (FRYJINGO)
Fryer, England, 1985

This rose was named after a magazine published for British housewives. I haven't seen the magazine, but the rose—honey yellow rimmed with salmon pink—is very good. 'The Lady' dispels a lot of misconceptions about yellow-apricot hybrid teas—specifically, that they are winter tender, disease prone and lack vigor. While there were exceptions, those were easy generalizations to make about roses in this color range introduced up to the 1970s. Of course, if you buy those same old varieties today it will still be true.

There are few absolutes about rose culture. As I have often said, "There is no one right way to grow a rose." But there is no getting past selecting the right variety. No amount of good culture can reform a disease-prone rose, make a scentless one

Vigorous, healthy and winter hardy, 'The Lady' marks a breakthrough in yellow-apricot hybrid teas.

fragrant or give vigor to a rose that simply does not want to grow. But start with a rose that laughs at winter and isn't going to be knocked down by the first disease spore that comes floating by, and everything about growing it becomes easier.

Right now, 'The Lady' is available in the United States only from specialized mail-order nurseries, at a cost of what could be 75 percent more than what you would pay for "any old apricot rose" at your neighborhood garden center. Amortize that added initial investment over a 15- or 20-year life for the rose and offset it against all

Since its introduction in the mid-1980s, 'Touch of Class' has set new standards for exhibition hybrid teas.

the extra you might spend on chemicals (or organic treatments) to get the same performance from a rose predisposed to disease, the reduced bloom production of a weaker cultivar, and the replacement cost for a plant that dies over winter. You will see what a bargain it really is to buy a better rose in the first place.

'TOUCH OF CLASS' (KRICARLO)
Kriloff, France, 1984

The top exhibition hybrid tea in the United States, and a rose that set new standards for classic, high-centered form, 'Touch of Class' is an excellent garden performer whether or not you are interested in exhibiting roses. Its blossoms are coral-orange when fresh, holding their form to finish as salmon pink. You will need to watch for

powdery mildew if that is a problem in your area.

'Touch of Class' is much more popular in the United States than it is in its native France, where it is known as 'Maréchale LeClerc'. One can never know when a rose will strike a nation's fancy. A transatlantic example in reverse is the bright orange miniature rose 'Hula Girl', raised in Texas in 1976. While it has now almost disappeared from commerce in the United States, it has achieved almost inexplicable popularity in Britain, and it is hard to find a British nursery catalogue that doesn't offer it.

'Touch of Class' has been disappointing as a parent rose. But just as the commercial success of 'Just Joey' spawned numerous other "Just" roses, 'Touch of Class' has sparked a somewhat wearying run of "Touch" names, including 'Touch of Elegance', 'Touch of Fire', 'Touch of Raspberry' and, from New Zealand, 'Touch of Kiwi'.

The easy-growing 'Trojan Victory' is an underrated red hybrid tea.

'TROJAN VICTORY' (KORPERKI)
Kordes, Germany, 1986

Here is a rose that fell through the cracks. Jackson & Perkins owned the American rights to this variety at a time when 'Olympiad' was brand new, and no one was paying any attention to any other red hybrid tea. So they sold it off to a University of Southern California alumnae association. That group named the rose in honor of their school's success at athletics and marketed it for one year as a fund-raising project. It has recently been reintroduced by two small nurseries.

'Trojan Victory' is a tall plant that produces glowing red blooms on long stems. Although opening more quickly, these blooms achieve better form than 'Olympiad' usually does. The glossy foliage is very large, and if 'Trojan Victory' can be faulted it would be for leaves that are too large in proportion to the bloom. Going easy on fast-acting liquid fertilizers will help to minimize this trait. 'Trojan Victory' is not better than 'Olympiad'. Still, it is one of the best recent red hybrid teas and deserves to be more widely grown.

I also recommend the following hybrid teas, some more unreservedly than others:

'American Dream'
(WINbur; Winchel, USA, 1987)

This dark red hybrid tea is a good garden rose that is especially successful in the South. In 1986,

'American Dream' became the first gold medal certificate winner at the American Rose Center trial grounds in Shreveport, Louisiana. It has not lived up to its promise, however; coincidentally, or not, all of the plants introduced into commerce have been infected with mosaic virus. One can only wonder how much better 'American Dream' would be if it weren't sick.

'Aotearoa-New Zealand'
(MACgenev, 'New Zealand'; McGredy, New Zealand, 1990)

The light coral-pink color of this rose deepens in cool weather. This all-around outstanding hybrid tea combines good health and great vigor with large blooms and intense fragrance. When this variety was introduced in connection with Queen Elizabeth's state visit to New Zealand in 1990, hybridizer Sam McGredy told the New Zealand press that he wanted everyone who thought that roses were losing their fragrance to bury their nose in this one. He described its fragrance as "really too strong. If you put a few blooms in a room it will just stink the room out," he said. "It has an almost nauseating fragrance." In my experience, 'Aotearoa-New Zealand' has a scent every bit as excellent and healthy as Sam McGredy's knack for getting publicity for his roses. *Aotearoa* is the Maori name for New Zealand and means "land of the long white cloud."

'Asso di Cuori'
(KORred, 'Ace of Hearts', 'Toque Rouge'; Kordes, Germany, 1981)

This scentless, crimson crossover rose is successful in the garden as well the greenhouse for which it was bred. Under glass or outdoors, 'Asso di Cuori' is a predictable, consistent producer of superbly shaped long-stemmed blooms. Its breeding as a florist's rose means that you can take long stems without sending the plant into shock.

'Beryl Bach'
(HARtesia; Harkness, England, 1985)

In muted blends of yellow and pink, this tough, healthy rose produces masses of bloom in regular

---

Mosaic Virus

Mosaic virus produces a pale green or yellow oak-leaf pattern on mature rose foliage. An infected plant may show many symptomatic leaves or only a few; the pattern with which the disease marks a leaf may disappear when the plant is growing well and increase when it is stressed. The overall vigor of infected plants is reduced, although sometimes only slightly.

There are a lot of misconceptions about mosaic virus. This virus is not spread by insects or pruning implements. One plant in your garden cannot catch it from another. The virus is transmitted only in the propagation process. In practical terms, it is spread only by nurseries.

Mosaic virus is spread by using infected budding eyes or infected understocks in propagation. Any budwood grafted onto an infected understock will result in an infected plant.

Likewise, infected budwood grafted onto clean understock will also result in an infected plant. Understocks will be virus free if they are grown from seed rather than cuttings. Unfortunately, many nurseries still grow their understocks from cuttings that are not virus free. And even nurseries that use only seed-grown understocks may still have infected budwood. Even if all known plants of a variety are infected with mosaic virus, there is a cure. Budding eyes can be purified by exposure to heat under laboratory conditions.

There is really no excuse for nurseries to continue offering virus-infected plants. On the other hand, cleaning up virus-infected stock can take a long time, and nurseries that are making a genuine effort to eliminate mosaic virus deserve our patience.

cycles. Not a hybrid tea to disbud, it is most effective when seen as a spray.

'Brandy'
(AROcad; Swim & Christensen, USA, 1982)

An entrancing rich apricot color, this rose is often perfectly formed. Its leaves will benefit from foliar feeding; the plant requires conscientious winter protection in the North.

'Bride's Dream'
(KORoyness, 'Fairy Tale Queen', 'Märchenkönigin'; Kordes, Germany, 1986)

The bush combines vigor and balance, producing clean, perfectly formed, light satin pink blooms on top of long, straight stems. This is the one of the best hybrid teas for cutting. Bred from 'Royal Highness', it lacks its parent's glossy leaves but offers greatly improved hardiness.

'Canadian White Star'
('C.W.S.', 'Dr. Wolfgang Pöschl'; Mander, Canada, 1980)

This rose produces perfectly formed, absolutely white, star-shaped blooms on a bush that is happiest in northern gardens.

'Caroline de Monaco'
(MEIpierar, 'Cameo Cream'; Meilland, France, 1988)

This hybrid tea has big, very light yellow blooms on a robust plant and is vaguely reminiscent of 'Peace'. Indeed, 'Caroline de Monaco' was bred from the 'Peace' mutation 'Chicago Peace'. (Breeding from mutations has been a somewhat neglected strategy among the world's hybridizers. One can only wonder if whatever factor caused a rose to mutate could remain in the background, prompting unexpected characteristics in a population of seedlings.)

The waxy blooms of 'Caroline de Monaco' can have outstanding high-centered form. This is one of many roses the Meillands have named for their friends the Grimaldis of Monaco.

'Cary Grant'
(MEImainger, 'Bushveld Dawn'; Meilland, France, 1987)

The blooms are a mouthwatering orange color; the foliage is lush and close set with dangerous thorns. A great grower in hot weather, this rose may be slow to get off the ground in the North.

Gardeners are often warned not to plant orange roses, such as 'Cary Grant', next to deep pink roses, such as 'Elizabeth Taylor'. These colors do clash, but unless you are planting large beds of single varieties the effect is unlikely to horrify anyone. Most home rose gardens are a hodgepodge of color, and the better for it. It is very difficult to synchronize colors in the rose garden because, after the initial explosion of bloom each spring, every variety will operate on its own repeat cycle, unlikely to be the same as that of its neighbors.

'Chablis'
(Weeks, USA, 1984)

This hybrid tea produces gorgeous, large, well-formed, off white flowers. The plants may be disappointingly short-lived, but are worth growing if you like the subtle color.

'Color Magic'
(JACmag; Warriner, USA, 1978)

This AARS winner has fantastically large, perfectly formed blooms in a blend of pink and cream on a bush that cannot stand up to northern winters. You may find it alluring enough to warrant planting as an annual.

'Confidence'
(Meilland, France, 1951)

With blooms of soft pink blended with creamy yellow, this is one of the best of the first-generation descendants of 'Peace'. It is a big rose on a strong bush that gives its best in the heat of summer. It is spectacular in the South, but cannot tolerate wet weather.

'Crystalline'
(ARObiby; Christensen & Carruth, USA, 1987)

This rose's very white, waxy blooms have unusual but attractive high-centered form. Bred as a florist's rose, this variety is rewarding to grow outdoors in a dry climate; blooms will waterspot in cool, damp weather. Its foliage is unusually textured and rugosalike for a hybrid tea and shows excellent disease resistance.

'Double Perfection'
(BURwin; Winchel, USA, 1987)

Bred for exhibitors, the effect of this red and custard rose is similar to 'Double Delight' (page 4). The rich, spicy fragrance of that great rose is missing here, but so are the split centers that exhibitors cannot stand. Exhibitor or not, you may find this rose worthwhile for its spectacular blend of colors. The bush may be happiest in hot weather, but the blooms are at their best when it's cool.

'Elegant Beauty'
(KORgatum, 'Delicia'; Kordes, Germany, 1982)

The soft yellow, double (but just barely) blooms may appear to explode open in summer's heat but will open easily in autumn when roses with more petals get stuck. Unfortunately, this gorgeous, profuse rose is not winter hardy.

'Elizabeth Taylor'
(Weddle, USA, 1985)

This rose bears a profusion of well-formed, deep pink blooms that are excellent to cut or to exhibit. This is a true hybrid tea, always producing its blooms one-to-a-stem. New plants may be troubled with white-streaked blooms, a problem that diminishes as the plant matures. Established bushes of 'Elizabeth Taylor' produce larger blooms.

'Elmhurst'
(Astor Perry, USA, 1985)

A blend of pink and yellow; the overall effect of these blooms is close to apricot. The best of Astor Perry's roses for general garden use, it's a dependable producer of globular yet high-centered blooms. This rose starts out well and improves with age.

'Esther Geldenhuys'
(KORskipei; Kordes, Germany, 1987)

This variety is a profuse producer of pinpoint-perfect, orange-pink blooms. The blooms are, however, considerably smaller than the typical hybrid tea. It is named for a former president of the South African Rose Society.

'First Prize'
(Boerner, USA, 1970)

The top exhibition pink blend hybrid tea in its day, this rose is still capable of producing enormous, perfectly formed blooms. The somewhat squat-looking bush is not reliably winter hardy in the North.

'Forgotten Dreams'
(Bracegirdle, England, 1981)

Perfect but short-lived dusky red blooms appear monthly throughout the growing season on this healthy, vigorous, underrated rose with an intoxicating scent.

'Fragrant Cloud'
(TANellis, 'Duftwolke', 'Nuage Parfumé'; Tantau, Germany, 1966)

Vigorous and free-blooming, it is more useful, I find, for its impressive coral-red hybrid tea sprays than for its scent, which is too rich for my nose and distressingly similar to that of turpentine.

'Freedom'
(DICjem; Dickson, N. Ireland, 1984)

The perfect chrome yellow hybrid tea for bedding, 'Freedom' grows low and is densely clothed in deep green, disease-resistant foliage. Its blooms, which usually appear one per stem, are small for a hybrid tea but are borne in great profusion. More effective than most yellow floribundas in providing garden color, this rose thrives in cool weather and continues its heavy bloom production right up to the first killing frost.

'Frohsinn'
(TANsinnroh; Tantau, Germany, 1984)

The apricot color, sparkling with pink and golden highlights, is so enchanting it's hard to do without this one, despite low bloom production. The foliage is excellent, and its form can be superb. This rose requires full sun in the summer and generous protection in the winter. (The German name *Frohsinn* means "cheerfulness" and not "fresh sin" as reported elsewhere.)

'Gina Lollobrigida'
(MEIlivar, 'The Children's Rose'; Meilland, France, 1989)

Egg-shaped buds open to scrambled egg–shaped, intense yellow blooms. 'Gina Lollobrigida' is colorfast, even in heat, which makes it a valuable hybrid tea for southern gardens.

'Granada'
('Donatella'; Lindquist, USA, 1964)

A fantastic blend of rose, red and yellow, this rose has been admired by visitors ever since I started growing roses, has been mother to 'Double Delight' and has even been classified as a grandiflora. The blooms, which appear on good cutting stems, are small by hybrid tea standards. This vigorous upright grower needs to be watched for mildew.

'Great Scott'
(Ballin, USA, 1991)

A rose that grows easily and well, it produces a continuous supply of well-formed, substantial, rich pink blooms.

'Helmut Schmidt'
(KORbelma, 'Goldsmith', 'Simba'; Kordes, Germany, 1979)

'Helmut Schmidt' is well named, for it blooms liberally and democratically. Its compact, rounded habit and continuity of butter yellow blooms makes this one of the very best hybrid teas for growing as a standard (tree) rose.

'Hinrich Gaede'
(Kordes, Germany, 1931)

This is one of the original orange-red roses. Because the orange-red classification was in later decades applied to roses such as 'Montezuma' and 'Tropicana', which ultimately fade to pink, our perception of what an orange-red rose should be has been altered. Some may find the nasturtium red of 'Hinrich Gaede' closer to what orange-red really should be.

'Honor'
(JAColite, 'Michèle Torr'; Warriner, USA, 1980)

A favorite in southern California, it hangs on in Ohio by its AARS tag, which entitles it to be entered in special AARS categories at rose shows. This rose is part of Jackson & Perkins's 'Love', 'Honor' and 'Cherish' AARS winners introduced in 1980. Before 'Love' and 'Cherish' came along, 'Honor' was tentatively named 'Silhouette', a name later given to another Jackson & Perkins white hybrid tea.

'Ingrid Bergman'
(POUlman; Poulsen, Denmark, 1985)

Completely dependable as a garden rose, this clear crimson rose is good to cut. One of the most honored roses of the 1980s, 'Ingrid Bergman' received gold medals at trial grounds in Belfast, Madrid and The Hague. Healthy and hardy, it lacks only fragrance and truly elegant form.

'Jardins de Bagatelle'
(MEImafris, 'Sarah'; Meilland, France, 1986)

This great grower produces long-stemmed, white shaded with pastel pink blooms of excellent form with precise regularity. It is one of the few strongly scented hybrid teas that also offers a high degree of mildew resistance.

'Joanne'
(Poole, Wales, 1985)

Although not a cross between 'Folklore' and 'Touch of Class', this hybrid tea is just what you might hope to get from such a match. A great grower (to 5 feet in Ohio) with every orange-pink bloom of perfect form.

'Kardinal'
(KORlingo; Kordes, Germany, 1986)

This profuse variety is excellent for use in arrangements. Perhaps the healthiest of all red hybrid teas, this rose's blooms are smaller than average. Reference to the code name KORlingo is necessary to distinguish this one from an earlier variety also called 'Kardinal'.

'King of Hearts'
(McGredy, N. Ireland, 1968)

Until the introduction of 'Olympiad', this was the best red hybrid tea for garden display. It is still worth growing and is one of the best roses for aspiring hybridizers to begin with, producing a high proportion of red and white, and red and yellow bicolored seedlings. 'King of Hearts' is difficult to find today only because its many thorns are a nuisance to nurserymen.

'King's Ransom'
(Morey, USA, 1962)

Most attractive as an urn-shaped bud, this is still one of the best golden yellow hybrid teas. Its winter tenderness is offset by amazing vigor, and even plants that appear to be dead first thing in the spring usually come roaring back.

'Lady Rose'
(KORlady; Kordes, Germany, 1979)

This rose combines the profusion of a top-rate floribunda with the elegance of a hybrid tea. The rounded bush is packed with smoky orange-red blooms, each on its own cutting-length stem. It is super as a tree rose.

'Lady X'
(MEIfigu; Meilland, France, 1965)

With long stems, ideal form and good fragrance, 'Lady X' would have been a great rose in almost any color other than its insipid pale lavender. However, it remains one of the most productive hybrid teas in the mauve color class.

'Madame Violet'
(Teranishi, Japan, 1981)

This hybrid tea produces well-formed, good-sized, mauve blooms on a healthy, vigorous plant. It is technically excellent, but can appear stiff and unnatural in the garden.

'Madras'
(Warriner, USA, 1981)

A well-rounded bush, this rose is one of the first hybrid teas to bloom in spring, producing flowers of cerise with a soothing light pink and white reverse. This fine rose is very difficult to find today, despite its introduction as Jackson & Perkins's "Rose of the Year" in 1981 and its later rating of 7.5 by the American Rose Society.

Numerical Ratings

The American Rose Society attempts to assign all roses in American commerce a numerical rating between 0 and 10. In reality, 90 percent of the ratings fall between 6.5 [Fair] and 8.0 [Excellent]. Therefore, it may be useful to assign these ratings, published in the ARS's annual *Handbook for Selecting Roses*, mathematical qualities similar to those of the ratings used in the Richter scale of earthquakes. By these standards, 'Madras', rated at 7.5, would be 31.5 times greater than a rose rated 6.5.

'Mikado'
('Koh-Sai'; Suzuki, Japan, 1987)

This AARS winner has intense red blooms with a pale yellow reverse and base. The plant, which is short for a hybrid tea, boasts beautiful foliage and is one of the most dependable producers throughout the rose season.

'Mister Lincoln'
(Swim & Weeks, USA, 1965)

Dark red, powerfully fragrant, and tall, this rose's tulip-shaped buds mature into large, attractive open blooms. This is an all-around excellent garden performer that is at its very best in the heat of summer.

'Mon Cheri'
(AROcher; Christensen, USA, 1982)

This colorful red and pink blend relative of 'Double Delight' provides near-constant garden color and a light, refreshing spicy scent. The rather short plant is not eager to provide long cutting stems.

'Narzisse'
(Krause, Germany, 1942)

This great and neglected rose produces large, exquisitely formed, maize yellow blooms regularly on a tough, leathery leaved, winter-hardy plant. People who see this variety for the first time think it must be something new, which must be the ultimate compliment for a "classic" hybrid tea.

'Oklahoma'
(Swim & Weeks, USA, 1964)

Forget 'Black Beauty', 'Black Delight', 'Black Garnet', 'Black Knight' and 'Black Night', 'Black Lady', 'Black Pearl', 'Black Ruby', 'Black Satin' and 'Black Velvet'. 'Oklahoma' is still the blackest red hybrid tea of them all. It has large, fragrant blooms and was bred from the same cross that produced 'Mister Lincoln'.

'Ophelia'
(Paul, England, 1912)

Although this rose may be delicate looking by today's standards, it is amazingly productive and almost always in bloom. The soft pink blooms with a pale yellow base have a superb fragrance. It is a parent of many subsequent hybrid teas.

'Painted Moon'
(DICpaint; Dickson, N. Ireland, 1989)

Fascinating in bud, the platter-size, open blooms in an absurd yet beautiful blend of pinks and red on a creamy background will stop traffic. Its growth is bushy, robust, nearly shrublike. This rose has a good health record and is happy in Ohio.

'Peter Frankenfeld'
(Kordes, Germany, 1966)

Almost boring in its consistent excellence, deep pink 'Peter Frankenfeld' is among the first hybrid teas to bloom each spring and will cycle through more bloom flushes each summer than any other variety. Named for the Bob Hope of Germany, this rose is an excellent example of a rose that has succeeded based on its merits and despite an uncommercial name. Incidentally, Bob Hope also had a Kordes hybrid tea named for him in 1966; although still in commerce, 'Bob Hope' is a dark red rose that has never achieved much popularity.

'Polarstern'
(TANlarpost, 'Polar Star'; Tantau, Germany, 1982)

A super producer of stark white blooms to cut, this rose is held short of greatness by inconsistent form and leaves that illustrate various mineral deficiencies. In the 1980s, British rose growers set up trial grounds to select a British "Rose of the Year" to promote. They may have been rather chagrined when this German-raised rose won in 1985.

'Polly'
(Beckwith, England, 1927)

Pastel white with pink and yellow undertones, this classic hybrid tea has a strong, pure scent. It is super in the spring but likely to produce tiny, weak-necked blooms in the fall.

'Président Leopold Senghor'
(MEIluminac; Meilland, France, 1979)

This rose combines good fragrance and health. The large, currant red blossoms are just barely double; they are most attractive fully open, displaying striking golden stamens. Named for the poet and former president of Senegal, the idealistic leader of the negritude movement.

'Rebecca Claire'
(Law, England, 1986)

A treasure still undiscovered by many rosarians, this coral-pink rose with orange shading has perfect (if fleeting) form, intense fragrance and good growth habits.

'Red Lion'
(McGredy, N. Ireland, 1964)

Its massive, cherry red blooms take a long time to open despite a relatively low petal count and last surprisingly well for such a large rose. The form is classic, and the bush is productive.

'Royal Highness'
(Swim & Weeks, USA, 1962)

Admired for its perfect form and extraordinarily glossy, mirrorlike leaves, this light pink rose is unfortunately winter tender in the North.

'Savoy Hotel'
(HARvintage, 'Integrity', 'Violette Niestlé'; Harkness, England, 1989)

A superior bedding rose, it offers large blooms on relatively short, very healthy plants. The buds have a squashed look as they begin, but expand beautifully into classically formed blooms. Dark, glossy leaves make a striking backdrop for the delicately colored, pearlescent pink blossoms. Bred from 'Silver Jubilee' × 'Amber Queen', 'Savoy Hotel' appears—remarkably—to have taken only the best qualities from each of its parents.

'Secret'
(HILaroma; Tracy, USA, 1994)

A good grower, this rose produces lots of fragrant, light pink blooms edged with deeper pink in clusters of three or four. It is one of the best of the recent AARS winners.

'Selfridges'
(KORpriwa, 'Berolina'; Kordes, Germany, 1984)

Producing a massive display of perfectly formed, golden yellow blooms in spring, repeat bloom is unpredictable. It is extraordinarily hardy for a yellow hybrid tea. Named for a British department store, by growing to 10 feet it pays particular homage to the escalator.

'Sheer Bliss'
(JACtro; Warriner, USA, 1987)

A big rose on a big, sprawling bush, 'Sheer Bliss' produces a lot of white blooms with a subtle pink blush. Not a bedding rose, this one might be most effective in the shrub border. It is not a cutting rose either: The blooms lose substance rapidly when cut and can look puffy after just a short time indoors.

'Sheer Elegance'
(TWOby; Twomey, USA, 1991)

With good form and orange-pink color, this rose is often compared to 'Touch of Class', to which it is superior only in its disease resistance.

'Silver Jubilee'
(Cocker, Scotland, 1978)

Most roses are defined by their antecedents. Rosarians will describe a worthwhile new introduction as being "like 'First Prize', only hardier" or "like 'Pristine' with more petals." But 'Silver Jubilee' defies such definition, setting entirely new standards for health, compact habit and freedom of bloom in the hybrid tea class.

When I lived in the city, I planted a row of 'Silver Jubilee' out at the street, where it stood up bravely to road salt in the winter, skateboards in the summer and dogs every day of the year. Nothing seemed to trouble it. 'Silver Jubilee' is a rose that wants to grow.

Its perfectly formed blooms are coral-orange with creamy pink shadings. It can be a challenge to get a long cutting stem, and the dense, well-foliaged bush may behave more like a floribunda than a hybrid tea in hot climates.

'Silverado'
(AROgrewod; Christensen, USA, 1987)

This rose has silvery mauve blooms with a deeper edge, excellent fragrance and attractive maroon-tinted foliage. One of the most perfectly formed of all hybrid teas, 'Silverado' needs coaxing to achieve decent bloom size and extra protection to survive northern winters.

'Suffolk'
(Astor Perry, USA, 1983)

This variety produces outstanding, classically high-centered, exhibition-form blooms in cream with a broad pink border. Vigorous in its summer growth, it may need extra protection in the winter. This is one of three very similar, yet distinct, hybrid teas introduced in the United States in the 1980s. I have found 'Suffolk' to be the best of a lot that includes 'Dorothy Anne' (Winchel, 1985) and 'Thriller' (Bridges, 1986), both of which are also good roses.

'Sutter's Gold'
(Swim, USA, 1950)

A golden orange rose that fades to yellow and is bordered in pink and red, this is a timeless beauty. The first hybrid tea to bloom each spring, it appears on an upright, rather narrow bush that is eager to repeat bloom as well. It has few thorns and much fragrance.

'Swarthmore'
(MEItaras; Meilland, France, 1963)

Having perfectly formed, rich pink blooms with a charcoal border, this strong grower can be faulted only for a tendency to mildew. Named for Swarthmore College in Pennsylvania, it has been planted at Quaker outposts in other parts of the world as well. There is a fine light pink sport called 'Sweetie Pie'.

'Taxi'
(Poulsen, Denmark, 1978)

A carefree, pure, unfading crimson rose for cutting and garden display, this strong grower reaches 5 feet in the Midwest. Blooms appear both singly and in modest clusters on long stems. This rose is quite disease resistant and also has a good scent, which makes it an important step forward in red hybrid teas. It was bred in Denmark, where the winters are cold and the taxicabs are red.

'Tequila Sunrise'
(DICobey, 'Beaulieu'; Dickson, N. Ireland, 1989)

This hybrid tea does not reflex the way one would expect; it lasts forever at a flat two-thirds open, without ever actually reaching the fully open state. Stiff stems and dark green, leathery foliage make for a good contrast with the glowing yellow blooms edged in orange-red.

'The McCartney Rose'
(MEIzeli; Meilland, France, 1991)

This fuchsia pink rose is superb for three reasons: First, it is incredibly fragrant, more so than any other hybrid tea I grow. This perfume may lack the nuance of 'Margaret Merril', for example, or of many old garden roses, but it is all rose and all pleasing. Second, it is a healthy rose that grows

---

Echo Geographical Crosses

The creator of 'Utro Moskvy', rose hybridizer E. E. Shtankto (an employee of crazed Soviet agronomist T. D. Lysenko) rejected Mendelian genetics and made what were called echo geographical crosses—roses from France mated with roses from America, British roses with Dutch, and so on, all designed to create new cultivars with strengths from both climatic backgrounds. By this way of thinking, a rose from northern Germany such as 'Independence' crossed with a cultivar from southern Germany such as 'Frau Karl Druschki' would be expected to produce offspring with characteristics promoting success in both regions.

This misplaced faith in echo geographical crosses was part of Marxist orthodoxy until the death of Stalin and is really not too far removed from the belief held by millions of Americans that roses bought from nurseries located north of their garden will automatically be more winter hardy. In reality, winter hardiness is a matter of chromosomes, as are all characteristics of seedling roses. 'Utro Moskvy' will be hardy for you in Minnesota even if you buy your plant from Visalia, California, which is, in fact, the location of the only American nursery that sells it.

(and roots) like a weed. Finally, it is always in bloom, repeating more quickly than such famous producers as 'Sutter's Gold' and 'Pristine'. This variety has already won more awards for the Meillands than 'Peace' ever did. Its scrolled buds open flat, and it does not have the high-centered form exhibitors crave. This rose was purchased by Paul McCartney and named for himself.

'Utro Moskvy'
('Moscow Morn'; Shtankto, USSR, 1952)

This very double, rose pink rose is a good grower and bloomer as well as the only Russian-raised rose in American commerce. 'Utro Moskvy' was bred from 'Frau Karl Druschki' × 'Independence', roses created at opposite ends of Germany, in the hope that it would inherit the strengths from both climatic backgrounds.

'Veldfire'
(KORgust, 'Sunsation', 'Wurzburg'; Kordes, Germany, 1987)

The fantastic, bright orange-apricot blooms, alas, are too fleeting to cut, but this is a marvelous garden rose nonetheless.

'Victor Borge'
(POUlvue, 'Michael Crawford'; Poulsen, Denmark, 1991)

With a classic hybrid tea form, this rose is a very consistent producer of soft orange blooms with a pale reverse. The bush is compact, reaching only 3 feet in northern Ohio. This great rose is named for two great entertainers.

'White Masterpiece'
(JACmas; Boerner, USA, 1969)

These immense, well-formed, luminescent, white blooms appear to glow in the dark on a moonlit night. The healthy and productive plant is short and chunky and noted for its thick peduncles.

Grandiflora is the one truly American rose classification. Unfortunately, it represents a redundant class of roses, born in the optimism that 'Queen Elizabeth' was just the opening shot of what was expected to be a salvo of many similar varieties and sustained in the commercial advantage nurserymen found in having an extra classification in which to insert their extra seedlings. Rather than introduce two pink hybrid teas in the same year, enterprising nurserymen thought "Why not call one of them a grandiflora?" Horticulturally, the classification makes no sense. But it has been a success economically.

Ranging in size from the dwarf 'New Year' to the very tall 'Queen Elizabeth', there isn't any grandiflora that wouldn't be perfectly happy as either a hybrid tea or a floribunda. (Indeed, the rest of the world is equally divided in how to catalogue 'Queen Elizabeth'. It's a hybrid tea in continental Europe and a floribunda in most English-speaking countries.)

Genetically, today's grandifloras will have the same mixture of floribunda and hybrid tea parents as today's floribundas and hybrid teas. The often-repeated idea that grandiflora roses are any more hardy than other modern roses, are taller or have any other consistently distinguishing characteristics is patently false.

Concern about the illogic of the grandiflora classification should not, however, distract from the very real excellence of some of the roses that have been stuck into it.

'GOLD MEDAL' (AROyqueli)
Christensen, USA, 1982

Glowing golden yellow, flushed with orange, the best exhibition grandiflora and a great garden rose in warm climates, 'Gold Medal' is not hardy in the North without winter protection. When it was introduced in 1982, 'Gold Medal' was inadvertently mixed up with a dullish yellow hybrid tea called 'Candlelight'. Shadings will vary with the weather, but if your 'Gold Medal' is never flushed orange at its edges, it is not 'Gold Medal'.

You may notice pale yellow flecks on the foliage of 'Gold Medal'. This is not a symptom of virus or disease, just proof that 'Gold Medal' is a descendent of the floribunda 'Arthur Bell', a rose that has passed this unusual foliage characteristic on to numerous descendants.

Bearing its flowers in large sprays, the stalwart 'Queen Elizabeth' was the first grandiflora and is one of the easiest of all roses to grow.

'Gold Medal' is the best exhibition grandiflora and a great garden rose in warm climates.

'QUEEN ELIZABETH'
Lammerts, USA, 1954

The prototypical grandiflora is a powerful plant, bearing its cyclamen pink blooms in attractive sprays on long stems. Growing tall and not too wide, it makes an excellent hedge. The flowers are not grand, being slightly smaller than the average hybrid tea and larger than most modern floribundas.

If I had to choose one word to describe 'Queen Elizabeth', it would be *indestructible* rather than *graceful* or *elegant*. It is a good rose to recommend to people who say they have no luck with roses.

'Climbing Queen Elizabeth' is a particularly useless mutation. 'Blushing Queen' and 'Yellow Queen Elizabeth' are color sports. However, 'Scarlet Queen Elizabeth' is a descendent rather than a mutation.

'SONIA' (MEIhelvet, 'SONIA MEILLAND', 'SWEET PROMISE')
Meilland, France, 1974

Although some of the best greenhouse roses are only average performers outdoors, 'Sonia' is a notable exception. It produces armloads of salmon pink flowers to cut all summer long. It dislikes rain, requires extra winter protection in the far North and, like almost all florists' roses, lacks scent.

'TOURNAMENT OF ROSES' (JACIENT, 'BERKELEY', 'POESIE')
Warriner, USA, 1989

If the notion of a grandiflora started out with 'Queen Elizabeth' as a tall bush bearing hybrid tea–type blooms in large floribunda-type clusters, 'Tournament of Roses' shows how it has ended up. Today, if a plant is as short as a floribunda with blooms as big as those of a hybrid tea, it qualifies as a grandiflora.

Large flowered but short stemmed, 'Tournament of Roses' is a workhorse in the garden, growing into a well-rounded, perfectly foliaged plant that is almost always covered in bloom. It flowers singly and in well-proportioned sprays of up to seven florets. In cool weather its coral-pink blooms can pick up an extremely attractive almond tinting. The long-lasting blooms are excellent to cut and use in arrangements.

Here are a few other recommended grandifloras:

'Lagerfeld'
(AROlaqueli, 'Starlight'; Christensen, USA, 1986)

Growing powerfully and producing massive sprays of hybrid tea–shaped, mauve blooms, this

The elegant 'Sonia' is a grandiflora that has achieved great popularity with both florists and gardeners.

rose actually comes close to the grandiflora ideal. It has excellent fragrance for a grandiflora; one bloom can perfume a room.

'New Year'
(MACnewye, 'Arcadian'; McGredy, New Zealand, 1983)

This is the littlest grandiflora and is sold as a floribunda in the rest of the world. Its unique and pleasing apricot orange color, low bushy habit and excellent glossy leaves make it a good choice wherever a short bedding rose in a modern color is desired.

'Olé'
(Armstrong, USA, 1964)

Massive clusters of medium-sized, ruffled blooms appear with good regularity on a short, stocky plant. It provides a rich orange-red color impact that may benefit from placement near softer colors, especially buff orange.

'Pink Parfait'
(Swim, USA, 1961)

A floribunda registered and sold as a grandiflora, 'Pink Parfait' makes attractive sprays of neatly formed blooms, pink with a little bit of cream, all summer long. An easy rose to breed with, it has achieved more success as a parent in England than in its native land.

'Prima Donna'
('Tobone'; Shirakawa, Japan, 1984)

The plant is vigorous, the stems are long and its blooms are small, well formed and an unexciting deep pink. A dependable but unremarkable rose that may be at its best as a producer of cut flowers for indoors.

'Rejoice'
(McMillan, USA, 1985)

This tall-growing plant blooms in salmon pink blended with yellow sprays that are clean and well formed. It has all the vigor of its mother, 'Little Darling', and unfortunately some of the winter tenderness of its father, 'Color Magic'. It was raised by an amateur in Michigan and is the

---

Greenhouse versus Garden Roses

The interests of the backyard rosarian and the greenhouse rose grower converge in a well-shaped bloom that lasts a long time. Other than that, their requirements may be considerably different. Greenhouse roses are bred for production in a highly artificial environment. They must respond predictably to chemical fertilization, develop their true, best color under low light conditions and bloom dependably at particular temperatures. But they do not have to withstand very many degrees of frost.

Because florists sell buds and not blooms, greenhouse roses may start out more elegantly than they finish or, as is increasingly the case, freeze at the bud stage and never fully open. Roses grown for the florist trade are almost always smaller than their garden counterparts (the bold hybrid tea 'White Masterpiece' being a notable exception) and feature thick, crisp petals.

Greenhouse roses do not necessarily arrive on top of an attractive bush. Indeed, they are bred to produce a lot of bloom under cramped conditions, so if you want to find a rose that can add a flowing or "natural" effect to your landscape, do not go looking in the greenhouse.

winner of a gold medal certificate at the American Rose Center trial grounds in Shreveport, Louisiana. This variety may be hard to find, but is definitely worth the search.

'White Lightnin'' (Christensen, USA, 1981)

Quite short for a grandiflora, this rose is a free bloomer. It was the first white AARS grandiflora and remains, perhaps coincidentally, the best white grandiflora. It has a lemon-fresh scent reminiscent of the finest household cleaning products.

Floribundas

Floribundas were invented at the New York World's Fair in 1939 and have been reinvented every couple of decades since.

Before floribundas, there were polyanthas, roses offering small florets in huge clusters, usually flowering late in the season, with the onset of mildew sometimes more certain than the arrival of a worthwhile display of autumn bloom. As polyanthas were improved by crossing with hybrid teas, a new class of roses evolved. These featured larger florets and better repeat bloom and were called *hybrid polyanthas*. It was a logical but not particularly commercial designation, and members of the rose-buying public could be excused if they expected these roses to be just like polyanthas, only more so. One of these hybrid polyanthas, a currant red specimen from Germany called 'Minna Kordes', was elected one of the original All-America Rose Selections in 1939 and scheduled for introduction in 1940. The firm of Jackson & Perkins, then based in Newark, New York, seized the moment and the rose. They renamed the variety 'World's Fair', secured a booth at the fair and sold this one new rose as a whole new kind of rose, a *floribunda*.

It worked, and that was the end of hybrid polyanthas. By the 1950s, floribundas were boasting blooms with classic hybrid tea form, in clusters. Then, in the 1960s, with roses such as 'Sea Pearl' and 'Tiki', the clusters were gone, and any hybrid tea that looked smaller than ordinary was registered as a floribunda. In the late 1970s, Jackson & Perkins touted the term *flora-tea* as a definition for these roses, but it did not catch on.

Today, thanks to an infusion of fresh blood from miniatures and from shrubs, most new floribundas can be counted on to display their flowers in sprays. It could be said that the floribundas are a collection of highlights from all of the other modern rose classifications. Offering superb bedding habit, excellent cutting stems, fragrance and a full range of color and form, the class has emerged as the most versatile group of roses available. In general, no rose will give you more pleasure for less trouble than today's floribunda.

People often ask me, "What's your favorite rose?" I have a different answer every day. But four days out of five, it's a floribunda.

'ALICE PAT'
Jerabek, USA, 1981

This cheerful tricolor of red, pink and white is one of the first roses to bloom each spring. While maintaining a low, compact habit, it still manages to put enough stem under its large sprays to satisfy rose exhibitors and flower arrangers.

Since the death of Jackson & Perkins's Eugene Boerner (known as "Papa Floribunda") in 1966, no American professional rose breeder has devoted his or her primary focus to floribundas.

One of the best floribundas for exhibition, 'Harkness Marigold' produces large, perfectly arranged natural sprays, showing all stages of bud and bloom at one time.

Fortunately, amateur enthusiasts such as Paul Jerabek have picked up the slack, with numerous excellent introductions, such as 'Alice Pat'.

'ANABELL' (KORBELL)
Kordes, Germany, 1972

Originally bred for florists' use, 'Anabell' is a hot-house rose that can stand up to the rigors of the great outdoors. It shrugs off winter and produces spray after well-proportioned spray all summer long.

Its blooms are orange with a silvery gold reverse. As one would expect from a florist's rose, they last a very long time. Cut roses generally last longest if cut first thing in the morning or between 4 and 6 P.M. Aspirin, nondiet lemon-lime soda or commercial floral preservative can all extend a bloom's vase life, but the most important thing is to recut its stem every second day. Cut at an angle while the stem is under fresh water, using clean, strong pruning shears with a curved blade.

'ANISLEY DICKSON' (DICKIMONO, DICKY)
Dickson, N. Ireland, 1984

Perhaps the greatest floribunda of the 1980s, 'Anisley Dickson' has set new standards for health, vigor, habit and production of sprays. Its color is a clear reddish salmon; its form reaches for classic hybrid tea symmetry without any hint of stodginess. Culturally, 'Anisley Dickson' is undemanding, except for insisting on total sun.

Named for Anisley, the wife of rose breeder Pat Dickson, this and 'Alice Pat' are two happy exceptions to the Wife Rule, which states that

The low-growing 'Alice Pat' is one of the first floribundas to bloom each spring.

'Anabell' is a floribunda that produces long-lasting cut flowers.

Theme Names

Most rose nurseries have at one time or another introduced a series of roses named around a common theme. In England, Harkness featured 'King Arthur', a salmon pink floribunda, and the Knights of the Round Table (and 'Guinevere'). Perhaps lacking such chivalric icons in Dutch history, de Ruiter introduced seven polyanthas named after the Seven Dwarfs (and that is why there is a rose named 'Dopey'). The American E. D. Williams has made miniatures ending with *glo* (such as 'Dreamglo' and 'Starglo') his trademark. For a while, Californian Ollie Weeks was naming hybrid teas after (mostly southern) states of the Union. The desire to popularize groundcover roses has led to separate series named after both game birds (including 'Grouse' and 'Pheasant') and the counties of England (including, to the certain amusement of those who remember *Monty Python's Flying Circus*, 'Rutland'). Jackson & Perkins have introduced at least seven roses with *Sun* as part of their name, and since leaving Ireland for New Zealand, Sam McGredy has made ample use of Maori names such as 'Matangi', 'Kaikoura' and 'Waitmata'. (But his deep yellow hybrid tea 'Yabadabadoo' still owes more to *The Flintstones*.)

Coloration of the tall-growing floribunda 'Festival Fanfare' is variable but often spectacular.

Introduced in the 1940s, 'Dusky Maiden' is a floribunda of timeless beauty.

roses named by breeders for their wives tend to be disappointingly ordinary. (It would be too cruel to recite all of the proofs of this rule. Until the 1980s, the one notable exception was the 1929 hybrid tea 'Mrs. Sam McGredy'. In that case, Mrs. McGredy went through all of her husband's seedlings and picked out her namesake rose herself.)

'DUSKY MAIDEN'
LeGrice, England, 1947

This rose of timeless beauty has wide crimson petals that enclose perfectly formed, long-lasting stamens. It repeats well, has excellent fragrance and is happier in really hot weather than many roses from England.

'Dusky Maiden' is part of a series of single-petaled floribundas introduced by E. B. LeGrice in the 1940s and 1950s that contain the word *Maid*. These include the free-blooming pink 'Dainty Maid' and the stalwart ivory-yellow 'Dairy Maid'.

'FESTIVAL FANFARE' (BlestOGIlvie, 'ST. JOHN OGILVIE')
Ogilvie, England, 1986

Exuberant, healthy and striped, 'Festival Fanfare' is a mutation of the floribunda climber 'Fred Loads', which is known for its vigorous growth and clear orange, single-petaled blooms. Its sport produces blooms ranging, in response to the weather, from pink to orange and striped in lighter tones. Sometimes the stripes are a stark, spectacular white. The bush grows tall and can be somewhat rangy in habit. The blooms usually appear only at the top of the plant, which makes it a good choice for planting behind something else.

This mutation was discovered by Mr. W. D. Ogilvie, who promptly named it 'St. John Ogilvie' after his ancestor the saint. It soon attracted the attention of a nursery, who renamed it for commercial introduction at a garden festival in Liverpool.

Striped Roses

Striped roses are as old as cultivation, appearing as mutations throughout recorded rose history. Mutations (or sports) can appear at any time, although there is some evidence that they are more likely to materialize when the plant is stressed, especially when it has a severe case of powdery mildew. Sports can affect growth (and that is how we got 'Climbing Peace' and many other climbing forms of bush varieties), form (in these mutations, a variety will gain or lose some petals) or, most commonly, color. Color sports usually represent a loss rather than an addition of genetic material. For this reason, most sports are lighter in color than their parent. Stripes occur as a variation on this model, with some color lost on each petal.

In India, where striped roses are particularly prized, scientists have had some success in producing striped mutations by bombarding propagating material with atomic radiation. Needless to say, one should not try this at home. But if you grow a lot of roses over several years, you are almost certain to find a color sport, maybe even a striped one. While few of these will have any commercial worth, no one knows how many potentially valuable sports have appeared over the years only to be lost through lack of observation or action.

It is important to try to propagate a sport — by rooting cuttings or bud-grafting — during the same summer in which it appears. If the sport is not propagated, and if winter kills the mutated cane, the new variety will be lost. When a basal cane produces a sport, and all of the flowers produced on that cane share the new characteristic, it will usually propagate true to its new type. But a sport appearing on only one of a basal cane's lateral branches will rarely persist through propagation. If you take budwood or cuttings from such a stem, you will usually find the resulting plants to be of the original variety and not the new one. This kind of sport is called a chimera.

Sometimes you may find a plant that sports over and over again. 'Festival Fanfare' remains somewhat unstable, and secondary mutations are common. Recently, California rosarian Kim Rupert found and selected a particularly fine clear pink sport to be called 'Festival Pink'.

'GEORGETTE' (INTerorge)
Ilsink, The Netherlands, 1983

Double, white, frilly petaled blooms open quickly to show off bright yellow stamens. This rose will repeat bloom in full sprays more quickly than any floribunda I know. But it can also produce a disconcerting number of blind basal shoots, which produce no flowers at all. Out of curiosity, my wife bud-grafted some eyes from one of these blind shoots, and they grew into perfectly normal plants of 'INTerorge' (as it is known to avoid confusion with a miniature rose called 'Georgette'). This floribunda grows wider than it does tall and makes an interesting low hedge.

'GLAD TIDINGS' (TANtide, 'LÜBECKER ROTSPON', 'PETER WESSEL')
Tantau, Germany, 1988

There are incredible depths to the crimson red color of this floribunda, which can appear different, and new, in every light. The plant stays healthy under all conditions, maintaining an excellent bushy habit. The blooms, which are large for a floribunda, usually appear in sprays of three or five.

There is no telling where this intriguing color came from because Herr Tantau rarely reveals the parentage of his introductions, which include some of the greatest hybrid teas of the 1960s. Modern

The Dutch floribunda 'Georgette' offers remarkably swift repeat bloom.

The floribunda 'Glad Tidings' displays extraordinarily rich shades of crimson.

roses have such a complex gene pool that it has been estimated that one would have to raise seventeen million seedlings from the same cross before getting the same result twice. And the fact that professional hybridizers work ten or more years ahead of the marketplace guarantees a huge head start on anyone wanting to duplicate a particular cross.

It is unlikely that Tantau has hybridized on such a large and successful scale without maintaining comprehensive records of his crosses. While it is possible that this breeder views his rose parents as proprietary information, the economic value of this data to any rival would be practically nil. It is hoped that all of Tantau's breeding records are tucked away somewhere and will be revealed to historians and students of the rose at some later date.

'GRACE ABOUNDING'
Harkness, England, 1968

This favorite of rose exhibitors presents perfect sprays of ivory-cream flowers very much like a slightly paler version of its hybrid musk parent, 'Penelope', on a plant of ideal floribunda proportions. In the days before commercial sponsorship of a new rose became an economic necessity, Jack Harkness gave some of the most pleasing, evocative names to his roses. In addition to 'Grace Abounding', there were 'Compassion', 'Judy Garland', 'Lake Como' and 'Yesterday'. Some of the more recent Harkness roses, such as 'International Herald Tribune', 'Spirit of Pentax' and 'Radox Bouquet', might be just as good. They just don't sound as good.

'HARKNESS MARIGOLD' (HARTOFLAX)
Harkness, England, 1986

Here is an example of what can happen when you start letting members of the public give names to roses. Naming rights for this variety were offered at a charity auction in England, where the successful bidder was a Mrs. Marigold Somerset. She decided to name the rose after the breeder and herself—'Harkness Marigold'. Because this violates the rules for naming roses, rose show exhibitors must use its code name of 'HARtoflax'.

'Harkness Marigold' is one of three closely related floribundas from Harkness, all of which produce spectacular, long-stemmed natural sprays, showing all stages of bud and bloom at one time. They appear on tall, upright plants that bloom later than most roses in the spring. Thus, they provide bloom while most of the rose garden is resting; the downside is that they take a good long time before blooming again in the fall. To encourage quicker repeat bloom, do not cut the bush back too severely.

'Harkness Marigold' is a wonderful coppery salmon color, unique in my experience. The other two roses in this series are the apricot 'Anne Harkness' and the bright yellow 'Princess Alice' (also sold as 'Brite Lites'). ('By Appointment', an

'Grace Abounding' combines the refined sprays of the hybrid musks with the easy-to-manage habit of the floribundas.

The floribunda 'Hiroshima's Children' is like a smaller, streamlined version of 'Peace'.

apricot floribunda from Harkness introduced in 1989, presents these same natural sprays on shorter plants that bloom earlier in the season.)

'HIROSHIMA'S CHILDREN' (HARMARK)
Harkness, England, 1985

Creamy yellow with a coral-pink border, this rose is like a smaller, streamlined version of 'Peace'. Perfectly formed blooms appear one to a stem and are splendid for cutting. Sprays are rare, which is just as well because they are also wildly asymmetrical.

'Hiroshima's Children' is a rose that rewards good culture, and even the most pampered plants may show some deterioration after three or four years. Roses that decline like this force the rosarian to reaffirm his faith in the variety or to abandon it for something new. On my third planting, I still have faith in 'Hiroshima's Children'.

This rose was named in honor of Dr. Tomin Hamada, who dedicated his life to caring for the radiation victims of Hiroshima. Although the

'Jubilee Celebration' is a floribunda whose blooms are most attractive when fully open.

parents of 'Hiroshima's Children' have never been officially recorded, raiser Jack Harkness believed that the cross may have been between two of his earlier floribundas, 'Bobby Dazzler' × 'Princess Michael of Kent'.

'JUBILEE CELEBRATION'
Smith, England, 1977

Although not bred from 'Dainty Bess', this floribunda can provide the same garden effect on a shorter plant, simulating the spectacular purplish stamens with cerise-streaked petaloids centered in a creamy coral-pink bloom. Not counting the petaloids, there are only twelve proper petals, which open quickly to reveal their full beauty. A particularly clean, refreshing rose fragrance is an added bonus. 'Jubilee Celebration' is of medium height and can sometimes be faulted for lack of vigor. It is a rose worth coaxing.

'LITTLE DARLING'
Duehrsen, USA, 1956

Ultra-vigorous, reaching shrublike proportions in mild climates, 'Little Darling' was one of the few

'Little Darling' is a good tall-growing floribunda and a parent of many modern miniature roses.

floribundas of its generation to offer good scent. Its hybrid tea–shaped flowers are yellow, blended with soft salmon pink, and appear in wide sprays. Although still available from many nurseries, 'Little Darling' is not as widely grown as it once was. But it will live on forever in its countless descendants, including almost all American-raised miniature roses that boast classic hybrid tea form. 'Little Darling' is a good rose and a great parent.

'MARGARET MERRIL' (HARkuly)
Harkness, England, 1978

As close to a perfect rose as you are likely to find, 'Margaret Merril' makes blush-white blooms in great profusion. These are classically formed and have an outstanding scent redolent of lemon and rose. The flowers usually appear singly or in small clusters, but because there are so many of them

Wonderfully fragrant and perfectly formed, the floribunda 'Margaret Merril' is as close to a perfect rose as you are likely to find.

Bred by the father of the modern miniature rose, Ralph Moore, the floribunda 'Playgirl' is a continuous bloomer.

'Margaret Merril' can equal the garden impact of a floribunda that makes big sprays. Unlike some of those roses, which throw all of their energy into a big burst of bloom, and then sit, exhausted, without flowers for a month or two, 'Margaret Merril' is almost always in bloom.

The plant grows to 4 feet in Ohio, making it taller than the typical floribunda. It associates very well with hybrid teas, its soft yet clear color brightening the reds around it and drawing out the mauves. 'Margaret Merril' is named for the "beauty advisor" for Oil of Olay, a fictitious advertising character along the lines of Amos Pettingill

or Mr. Clean. Subsequent to its introduction, three real-life Margaret Merrils have been discovered, and all report growing and enjoying their namesake rose.

'PLAYGIRL' (*MORPLAG*)
Moore, USA, 1986

This is one of the first floribundas to bloom each spring; only frost stops it in the fall. Hot pink with brilliant gold stamens, the single-petaled, slightly ruffled 'Playgirl' recycles its bloom with incredible speed. Florets usually appear in sprays of three to five; they make interesting cut flowers if taken just before opening.

Bred from 'Playboy', a remarkably healthy scarlet and gold floribunda that has also produced 'Playmate' and 'Playtime', 'Playgirl' has in turn been used to breed 'Playfair'. But 'Playgroup Rose' is, amazingly, completely unrelated.

'PURPLE TIGER' (JACPUR, 'IMPRESSIONIST')
Christensen, USA, 1992

Resulting from mutation, striped roses have traditionally appeared without warning, like lightning on the rose horizon. Finally, in the early 1970s, California rose breeder Ralph Moore captured lightning in a bottle. Moore successfully introduced stripes from the hybrid perpetual 'Ferdinand Pichard' into his family of miniature roses. It was now possible to hybridize striped roses instead of waiting for—or trying to induce—mutations (see also page 50).

It was only a matter of time before larger striped roses would be hybridized. Working at Armstrong Roses in the 1980s, Jack Christensen came up with numerous striped floribundas, including the one we now know as 'Purple Tiger'. Then disaster struck. While rose breeders of earlier generations found their work disrupted by world wars, in the 1980s Christensen faced an outbreak of corporate takeovers. Armstrong was passed from one giant corporation to another, and the striped floribundas got lost in the shuffle. Finally, what was left of Armstrong was purchased by the same Japan-based multinational corporation that also owns Bear Creek Nurseries and Jackson & Perkins. Mosaic virus infection had always been a problem at Armstrong, and to its great credit, Jackson & Perkins took the time to rid Armstrong stock of virus before introducing it. Even free of virus, 'Purple Tiger' is not a strong plant. However, it flowers freely, and nothing can match its bizarrely original blooms, which are purple and boldly striped and randomly flecked with

The amazing 'Purple Tiger' is one of the first striped floribundas to arise from deliberate hybridization rather than chance mutation.

white and mauve. Like snowflakes, no two are exactly alike, and 'Purple Tiger' never fails to attract attention. It is an ideal floribunda for growing in a tub on a patio or deck, where people can enjoy it up close.

'SEXY REXY' (MACREXY, 'HECKENZAUBER')
McGredy, New Zealand, 1984

Introduced to a frenzy of media attention in New Zealand, including bumper stickers asking "Have you Sexy Rexy in your rose bed?," this variety received a less enthusiastic welcome in England, where newspapers saw its name as just one more example of deteriorating standards and, perhaps, impudent antipodeans. Several British nurseries were slow to stock this rose, and one still catalogues it only under its code name of 'MACrexy'. American nurseries have had no such qualms, and

'Sexy Rexy' has enjoyed rapid acceptance in this country.

With or without a controversial name, it is one of the very best floribundas. Producing soft pink, many-petaled blooms in humongous sprays, 'Sexy Rexy' marks a return to the free-blooming ideals of the floribunda class. It flowers late in the spring and requires diligent deadheading for good repeat bloom. 'Sexy Rexy' is very winter hardy and rarely shows any sign of disease. One could only wish that it were fragrant or that it came in every color.

'SHOWBIZ' (TANWEIEKE, 'BERNARD DANEKE ROSE', 'INGRID WEIBULL')
Tantau, Germany, 1981

Not the run-of-the-mill northern European red floribunda, 'Showbiz' is enlivened by the subtlest of orange shadings in its scarlet blooms. These appear in tremendous trusses that stay fresh for a long time. The plant keeps a compact, rounded habit that makes it ideal for growing in a tub. It is also particularly attractive budded as a half-standard (or tree rose) at about 24 inches.

Floribunda 'Sexy Rexy' in its full bloom, with climber 'Altissimo' in the background.

The well-rounded floribunda 'Showbiz' is an excellent subject for pot or tub culture.

'STADT DEN HELDER' (INTERHEL)
Ilsink, The Netherlands, 1979

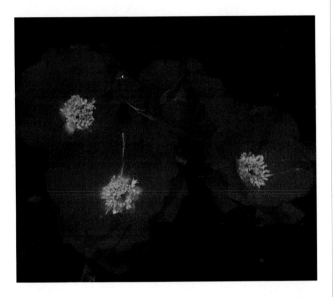

Rare among red floribundas, 'Stadt den Helder' enjoys excellent health and good weather resistance.

What are the problems with red floribundas? First, they make unwieldy trusses of bloom that cannot stand up to wind or rain. Second, they take a long time to repeat bloom. Finally, they are prone to mildew. 'Stadt den Helder' smashes all three stereotypes in a glorious display of color that holds its brilliant red sprays up against almost any weather, on a healthy plant that makes an excellent 5- to 6-foot hedge in the Midwest.

Dutch rose hybridizer Peter Ilsink started out by breeding conifers and other trees. His roses are all noted for their excellent health, and he has a sensibility about picking plants that look tidy even when they aren't blooming.

'SUMMER DREAM' (FRYMAXICOT)
Fryer, England, 1990

In the "And now for something completely different" department, 'Summer Dream' offers tight clusters of many-petaled pale apricot blooms on a short, stocky plant. The blooms make long-lasting cut flowers and have a pleasant scent reminiscent of raspberries.

Different Roses for Different Countries

In my work with Beverly Dobson in compiling and editing the *Combined Rose List*, I have occasion to see more rose catalogues than anyone else in the world (at least anyone other than Bev). I'm not sure whether you can tell anything about a country by the roses it likes, but you can certainly tell that different countries like different roses. I was surprised to find that Australian nurseries offer a much higher proportion of white and pastel roses than nurseries in the rest of the world. In America, it's red and red blend hybrid teas that are most abundantly offered. In France, it's apricot and orange hybrid teas. Italian nurseries offer an extraordinary proportion of blackish red roses. German rose catalogues feature page upon page of red floribundas.

The many-petaled 'Summer Dream' demonstrates the great diversity of bloom form found in contemporary floribundas.

'Sweet Vivien' is a floribunda especially well suited to California and the South.

'Summer Dream' goes about growing and blooming without any special demands and almost always attracts attention from garden visitors. Its petal-packed form is an excellent example of the universality of floribundas. This floribunda should not be confused with 'Summer Dream' (JACshe), an excellent free-blooming, apricot hybrid tea from Jackson & Perkins.

'SWEET VIVIEN'
Raffel, USA, 1961

Pretty as a picture every time, 'Sweet Vivien' must be one of the most photogenic roses ever bred. Semi-double, it is bright pink with a creamy yellow center and lively stamens.

'Sweet Vivien' makes wiry stems on a short, compact plant. While thriving in California and the South, it requires special protection to make it through rough midwestern winters. The father of this floribunda is often mistakenly reported to be the seminal China rose *R.* × *odorata*. In fact, 'Sweet Vivien' is a result of a cross between the floribunda 'Little Darling' × 'Odorata', a hybrid tea introduced in Holland in 1928.

I also recommend the following floribundas:

'Amber Queen'
(HARroony, 'Prinz Eugen von Savoyen'; Harkness, England, 1984)

This amber rose is wonderfully leafy, healthy and fragrant. It boasts perhaps the most perfect foliage ever bred to a rose. 'Amber Queen' makes modest sprays. An incredibly fertile rose, it is so eager to set hips that earnest deadheading is required to ensure prompt repeat bloom.

'Amberlight'
(LeGrice, England, 1961)

This is described by its creator as "Egyptian buff"; I think of this semi-double rose as a yellowish tan. This upright, somewhat wiry-looking plant makes impressive sprays that drip with honey fragrance.

'Betty Prior'
(Prior, England, 1935)

This pink, single-petaled rose has a "wild rose" appearance in its simple flowers and twiggy growth. Profuse, tough and extremely winter hardy, 'Betty Prior' will thrive with minimal care.

'Class Act'
(JACare, 'First Class', 'White Magic'; Warriner, USA, 1989)

This very good, white garden floribunda grows over several years to the size of a small shrub. Although some roses start out like gangbusters and go downhill from there, 'Class Act' does it right—starting slowly, perhaps, but building to excellence over several years.

'Escapade'
(Harkness, England, 1967)

This rose makes a big bush, throwing spray after wonderful-to-cut spray of bright lavender-pink blooms with white centers that are effectively single-petaled. The opening buds resemble butterflies perching on the bush. A lot of American rosarians found out about this superb floribunda by accident when a nursery somehow got budwood of it mixed up with 'Keepsake', a hybrid tea that exhibitors were eager to grow. Even though 'Escapade' was far from what they were expecting, I doubt if very many have discarded it. This is a rose that makes you smile. Floriferous, healthy and polar hardy, 'Escapade' is a rose unlike any other.

'First Edition'
(DELtep, 'Arnaud Delbard'; Delbard, France, 1976)

This variety produces outstanding sprays of salmon orange, hybrid tea–shaped blooms. It is a very good floribunda in all respects; 'Anisley Dickson', however, is a superior floribunda in this color range.

'French Lace'
(JAClace; Warriner, USA, 1982)

This rose produces large, perfectly formed, ivory blooms with subtle apricot tints. An elegant, appealing rose that is much more like a short hybrid tea than a floribunda, it requires winter protection north of Zone 7.

'Gene Boerner'
(Boerner, USA, 1969)

This old favorite is a great producer of medium pink, hybrid tea–shaped blooms to cut. Its growth is tall for a floribunda, and the plant is healthy but not very fragrant.

'Goldmarie'
(KORfalt; Kordes, Germany, 1984)

'Goldmarie' has the brightest yellow blooms I know in a rose. The glossy-leaved bush demonstrates no health or hardiness problems, and the blooms appear in modest but well-arranged sprays. A really happy rose that is almost always in bloom, this is the rose I've planted beside my back door.

'Greensleeves'
(HARlenten; Harkness, England, 1980)

Pink buds opening to green blooms, this remarkably novel plant grows upright, is somewhat coarse and will blackspot without protection. For best results, pick the buds when they are still pink and just beginning to unfurl. Taken at that stage, they will turn an extraordinary apple green indoors. Left outdoors, the green coloring is likely to be interrupted by weather spotting. Indoors or out, the semi-double blooms display stamens that age poorly. (This dead stamen effect has been described as "cigarette butts in a green ashtray.") Later attempts at a green floribunda have included 'Sheila MacQueen' (Harkness, 1988), a rose that begins as apricot and, with fully double petals, tastefully conceals its stamens. Unfortunately, it never turns quite as green as 'Greensleeves'. 'Peppermint Ice' (Bossom, England, 1991) is another semi-double. It begins a pale pinkish white and turns a pale green-yellow. While its stamens remain reasonably fresh, the startling color drama of 'Greensleeves' is still missing.

'H. C. Andersen'
('Hans Christian Andersen', 'America's Choice'; Poulsen, Denmark, 1986)

This bright, rich red rose stands apart from the crowded family of red floribundas by growing upright and supporting its large sprays of bloom—no matter how big they get or how much it rains. Many rosarians have found 'H. C. Andersen' to be a suitable replacement for the popular but over-planted old favorite 'Europeana'.

'Hannah Gordon'
(KORweiso, 'Raspberry Ice'; Kordes, Germany, 1983)

White with a deep pink edge, the blooms appear on a tall, leafy and thorny plant that can make an excellent hedge. The buds are disappointingly zinnialike, but quickly redeem themselves as spectacular fully open blooms. The flowers are good-sized, meaning that it does not take too many of them to make an impressive cluster.

'Iceberg'
(KORbin, 'Fée des Neiges', 'Schneewitchen'; Kordes, Germany, 1958)

This classic, white floribunda achieves shrublike proportions while still looking fresh and young. 'Iceberg' always seems to be sprouting new growth. Its informal blooms, which can be tinted pale pink in cool weather, appear in modest clusters all over the bush. This is one of the few floribundas suitable for use as a specimen shrub, that is, planted all by itself. It also makes an excellent standard (or tree) rose. Its one fault is a predisposition to blackspot. 'Iceberg' has been widely used as a parent and appears in the ancestry of some of

David Austin's finest English roses. A climbing form, introduced by the Cants nursery in England in 1968, it is a marvelous exception to the rule that climbing sports usually are not very good.

'Julie Cussons'
(FRYprincess; Fryer, England, 1988)

This produces eye-catching, bright orange, apricot and pink blooms on a healthy, free-blooming plant. The blooms have hybrid tea form and usually appear one to a stem. Julie Cussons, the person, is the granddaughter of Wendy Cussons, for whom a famous hybrid tea of the 1960s was named. The roses are not related.

'Lady of the Dawn'
(INTerlada; Ilsink, The Netherlands, 1984)

This rose's soft pink, semi-double blooms make large, airy sprays. Free-blooming and mildew resistant, 'Lady of the Dawn' has the vigor one would expect from a shrub and can be trained as a climber in mild climates. Classified and sold as a floribunda, it is a very good rose regardless of what you call it.

'Lavaglut'
(KORlech, 'Intrigue', 'Lavaglow'; Kordes, Germany, 1979)

The darkest red floribunda, this rose shows its nearly black blooms to good advantage against the shiny green foliage of a leafy, healthy bush. Best in dry weather (like many other red floribundas), 'Lavaglut' makes clusters so huge that they can't stand up to rain. This variety is sold in England as 'Intrigue', which has caused unnecessary confusion with a plum-colored Jackson & Perkins floribunda sold under the same name.

'Marina'
(RinaKOR; Kordes, Germany, 1974)

This rose came out of the European florist industry to win a AARS award in 1981. This prolific producer of small, long-stemmed, orange blooms makes nice bouquets.

'Matilda'
(MEIbeausai, 'Charles Aznavour', 'Pearl of Bedfordview', 'Seduction'; Meilland, France, 1988)

A great floribunda, this rose produces loads of incredibly long-lasting creamy white blooms with a pink border both singly and in attractive, perfectly proportioned clusters. The vase life of 'Matilda' as a cut flower has approached two weeks for me. It offers outstanding repeat bloom and no health problems. The good news for Charles Aznavour, the entertainer, is that he had one of the great roses of the 1980s named for him. The bad news is that nurseries in America, Australia and South Africa felt compelled to sell it under a more appealing name. The Americans and Australians did okay with 'Matilda' and 'Seduction', respectively. But 'Pearl of Bedfordview'?

'Nana Mouskouri'
(Dickson, N. Ireland, 1975)

A healthy grower that throws many sprays of well-formed, cream blooms, this rose would undoubtedly be more popular if there were not so many other excellent white floribundas.

'Natali'
(TANrotreili; Tantau, Germany, 1981)

These impeccable, medium pink, hybrid tea–form blooms fall just short of hybrid tea size. Not very floribundalike, this rose, however, is always eager to grow and usually great to cut. Its blooms may waterspot in cool, damp weather.

'Pleasure'
(JACpif; Warriner, USA, 1990)

If you don't want 'Sexy Rexy' in your garden, you can call it by its German synonym 'Heckenzauber'. However, if you really don't want 'Sexy Rexy' in your garden, you can plant 'Pleasure', the next best thing in profusely blooming pink floribundas. 'Pleasure' does not make the fantastically large sprays of 'Sexy Rexy', but it may offer speedier repeat bloom.

'Rosali 83'
(TANilasor; Tantau, Germany, 1983)

This is a shiny rose. Its foliage is so glossy you can almost see your reflection in it, and the apple blossom pink blooms just glisten. 'Rosali 81' blooms in well-proportioned sprays. While this rose is a great producer of basal breaks, its repeat bloom is not as strong as one would expect from established canes.

'Sheila's Perfume'
(HARsherry; Sheridan, England, 1985)

Essentially a small hybrid tea sold as a floribunda, this rose is notable for its upright, healthy growth (to 3½ feet in Ohio), good cutting stems and excellent fragrance. In roses, yellow and red combinations have a habit of ending up looking more like manila and rust, but these yellow blooms with a red border are an exceptionally clean combination that lasts quite well.

'Shocking Blue'
(KORblue; Kordes, Germany, 1985)

These blooms are bright mauve—not shocking and not blue—and boast an intense fragrance. Most arrive one to a stem, but you may also find some spectacular sprays if you plant this vigorous grower in full sun.

'Sun Flare'
(JACjem; Warriner, USA, 1983)

Disease-resistant but not blackspot-proof as reported elsewhere, this rose requires the same protection as any other modern floribunda. In return, it will display its perfectly formed, lemon yellow sprays all summer long. I like 'Sun Flare' better than the more widely grown 'Sunsprite' because it is a good source of cut flowers. 'Sun Flare''s distinctive fragrance has been compared to licorice and vermouth. It requires winter protection from Zone 5 northward. A climbing sport is marketed as 'Yellow Blaze'.

'Trumpeter'
(MACtrum; McGredy, New Zealand, 1977)

This short-growing, very tough and incredibly profuse rose is rarely out of its orange-red blooms from spring until frost. One of two floribundas Sam McGredy named for Louis Armstrong, 'Trumpeter' is an improvement over the first one, called 'Satchmo'.

The LeGrice nursery introduced a short, orange-red floribunda called 'Warrior' in 1977. It had the misfortune of having to compete with 'Trumpeter' and has now virtually disappeared from commerce. However, it is still a very good rose, and I recommend it.

HAND-PAINTED ROSES

When he was still working in Northern Ireland, Sam McGredy had the idea of using hybrids of *R. spinosissima* (the Scotch briar rose) to bring added winter hardiness to modern garden roses. What he eventually found was that the marbled coloring peculiar to *R. spinosissima* and its offspring could be captured, intensified and used to create a new family of roses that McGredy dubbed hand-painted.

Although it could be argued that they would most correctly be called dwarf shrubs, the first hand-painted roses were introduced as floribundas, and in that class hand-painting has reached its fullest potential. Hand-painted hybrid teas and miniatures have followed, with less obvious success, and today it is not uncommon to see hand-painted ancestry in roses that are not themselves hand-painted (for example, the AARS-winning shrub 'Bonica' [MEIdomonac]).

Hand-painted roses feature pale streaks and markings emanating from a central eye to agitate a bolder background. The effect, at its best, is random and beautiful. White-on-carmine is the most common combination, although the full range of reds, pinks, oranges and mauves appear as background colors, with markings in silver and finally yellow in addition to white. In all hand-painted roses, the color effect is most striking and dramatic in cool weather.

'CHAMPAGNE COCKTAIL' (HORFLASH)
Horner, England, 1983

'Champagne Cocktail' is the rose that brought yellow shadings into the family of hand-painted roses.

This is the rose that finally brought yellow into the hand-painted family, and it took an amateur to do it. 'Champagne Cocktail' is a flat yellow, speckled and marked in carmine pink. This variety is usually a muddled mess in summer's heat, but puts out a stunning display in the spring and fall. Like other hand-painted roses, it stands up well to winter but is particularly prone to blackspot.

The bush is exceptionally prickly, and does not benefit from severe pruning. 'Champagne Cocktail' can be a useful cut flower, but it is essential to take the flowers young, when the outer petals are just beginning to loosen.

'MAESTRO' (MACKINJU)
McGredy, New Zealand, 1981

'Maestro' was the first hand-painted hybrid tea, and it is still the most spectacular. It is well worth growing despite being somewhat stingy with its blooms.

Introduced in 1981, 'Maestro' was the first hand-painted hybrid tea. It is still the best.

'Maestro' has a habit very similar to many of the hand-painted floribundas and owes its classification as a hybrid tea solely to its fully double blooms. These show white sprinkles on a turkey red background in bud stage, but are most dramatic when fully open. Other hand-painted hybrid teas have been introduced, but none is nearly so sensational.

'PICASSO' (MACPIC)
McGredy, N. Ireland, 1971

Raised in Ulster by Sam McGredy IV, 'Picasso' was the original hand-painted rose.

This was the first hand-painted rose. Growing in fits and starts and clothed in unusually tatty foliage, it was soon superseded by better varieties. However, the unique white markings on its carmine red blooms pointed the way to something completely new in roses.

'Picasso' and its immediate successor, 'Old Master', gave hope that we would have a whole series of hand-painted roses unified by names from the art world. But it was not to be, and later introductions have been named for alcoholic beverages, wives of department store magnates and villages in Switzerland.

'PRISCILLA BURTON' (MACRAT)
McGredy, N. Ireland, 1978

Although highly variable in color, 'Priscilla Burton' can be the most spectacular hand-painted rose.

'Priscilla Burton' exemplifies everything that is beautiful about hand-painted roses, and everything that can be frustrating, too. At its best, there can be no rose more stunning than 'Priscilla Burton'. The blooms are semi-double (ten petals), in brilliant shades of carmine ranging almost to purple, and streaked and marked in white. Unfortunately, this rose is not consistent, and even when the season (autumn) and the temperature (cool) are right, the bloom can sometimes go wrong, ending up a disappointing dirty pink.

The bush is lanky and thorny and occasionally sends up gross, semi-climbing, nonflowering shoots. While quite resistant to mildew, 'Priscilla Burton' requires diligent protection from blackspot.

'REGENSBERG' (MACYOUMIS, 'BUFFALO BILL', 'YOUNG MISTRESS')
McGredy, New Zealand, 1979

The best all-around hand-painted rose, flowering well throughout the growing season and maintaining a short, compact habit that never gets out of hand, this is the only hand-painted floribunda that is really satisfactory when grown in a large pot or tub or budded as a standard (or tree) rose. Almost alone among the hand-painted roses, 'Regensberg' also demonstrates good resistance to blackspot.

The blooms are a combination of lilac pink and white. While not flamboyant, they are consistently pleasing. This rose's habit and health might have pointed the way to more landscape-friendly hand-painted roses, but its offspring have been disappointing. This rose was Sam McGredy's first success after emigrating to New Zealand.

Almost all hand-painted roses can be fun to grow, but some are more fun than others:

'Inner Wheel'
(FRYjasso; Fryer, England, 1984)

This variety produces scads of chiffon pink blooms with white markings all summer long. An outstanding hand-painted rose, 'Inner Wheel' has an excellent bushy habit and notable resistance to blackspot. Indeed, this is the first hand-painted rose to prove completely blackspot resistant in my garden. The blooms appear continuously in modest clusters above reddish green foliage. While this rose is not the most dramatic color combination found in the hand-painted roses, it is the healthiest plant. This is a seriously underrated rose from Cheshire's Gareth Fryer, perhaps the world's most underrated rose breeder.

'Little Artist'
(MACmanly, 'Top Gear'; McGredy, New Zealand, 1982)

This rose produces semi-double, creamy white blooms that are surrounded by and marked in red. The best hand-painted miniature, this vigorous grower can be marred by ugly, fast-fading stamens.

'Stretch Johnson'
(MACfirwal, 'Rock 'n Roll', 'Tango'; McGredy, New Zealand, 1988)

Despite an overabundance of orange roses, orange and white is still an under-used color combination in the rose world, and this introduction exploits the combination very successfully. It has nicely spaced clusters of bloom in the spring; however, nonproductive climbinglike canes appear in the fall. This rose has super foliage and is one of the healthiest hand-painted roses.

'Wapiti'
(MEInagre, 'Laurence Olivier', 'Striking'; Meilland, France, 1988)

With scarlet red blooms and silver and white markings, this rose is a return to the basic color scheme of the original hand-painted roses. However, this plant is much bushier and more attractive in the garden than the originals. Unfortunately, blackspot can still be a problem.

Perhaps the best of all the hand-painted roses, the low-growing 'Regensberg' combines continuity of bloom with excellent disease resistance.

Polyanthas

Polyanthas get no respect. If rosarians think about them at all, it is likely to be as some sort of primitive version of the floribunda. We may remember their tiny flowers and their mildew, but not the way that they bloom with abandon, smothering themselves with flowers each July while most other roses are either finished for the year or resting for the summer. Floribundas have supplanted the polyanthas, without offering any replacement for the breezy, ethereal effect they provide in the garden. While miniature roses also produce small flowers, few miniature roses come anywhere near to producing the amount of bloom one can expect from a polyantha.

Once, as a novice rose exhibitor, I took a nice spray of 'Fairy Changeling' to a rose show some fifty miles away only to be told by the show chairman that there was no place for it in his show schedule. "We're trying to get away from that sort of thing," he explained. Nurseries got away from polyanthas in the 1950s, and what was a flood of introductions in the early decades of this century has now slowed to what could only be described as a drip. With no fan clubs dedicating to saving them, no newsletters chronicling the rediscovery of lost polyanthas, no nurseries specializing in them and only one or two hybridizers still working with them, the future for polyanthas may not be bright. However, many remain worthwhile.

It is typical for polyanthas to bloom late in the spring in massive sprays. Genetically, polyanthas—descendants of *R. multiflora*—are one of the least diluted of all rose classes. While floribundas and hybrid teas, for example, are essentially interchangeable and classified only by subjective opinion (a hybrid tea is a hybrid tea only because someone, usually its introducer, thinks it is one), polyanthas are one horticultural classification that usually can be identified botanically: Polyanthas almost always have fringed stipules. Most polyanthas can be expected to grow between 2 and 2 ½ feet tall in the North.

'LULLABY'
Shepherd, USA, 1953

This rose produces small, pompom-type flowers that are in some ways reminiscent of the classic white damask 'Mme. Hardy'. However, these have shades of coral and pale pink that vary with the weather near the center of the sterile bloom. With

The polyantha 'Lullaby' is in some respects a dwarf version of the classic damask rose 'Mme. Hardy'.

Bred by Ann Bentall in 1932, the semi-spreading polyantha 'The Fairy' is the most widely catalogued rose in the world today.

good bloom throughout the season and excellent mildew resistance for a polyantha, 'Lullaby' benefits from light shade.

Roy Shepherd, of Medina, Ohio, took early retirement from the iron business to devote his life to roses. He created several remarkable roses, including 'Lullaby' and the shrub 'Golden Wings', and wrote *The History of the Rose*, the best rose book ever written by an American.

'THE FAIRY'
Bentall, England, 1932

'The Fairy' is hardy to the point of indestructibility. Even if you can grow no other rose, you can grow 'The Fairy'. It's a semi-spreader, with soft pink blooms against tiny green leaves, and looks particularly appealing planted around water. Blooming does not begin until July in the North, but continues right up to frost.

For many years this rose was incorrectly and somewhat improbably recorded as a mutation: a

---

Ann Bentall

How often has Ann Bentall been left off of lists of the world's great rose hybridizers? Has she been omitted because she was a woman? Or because she was a blue-collar hybridizer during a time in England when a lot of rose breeding was done by members of the leisured classes, often with sinecures in the Church? Or simply because she raised only a few roses? But what roses!

There are currently about eight thousand different roses in commerce. Of all of these, two varieties are catalogued more than any others by the rose nurseries of the world. One is 'The Fairy', and the other is the hybrid musk 'Ballerina'. Both were raised by Ann Bentall.

---

rambler that spontaneously got small and remontant and different in several other ways. Recent research by British gardener and author Hazel LeRougetel has demonstrated conclusively that 'The Fairy' was hybridized by Ann Bentall from a cross between the polyantha 'Paul Crampel' and the rambler 'Lady Gay'.

'ZENAITTA'
Jerabek, USA, 1991

A superb landscaping rose, it produces huge trusses of bright red blooms straight through the summer. 'Zenaitta' is rarely, if ever, out of bloom and demonstrates excellent disease resistance. The sprays of this variety are so gigantic that you will likely find withered blooms and unopened buds in the same cluster. This is a problem for rose exhibitors to contend with, but it only ensures a steady supply of color for everyone else.

Although 'Zenaitta' is registered with the American Rose Society, its parentage has never been recorded. Its raiser believes that it might be the result of a cross between 'The Fairy' × 'Starina'.

I also endorse the following polyanthas:

'Cécile Brünner'
('Mignon'; Ducher, France, 1881)

Famous as "The Sweetheart Rose," 'Cécile Brünner' produces tiny, light pink blooms of perfect hybrid tea quality on a short, sparsely foliaged plant. It may not have many leaves, but what leaves it has are healthy. A cross between a polyantha and a tea rose, 'Cécile Brünner' is sometimes classified as a China.

'Fairy Changeling'
(HARnumerous; Harkness, England, 1981)

The best of a series of "Fairy" polyanthas bred from 'The Fairy' by Jack Harkness in the late 1970s and early 1980s, this is a much more compact plant than its parent. While not as profuse, it makes sprays that are much more balanced in appearance than 'The Fairy' does. This rose is true

One of the few polyanthas bred in the 1990s, 'Zenaitta' is a superb landscaping rose.

to its name, and it is not uncommon to see florets ranging from blush to deep pink at the same time in the same spray.

'Marie-Jeanne'
(Turbat, France, 1913)

My favorite of the old polyanthas, this blush-colored rose produces sprays of more than one hundred florets each in early summer. It grows in a bushy habit to about 2½ feet; being thornless, it is excellent for planting along walkways. 'Marie-Jeanne' has only a little scent and needs protection from powdery mildew.

'Yesterday'
('Tapis d'Orient'; Harkness, England, 1974)

This rose produces semi-double, lilac pink blooms with prominent golden stamens. It makes a more substantial bush than most polyanthas, growing to 4 feet in my garden and enjoying good health every inch of the way. Sprays of 'Yesterday' provide exactly the airy effect that we most closely associate with polyanthas as well as modest but pleasing fragrance.

Miniatures

How to use miniatures? The 1964 Annual of England's National Rose Society suggests, "A little garden in a secluded corner, all laid out to scale in front of a doll's house...." The miniatures of this era, with names such as 'Tommy Tucker' and 'Midget', were more dwarf than most of the varieties we call miniatures today and could very possibly have given an acceptable performance in a miniaturized landscape. Most were heavily petaled and lacked the classic hybrid tea form and full range of rose colors available in contemporary miniatures.

Some miniature roses.

I am not as big a fan of miniature roses as some people, but I am relieved that miniatures have achieved their present popularity in the United States with no accompanying increase in the appearance of dolls' houses in American backyards. No class of roses can achieve complete success if it cannot harmonize with other roses and the garden as a whole. In its transformation into a tiny version of the hybrid tea, the miniature rose appears to have achieved this harmony.

Apart from completely miniaturized gardens, miniature roses are effective as low-growing borders and in pots and tubs. The shorter miniatures can be useful in window boxes. I do not recommend miniatures for edging beds of large roses — when this is done, no one notices the minis. Miniatures are often recommended for use in rock gardens. However, miniature roses have cultural requirements that are quite different from those of most alpine plants, and care must be taken to provide them with ample water and a humus-rich soil. Miniature roses require less fertilizing than large roses (less food in real terms, not just proportionally less after accounting for their smaller size). Too much food will result in miniature plants that grow to monster proportion while producing very little bloom. In general, the average miniature rose grows 12 to 18 inches high and is more winter hardy than the average hybrid tea.

Since the early 1980s, more than half of all roses introduced in the United States each year have been miniatures. There have been numerous explanations for this phenomenon. First, miniatures are easy to grow. Second, Americans have smaller gardens than they used to. Finally, because of their suitability to pot culture, people whose physical limitations prevent them from growing larger roses can grow miniature roses.

All of these reasons may be perfectly valid. But the real push for miniature rose introductions has come from rose exhibitors. After the American Rose Society elevated the miniature rose to the

The miniature groundcover 'Robin Redbreast' is a real landscaping asset.

The miniature 'Autumn Fire' is suitable for use in a hanging basket.

same plateau on which it has placed the hybrid tea, exhibitors who did not previously pay much attention to miniatures sprang into action. The ARS offers a "Queen of Show" award for both hybrid teas and miniatures (but floribundas and climbers, for example, are not eligible). There are a dozen miniature rose nurseries operating in the United States today who do almost no business outside of the universe of rose society members and exhibitors.

A check of your neighborhood garden center will show a much smaller percentage of miniature rose introductions, something more in line with miniatures' actual popularity with real people, before their value was inflated by an eligibility to win awards at rose shows. If you look beyond the almost endless parade of cookie-cutter miniaturized hybrid teas, you will find an exciting diversity in the miniature class, including some of the best single-petaled roses and the most recent moss roses (for more on moss roses, see page 119).

Miniatures are the one class of roses in which most of the noteworthy recent introductions have been made in America. Virtually all miniatures sold in the United States are grown from cuttings on their own roots.

'AUTUMN FIRE' (MORANIUM)
Moore, USA, 1982

Spreading but not unwieldy, this is one of the very best miniatures for growing in a hanging basket. The orange-red blooms appear in impressive sprays on stems that are usually both crooked and short.

In setting up a hanging basket, it is essential to balance the advantage of a lightweight, soil-less mixture such as ProMix, which will let you lift the basket up and down with ease, and the water-retaining qualities of traditional potting soil, which will require less frequent attention. Many gardeners are used to growing hanging plants on porches and other shady places; this will not do for roses, which must have sun.

I'm not sure that scent would be a big advantage in a hanging basket. Would it come wafting down, or would it be lost on those below? In this case, though, it doesn't really matter. Like most miniatures, 'Autumn Fire' is scentless.

'CHURCH MOUSE' (FOUMOU)
Jacobs, USA, 1989

This really fun rose has oversize blooms on a slightly straggly plant. The form is urn-shaped and somewhat loose. 'Church Mouse' is always a surprise, with rich tanish brown blooms fading to grayish brown. There is no other miniature like it. In very cool weather 'Church Mouse' will show some purple in its blooms. In the genetics of roses there is just a fine line between mauve and russet, and 'Church Mouse' was bred from two mauve roses, the floribunda 'Angel Face' and the miniature 'Plum Duffy'.

'Church Mouse' has a sweet fragrance. Unfortunately, it is not hardy in the North. Winter has defied my best protection strategies for this rose, so I have defied winter and ordered a new 'Church Mouse' each year, treating it as an annual.

'Church Mouse' is a novel mini, worth growing despite its winter tenderness.

The raiser of 'Church Mouse', California's Betty Jacobs, is a specialist in unusual colors. Among other introductions, she is also responsible for the vigorously growing, solemnly colored, white-gray 'Winter Magic'.

'OLYMPIC GOLD'
Nelson Jolly, 1983, USA

Clear yellow with a pink edge in cool weather, this perfectly shaped bloom is much too large to be an ideal miniature but far too small to be a hybrid tea. The plant grows tall too, beyond the bounds of what we could call a patio rose. The foliage of 'Olympic Gold' is not an asset, being dull and grossly oversized (one exhibitor of miniature roses disparages its leaflets as "elephant ears").

This top exhibition rose is an example of a perfect bloom on a less-than-perfect plant. But, if men ever start wearing rose buds in their buttonholes again, 'Olympic Gold' will be an excellent candidate.

'ORANGE SUNBLAZE' (MEIJIKATAR, 'ORANGE MEILLANDINA')
Meilland, France, 1981

A step back from slavish adherence to hybrid tea form, 'Orange Sunblaze' is one of the best of a whole family of Sunblaze and Meillandina roses, which were raised in France and noted for excellent health and outstanding bloom production.

You may find Sunblaze and Meillandina roses sold in the floral department of your neighborhood

Although large for a miniature, 'Olympic Gold' produces perfectly formed blooms.

Growing Miniature Roses Indoors

Miniature roses can be grown indoors, but they require abundant artificial light to bloom well and high levels of humidity to thrive. If insects or disease gain a foothold, it is almost impossible to bring them under control indoors. Roses are many things, but they are not houseplants.

However, if you want to try to grow them indoors anyway, carefully controlled conditions must be provided. Most houses can supply a temperature in the ideal 60 to 72° F. range, but contemporary centrally heated homes lack the humidity miniature roses require. To create this, you will need to grow your minis over trays of moist gravel or pebbles. Unless you have a conservatory or sun room, indoor miniatures need to grow under fluorescent lights to set buds and bloom. Special "grow lights" are not necessary; ordinary fluorescent lights work perfectly well. You will need a minimum of two 40-watt tubes to produce any amount of bloom; four tubes will give you much better results.

supermarket. If you bring one home, please do not hold it hostage on your kitchen windowsill. Set free outdoors, the Sunblazes will be certain to reward you. Indoors, absent the most extraordinary care, they will almost certainly die. For outdoor use, there is a climbing sport of 'Orange Sunblaze', which is unusually free-blooming and good. (The photo on page 166 shows 'Orange Sunblaze' grown as a standard [tree] rose.)

'ROBIN REDBREAST' (INTerrob)
Ilsink, The Netherlands, 1984

This miniature groundcover is unsurpassed for its landscaping versatility. A mature plant will produce thousands of flowers each summer. 'Robin Redbreast' grows wider than it does tall and can be kept quite low by cutting off any spiky shoots as they appear. If you leave the spiky shoots, 'Robin Redbreast' will eventually be weighted down by huge clusters of bloom, producing a cascading effect. The rather thorny plant enjoys excellent health.

At their freshest, blooms of 'Robin Redbreast' have been very successful in the rose show category calling for single-petaled miniatures. Other exhibitors often ask me for cuttings of this unpatented rose, which I am happy to supply. It's always fun to check back in a year or two, when they discover that 'Robin Redbreast' is a miniature that grows 1 foot high by 4 feet wide!

Although bred from 'Eyepaint', a hand-painted floribunda-shrub, 'Robin Redbreast' shows no hand-painted markings itself. Hand-painted characteristics will, however, show up in its seedlings. This variety is very easy to breed and will also give a fascinating range of offspring from self-pollinated hips.

'SCARLET MOSS' (MORcarlet)
Moore, USA, 1988

Not just an outstanding miniature mossed rose, this is the reddest of any moss rose. The

In addition to being an outstanding miniature mossed rose, 'Scarlet Moss' is the reddest of any moss rose.

The simple elegance of the miniature 'Simon Robinson' is appealing even to those who do not usually appreciate single-petaled roses.

combination of a crystal-clear red color, mossy buds and brilliant golden stamens in the heart of the seven- to ten-petaled blooms is unforgettable. Not a rose to tuck away somewhere, this is definitely a variety to plant where garden visitors can appreciate it in its entirety.

Young plants appreciate being babied until they're off to a good start. After that, 'Scarlet Moss' is trouble-free. Hardy enough in Ohio, it may prove tender in the far North.

'SIMON ROBINSON' (TRObwich)
Robinson, Channel Islands, 1982

An impossible miniature, this rose is reported to have been bred from the species rose *R. wichuraiana* and 'New Penny', a miniature. *R. wichuraiana* blooms only once a year and, according to the Mendelian principles of genetics, could produce repeat blooming offspring only after an intervening generation. It is possible that

'Simon Robinson' was bred from a first-generation self-seedling of *R. wichuraiana* that was nearly identical to its parent. Another possibility is that the breeder may have had his records confused.

In any case, 'Simon Robinson' supplies excellent repeat bloom and, in its leaflets, displays several wichuraiana characteristics, including a predisposition to the fungus disease anthracnose. Apart from this, the plant is trouble-free and especially winter hardy.

The clear pink, single-petaled blooms have attractive, wavy stamens. They appear in large,

perfectly arranged sprays all summer long. 'Simon Robinson' looks dainty, grows tough and has a surprisingly good scent for a single-petaled miniature. Even people who think they don't like single-petaled roses usually like 'Simon Robinson'.

'SNOW BRIDE'
Betty Jolly, USA, 1983

The best white miniature, it is outstanding among miniatures for being in perfect proportion. Habit,

The exquisite 'Snow Bride' makes a perfectly proportioned miniature plant.

foliage, stems and blooms all combine to make one unified and outstanding whole. The form is exhibition (meaning high-centered and hybrid tea–like), and 'Snow Bride' makes exceptional sprays as well as one-bloom-per-stem specimens.

Occasionally, you may find a plant of 'Snow Bride' that doesn't want to grow. It's worthwhile to try again because this rose is one of the most rewarding of all miniatures.

'STARINA' (MEIGABI, MEIGALI)
Meilland, France, 1965

Introduced in 1965, 'Starina' was the first miniature to exhibit truly high-centered hybrid tea form.

The landmark miniature on the road to duplicating hybrid tea form, 'Starina' remains the most widely sold miniature rose in the world today. It has shown little deterioration after three decades, and new buds never fail to look fresh and beautiful. 'Starina' has a slightly spreading growth habit and makes a good miniature standard (or tree) rose.

'STARS 'N' STRIPES'
Moore, USA, 1975

The first hybridized striped rose to be introduced, 'Stars 'n' Stripes' was bred from 'Ferdinand Pichard', a striped (i.e., mutated) hybrid perpetual. A vigorous, leggy grower, 'Stars 'n' Stripes' needs to be planted behind something bushy to avoid a straggly garden appearance. Some lanky roses can be made to bush out by cutting back their growing tips, thus forcing the growth of lateral canes. Unfortunately, 'Stars 'n' Stripes' is not one of them. No matter how you treat it, it will be spindly. Additionally, its flowers do not last very long.

The habit (and flower life) of 'Stars 'n' Stripes' has been improved in later striped miniatures introduced by Ralph Moore, Sam McGredy and others. However, none completely matches the bizarre, exuberant effect of 'Stars 'n' Stripes'.

'WINSOME' (SAVAWIN)
Saville, USA, 1985

This bushy plant, covered with bloom, is larger than usual for a miniature, and 'Winsome' could easily be considered a patio rose. But because its breeder does not call it one, I won't either.

While a mature hybrid tea plant grown from a cutting will produce the same size blooms as a bud-grafted plant, this is not the case with miniatures. All of the varieties introduced from Europe as patio roses are bud-grafted onto a rootstock, and I am certain that more than a few of them

Despite its unwieldy, leggy growth, 'Stars 'n' Stripes' is worth growing for its bizarre, exuberant blooms.

Larger than the average miniature, the fragrant 'Winsome' is a free bloomer that is a good producer of cut flowers.

would shrink to miniature proportions if they weren't. Conversely, 'Winsome' and almost all other American-raised miniatures are sold on their own roots, and many of them could be expected to gain greater size—in both the bush and the bloom—as budded plants. Its mauve-pink blooms are excellent to cut and have unusually good fragrance for a miniature.

There is a glut of miniature rose varieties in the market-place, with an astounding number of inconsequential varieties. The following are noteworthy exceptions:

'Acey Deucy'
(SAVathree; Saville, USA, 1982)

This rose is a profuse producer of hybrid tea–shaped blooms in a shade of red deeper than it is bright. Its spreading habit makes it an ideal miniature standard (or tree) rose.

'Adam's Smile'
(SAVarend, SAVasmile; Saville, USA, 1991)

This compact, disease-resistant plant is excellent for low-growing garden color. The deep pink blooms with a creamy yellow base have good, consistent form.

'Angel Darling'
(Moore, USA, 1976)

An otherwise dull, dusty mauve color is brought to life by spectacular golden stamens. The ten-petaled blooms have a good fragrance.

'Anytime'
(McGredy, New Zealand, 1973)

This salmon orange, semi-double variety has a unique purple eye at the center of its petals, making it both an interesting novelty and an intriguing parent for hybridizers trying to reverse the usual pattern of rose eyes being only white or yellow. Purple in the center of a salmon rose is interesting. A purple eye in the center of a white or yellow rose would be spectacular. Unfortunately, the plant's habit is rangy and uneven.

'Beauty Secret'
(Moore, USA, 1965)

This old favorite produces profuse, cardinal red blooms on a compact 10-inch plant. Extremely rapid repeat bloom makes this one of the very best miniatures for edging or growing in a pot. It has good fragrance for a mini. While high-centered, the double blooms lack true hybrid tea form, displaying pointed petal ends that are characteristic of many early miniatures.

'Black Jade'
(BENblack; Benardella, USA, 1985)

This has the blackest red of all modern roses; flower arrangers have found that this rose gets even blacker when stored in the refrigerator.

'Chelsea Belle'
(TALchelsea; P. & K. Taylor, USA, 1991)

These perfectly formed, red and white blend blooms are large (for a miniature) and last a good long time. The Taylors named this one after their dog, and it may well be the best rose ever named after a dog.

'Debut'
(MEIbarke, 'Douce Symphonie', 'Sweet Symphony'; Mouchette, France, 1988)

This semi-double, red with ivory rose is always in bloom. Its low, slightly spreading habit suggests its use for edging walkways or as a miniature standard (or tree) rose. Its color is most vivid in cool weather.

'Dee Bennett'
(SAVadee; Saville, USA, 1989)

This vibrant orange rose lacks truly classic hybrid tea form, but is an easy grower that makes good sprays. Named in memory of the Australian-American breeder of 'Jean Kenneally', 'Irresistible' and other excellent miniatures.

'Dreamglo'
(E. D. Williams, 1978, USA)

This is a reliable producer of both sprays and one-bloom-per-stem exhibition specimens. Fifteen years is a long run for a miniature rose, but this is still the best red and white miniature with hybrid tea form.

'Fairhope'
(TALfairhope; P. & K. Taylor, USA, 1989)

This rose produces absolutely flawless, light yellow blooms on a plant that, ideally, would bloom more than it does.

'Fancy Pants'
(KINfancy; King, USA, 1987)

Fantastic, ever-changing color, hybrid tea form and good bloom frequency have made 'Fancy Pants' a favorite with gardeners and exhibitors alike. The blooms are deep pink on a golden base and edged in red.

'Figurine'
(BENfig; Benardella, USA, 1992)

This tall-growing plant has long, pointed, classically shaped buds that hold their shape longer than this variety's low petal count would lead you to expect. One plant can produce an incredible harvest of porcelain pink cut flowers.

'Irresistible'
(TINresist; Bennett, USA, 1990)

White, with a greenish cast that occasionally envelops the opening bloom, and heavily petaled, this rose is eager to grow and bloom with a minimum of special attention. However, one must be especially careful not to overfeed this rose.

'Jean Kenneally'
(TINeally; Bennett, USA, 1986)

The best exhibition miniature, this light apricot rose is also an excellent, rather tall-growing (to 3 feet in Ohio) garden rose.

'June Laver'
(LAVjune; Laver, Canada, 1988)

This variety is the most intensely deep yellow miniature introduced to date. Its blooms are hybrid tea form, and its foliage is small in proportion to the bloom. It is difficult to coax cutting stems from this variety. 'June Laver' is somewhat tender despite its Canadian heritage.

'Lavender Jade'
(BENalav; Benardella, USA, 1987)

This rose has lovely pastel lavender blooms with a cream reverse, great fragrance, steady production and dependable form. The bloom can be large for the size of the plant, which does need watching for disease.

'Linville'
(Bridges, USA, 1990)

This miniature features large, perfectly formed, very light pink (fading to white in hot weather) blooms. Unlike other large-bloomed miniatures, however, 'Linville' has leaves that look as if they were made for the plant and not left over from some floribunda or hybrid tea.

'Magic Carrousel'
(MORroussel; Moore, USA, 1972)

The classic, creamy white blooms with red picotee edge are stunning as an open bloom. This plant is vigorous and nearly shrublike.

'Minnie Pearl'
(SAVahowdy; Saville, USA, 1982)

A pink and coral blend, this all-around excellent miniature is recommended for garden, cut flowers and exhibition.

'Mother's Love'
(TINlove; Bennett, USA, 1989)

The barely double, pastel pink blooms with a soft yellow base are flawless but ephemeral. This rose is unusual among miniatures because it requires extra winter protection.

'My Sunshine'
(TINshine; Bennett, USA, 1986)

This miniature is not a heavy bloomer, and it almost never makes sprays, so its garden value is limited. However, individual medium yellow blooms are absolutely perfect and surprisingly long-lasting for a single-petaled rose.

'Near You'
(SEAnear; McCann, Ireland, 1991)

These lightest yellow blooms have hybrid tea form; the plant grows tall. With this variety, the great hybrid tea 'Elina' puts its genetic footprint into the miniature bed.

'Party Girl'
(Saville, USA, 1981)

This yellow-apricot blend rose is an especially useful hybrid tea–formed miniature because it produces excellent miniature sprays. 'Party Girl' has become an important parent of miniature roses.

'Pierrine'
(MICpie; Michael Williams, USA, 1988)

This rose's rich coral-pink, hybrid tea–form blooms are excellent for both long-lasting cut flowers and overall garden display.

'Pink Petticoat'
(Strawn, USA, 1980)

This strong growing miniature approaches shrub proportions. Its cream blooms edged with coral-pink are plentiful and almost always in sprays. The plant is extremely winter hardy.

'Rainbow's End'
(SAValife; Saville, USA, 1986)

This rose is yellow with an edge that is more or less red depending on the amount of sun it receives. The healthy, well-proportioned plant is very easy to grow. Craft alert: 'Rainbow's End' is one of the best miniature roses to dry and use in everlasting arrangements.

'Raindrops'
(SAVarain; Saville, USA, 1989)

Most lavender miniatures are decidedly on the large side. If you want a small mauve rose with good form, this is it. Its only major fault is slow repeat bloom.

'Red Beauty'
(Ernest Williams, USA, 1981)

Although its performance can vary from garden to garden, this is still the best red miniature with hybrid tea form.

'Rose Gilardi'
(MORose; Moore, USA, 1987)

This low-growing, bushy, free-blooming plant is fun to grow. It has cerise red blooms with purplish pink stripes on a pale pink background. This mini is mossed too, but not nearly as heavily as it is striped.

'Ruby Pendant'
(Strawn, USA, 1979)

A fast growing miniature that displays lots of red-purple, hybrid tea–shaped blooms on a tall, healthy bush. It produces an intriguing proportion of thornless canes.

PATIO ROSES

It has taken the rose world a while to settle on a name for those varieties that are too big to be miniatures and too little to be floribundas. Numerous names were suggested, bandied about and even trademarked. Various nurseries promoted maxi-minis, mini-floras, sweethearts, short-n-sweet roses and, perhaps least creatively of all, big miniatures. The World Federation of Rose Societies, composed of people who do not actually have to sell roses for a living, decided these plants should be called dwarf cluster-flowered roses. But this was for the most part ignored, and in the end, these in-between varieties have achieved commercial success as patio roses.

'Emily Louise' is a steady bloomer and a sight to see when its blooms are fresh.

The long, quilled petals in the blooms of 'Cosette' are quite unlike those of any other modern rose.

Describing how the rose is to be used, rather than how the rose looks (e.g., miniature, large-flowered climber) or where it comes from (e.g., Bourbon, China), can be limiting because patios are only one of any number of places where compact, profuse-blooming roses can be effective. But deck roses? Balcony roses? Tub roses? Patio rose is as good a name as any other.

Patio roses should be expected to bloom constantly or nearly so. They should maintain a compact habit that is attractive in a container. And they should have blooms in proportion to the rest of the plant, a requirement that rules out low-growing floribundas with oversized blooms, such as 'Strawberry Ice' (a fine rose, but not a patio rose). Tall miniatures with tiny blooms are also disqualified and should not be seen outside of the climbing miniature class (if they should be seen at all).

Because patio gardeners may have limited garden space, they might also lack the usual arsenal of garden supplies. Thus, patio roses should thrive without extraordinary care and show excellent disease resistance.

'COSETTE' (HARQUILLYPOND, 'BLUE CARPET')
Harkness, England, 1983

A true novelty, its blooms are a mass of long, quilled petals, quite unlike those of any other modern rose. The plant—a healthy and hardy grower—maintains an excellent low habit. This is the kind of rose that can always be expected to display a bloom or two; after its first spring flush, however, it will not display a lot of bloom at any one time.

'Cosette' blooms a dusky medium pink, with no trace of lavender (let alone blue); nurseries that advertise it as 'Blue Carpet' are misleading their customers. This rose looks as though it should be fragrant. Unfortunately, it is not.

'EMILY LOUISE' (HARWILLA)
Harkness, England, 1990

This leafy plant is shrubby, hardy and always compact. Simple five-petaled blooms open as rich yellow, fading to what rose catalogues call "fawn yellow" and what you may call dirty brown. It is a sight to see when its blooms are fresh, which will be monthly throughout the growing season. 'Emily Louise' is mildew-proof but may need occasional protection from blackspot.

'HAKUUN'
Poulsen, Denmark, 1962

One of the toughest of all roses, 'Hakuun' is untroubled by insects, disease or northern winters.

This remarkable little rose produces exhibition stems on a dwarf plant and gigantic trusses of perfectly proportioned ivory-yellow buds that open to cream-colored florets. Selectively disbudding florets that are about to open can cause the spray to grow bigger and bigger. 'Hakuun' is untroubled by insects, disease or northern winters.

This variety was raised more than thirty years ago in Denmark from an unnamed seedling that had been rejected for introduction in California, given a Japanese name (*Hakuun* means "white cloud") and for many years sold only in England. 'Hakuun' is a survivor. Before the emergence of patio roses, 'Hakuun' was something of a rose without a classification. It remains a seriously underrated variety that deserves to be more widely grown.

'LAURA ASHLEY' (CHEWARLA)
Warner, England, 1991

Registered with the authorities as a climbing miniature, this is a rose that sprawls but does not climb. It can perhaps best be thought of as a cascading patio rose. 'Laura Ashley' is ideal for

A cascading patio rose, the delicate-looking 'Laura Ashley' is ideal for growing in a tub or large basket.

growing in a tub or large basket and is one of the first varieties I think of when people ask what rose they should plant in their rock garden.

Tiny, purplish blooms almost swamp the small, dense, polyanthalike foliage. And bright golden stamens really do swamp the tiny, single-petaled blooms. The rosarian will not find shorter petals anywhere. Described as remontant in England, this fascinating introduction has offered no repeat bloom in my garden.

I also recommend the following patio roses:

'Anna Ford'
(HARpiccolo; Harkness, England, 1980)

This deep orange, semi-double rose was the winner of the Royal National Rose Society's highest award in 1981, thus launching patio roses as a commercial attraction. It was slow to catch on in the United States, but has now become quite popular with collectors in the South and is spreading into the North (where it will require winter protection). It was named for a BBC television news anchor.

'Boy Crazy'
(DICrevival; Dickson, N. Ireland, 1992)

This deep pink patio rose grows well to 15 inches, has a neat habit and smothers itself in bloom at

regular intervals. In addition to its suitability for growing in a tub, this is one of the very best patio roses for planting as a more permanent replacement for annual bedding plants.

'Brass Ring'
(DICgrow, 'Peek a Boo'; Dickson, N. Ireland, 1981)

A proto-patio rose, this apricot rose was introduced before the class had been adequately defined. It is bushy, profuse and slightly sprawling. 'Brass Ring' is among the best of the class for budding as a half-standard.

'Cider Cup'
(DICladida; Dickson, N. Ireland, 1988)

With perfect hybrid tea–formed, deep apricot blooms on a healthy, branching plant, this rose is good in a tub and great to cut.

'Conservation'
(COCdimple; Cocker, Scotland, 1988)

The semi-double, orange blooms with a pale yellow eye are long lasting and nonfading. I only wish the bush produced more of them.

'Dorola'
('Benson & Hedges Special', 'Parkay'; McGredy, New Zealand, 1983)

Healthier than a cigarette, more yellow than margarine, this rose makes up for what it lacks in superior form and perfect habit in vigor and profusion.

'Majorette'
(MEIpiess; Meilland, France, 1986)

This rose produces rich, currant red blooms with underlying silver tones. This is the one patio rose I grow that is never out of bloom from Memorial Day to killing frost. Watch for blackspot in wet weather and pretty petal markings in cool weather, both evidence of 'Majorette''s hand-painted heritage.

'Minilights'
(DICmoppet, 'Goldfächer'; Dickson, N. Ireland, 1988)

'Minilights' produces primrose yellow, semi-double flowers on a procumbent plant. Its soothing color in the landscape makes it a particularly outstanding companion for the very purple 'Laura Ashley'. Repeat bloom is very good.

'Pandemonium'
(MACpandem, 'Claire Rayner'; McGredy, New Zealand, 1988)

This novelty rose has fantastically colored yellow blooms with orange-red stripes on a well-rounded, bushy plant. It grows to 30 inches, taller than most patio roses. 'Pandemonium' is a very modern-looking rose that can overpower its neighbors if allowed.

'Rosabell'
(COCceleste; Cocker, Scotland, 1988)

The classically quartered, rose pink blooms appear just like little versions of David Austin's English roses on a well-mannered dwarf plant. Unfortunately, reports of its fragrance have been greatly exaggerated.

'Sweet Chariot'
(MORchari, 'Insolite'; Moore, USA, 1984)

This purple rose has many of the characteristics of a polyantha and a low, spreading habit that has prompted some nurseries to merchandise it as a groundcover (but growing only 2½ feet wide, it won't cover much ground). I have found 'Sweet Chariot' outstandingly effective planted in an old hollowed-out tree stump, where it puts on spectacular spring and autumn blooms, with scattered flowers in between. It has superior fragrance and is extraordinarily hardy.

'Tear Drop'
(DIComo; Dickson, N. Ireland, 1989)

This remarkably floriferous rose has single-petaled, pure white blooms that appear singly and in attractive small sprays. The petals are "self-cleaning," which means that they do not last very long.

CLIMBING MINIATURES

Excuse me if I don't quite grasp the concept of climbing miniatures. Miniature roses are ideal for all of the spaces where larger roses won't fit and all of the applications where larger roses won't work (such as edging beds of perennials and growing in small containers). But miniature climbers are plants that reach the same dimensions as a hybrid tea, or sometimes a shrub, except they have tiny blooms. What's the point? If a gardener can spare the space for a full-size plant, why wouldn't he want full-size blooms? I would. But just in case you don't, I can recommend three climbing miniatures.

'JEANNE LAJOIE'
Sima, USA, 1975

Far and away the best climbing miniature, this rose is unequaled for its sheer profusion of bloom. The flowers are medium pink, and by themselves not particularly interesting. But hundreds—or sometimes thousands—of them blooming at one

The profuse 'Jeane Lajoie' is far and away the best climbing miniature.

time make a magnificent sight. 'Jeanne Lajoie' was named for a little girl in Texas, namesake of a Roman Catholic missionary to the native inhabitants of Quebec and not, as erroneously reported elsewhere, for the most notorious prostitute in all of Paris.

'NOZOMI'
Onodera, Japan, 1968

This dainty-looking plant with tiny foliage is as eager to trail along the ground as it is to climb. It has one long annual bloom of single-petaled, pearl white flowers. Its abundant, trailing growth makes it one of the most spectacular standard (or tree) roses. *Nozomi* means "hope" in Japanese.

'WARM WELCOME' (CHEWIZZ)
Warner, England, 1991

In a rich, autumnal orange color, 'Warm Welcome' is more compact in habit and sends out fewer meandering blind shoots than some other recent climbing miniatures. Hybrid tea–shaped buds appear in widely spaced sprays and open quickly. 'Warm Welcome' has shown excellent resistance to disease in my garden.

The rap against climbing roses of all kinds is that they either climb or repeat bloom. Like 'Jeanne Lajoie', 'Warm Welcome' is a miniature climber that does both.

Climbers

To look at all of the pictures of antique cottage gardens and Victorian vistas festooned with climbing roses, one would think climbers have been with us forever. But the appearance of climbing garden roses is a relatively recent phenomenon, dating to the 1890s and early 1900s.

There is nothing that specifically makes a rose a climbing rose, except that it is taller than other roses. While any tall rose can be called a climber, most new hybrid climbers are descended in one way or another from *Rosa multiflora* and *R. wichuraiana*, rambunctious species roses discovered by Europeans in Asia in the second half of the nineteenth century. Their initial, once-flowering offspring were called ramblers; the climbers being introduced today are technically classified as large-flowered climbers.

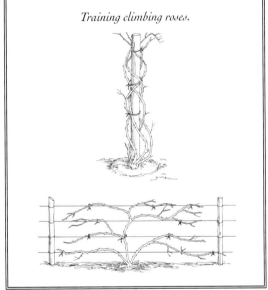

Training climbing roses.

Ramblers were as stylish in the early 1900s as miniature roses are now, outselling all other classes of roses in the years prior to World War I and forming the skeleton of many of the large American estate gardens that flourished in the first third of this century. Since then they have evolved from rampageous plants bearing immense clusters of tiny flowers in midsummer to a diverse family of roses that is, as a whole, more restrained in growth and larger in flower than the ramblers our grandparents knew. Sheer multitude of bloom has been exchanged for continuity, but I am not sure this has been an entirely fair bargain. Today's repeat-blooming climbers, while offering some flowers each month, cannot in a year match the total number of blooms a rambler can produce in its one month of glory. It is true that ramblers, with their nonremontant, space-invading ways, nod a little to the past. But no rose of the present can produce so much bloom all at once.

Space considerations limit the use of ramblers in today's city and suburban gardens. However, there are numerous large-flowered climbers suitable for growing in even the smallest garden, where they make economical use of vertical space, adding height to what could otherwise be a flat situation.

Lacking tendrils or other means of attachment, climbing roses do not actually climb, of course, unless the gardener trains them to. The shorter varieties work especially well entwined around pillars, and most climbers can be guided very easily through latticework. It is, however, essential to remember that every pliant young shoot you train will someday have to be removed as a large and probably thorny piece of dead growth. Like all other roses, climbers will bloom best when their canes are allowed to grow laterally. Thus, to encourage the most bloom possible, employ a strategy of training climbers up, and then out, rather than just straight up.

Many bush roses look good when planted in clusters or groups of three or more. Climbers can work very well in tandem (one on each side of an arch or one on either side of a window, for example), but clumping them is hardly necessary, even if a nursery is offering you a discount to buy three at a time. Because climbers range in height from 6 feet to more than 40 feet, there can be no firm rule about how far apart to plant them. Care should be taken to not put them too close together or to install bush roses in their shadow, or what will become their shadow. Even the best climbers will take three years to become established, and, in many cases, several more years to hit a stride of peak performance.

In addition to all of the climbers that have been raised on purpose, there are also a great many climbing sports, mutations of bush varieties (such as 'Climbing Peace' and 'Climbing Queen Elizabeth'). With very few exceptions these mutations offer little more than the famous name of the bush from which they sprang, with the addition of vegetative growth and the subtraction of flowers; many are notoriously poor garden performers.

'ALTISSIMO' (DELMUR)
Delbard-Chabert, France, 1966

This spectacular, single-petaled rose displays seven petals instead of the usual five in its 5- to 6-inch blooms. Remarkable for its constant bloom, the brilliant blood red 'Altissimo' grows with more vigor than grace, stiffly to about 7 feet in the Midwest. While it can look rather awkward all by itself, this climber is easy to wrap around a pillar or fan out along a short fence.

'Altissimo' is very healthy and hardy but not very fragrant. The name *Altissimo* is the subject of a trademark dispute in Canada, so Canadians, and the many Americans who buy their roses by mail from Canadian nurseries, may have to look for this variety under its code name of DELmur or the bastardized name "Altus."

'BUTTERSCOTCH' (JACTAN)
Warriner, USA, 1986

'Butterscotch', the only climber of its color, is a novelty rose that is also easy to grow.

This rose is a novelty climber. Its blooms spread across the entire mustard spectrum from yellow to gray to brown. I do not like it at the Poupon stage, but at its best it is an even shade of creamy light brown, the color of Stadium mustard. Unlike many curiosity roses, 'Butterscotch' is also a good grower. Its loosely formed blooms appear continuously throughout the summer, but the plant may not be hardy enough to survive a severe winter without extra protection.

'Butterscotch' was a favorite of its creator, the late Jackson & Perkins hybridizer William Warriner. After creating it in the early 1970s, he waited a dozen years to see it introduced. Warriner's corporate bosses did not believe a climber of this color could be a commercial success. Alas, they were right. Reference to the code name JACtan is necessary to distinguish this rose from an old hybrid tea called 'Butterscotch'.

'CHEVY CHASE'
Hansen, USA, 1939

Producing showers of bright crimson flowers for a month every summer, this is the one red rambler that will not mildew. One of innumerable twigs on the rose family tree, 'Chevy Chase' comes from a breeding line completely different from other ramblers, a cross between *Rosa soulieana* and the polyantha 'Eblouissant'. *R. soulieana* is a rampant, white species rose native to western China.

You may find 'Chevy Chase' more eager to spread out than to grow upright. In the far North, it is not as hardy as most of the wichuraiana and multiflora ramblers. But for anyone wishing to grow a healthy red rambler without spraying fungicides, 'Chevy Chase' is the answer.

Rosarians cannot say that nothing good ever came out of Washington, D.C. 'Chevy Chase' was bred in our nation's capital and named for one of its Maryland suburbs.

healthy foliage. It's a limber grower and quite winter hardy. It blooms in spring for a long period, but rarely offers repeat bloom in my garden. The 3- to 4-inch blooms are quite large for a rambler. There is a pungent fragrance.

Sometimes erroneously called "City of New York," or supposed to have been named after York, England, this variety commemorates York, Pennsylvania, a town near the headquarters of its American introducer, Conard-Pyle Roses.

Only thirteen roses have won the American Rose Society's Gold Medal Certificate for Outstanding Performance over a five-year period. 'City of York' is the only climber among them. Fifty years after its introduction, it remains the showiest white climber.

'CITY OF YORK' (DIREKTÖR BENSCHOP)
Tantau, Germany, 1945

As clean a climber as you will find, 'City of York' features striking semi-double flowers of creamy white against waxy green and exceptionally

'COMPASSION' (BELLE DE LONDRES)
Harkness, England, 1973

This is the best climber—large-flowered or small—that I have ever grown. One could not ask for more from a climbing rose.

'City of York' combines clean, healthy growth with showy white blooms.

Michael Horvath's 'Doubloons', growing in the rose garden named in his memory at the Ohio Agricultural Research and Development Center, Wooster, Ohio.

'Compassion' is the ideal climbing rose for contemporary gardens.

First, 'Compassion' climbs. It doesn't wait a few years to find its way; it doesn't sulk. It climbs (to 9 feet in Zone 6). Second, it blooms. From the first year onward, 'Compassion' produces a wealth of bloom throughout the summer. Third, it is a great producer of basal breaks. Because it constantly renews itself, 'Compassion' is one climber certain to never look spindly. Fourth, the large apricot-pink blooms are lovely against the dark green foliage and excellent to cut as well. Fifth, it is very healthy. And, finally, 'Compassion' is wonderfully fragrant.

There is an equally vigorous and fragrant pale yellow sport called 'Highfield'. Apart from the color change, its petals also appear to be slightly less elegantly formed.

'DOUBLOONS'
Horvath, USA, 1934

This is one of a series of climbers bred from the native American species *Rosa setigera* by Michael Horvath in Mentor, Ohio. Even though Mentor is not a particularly swashbuckling kind of place, Horvath gave his setigera hybrids pirate names. The others include 'Captain Kidd', 'Jean Lafitte' and 'Long John Silver'.

Golden yellow buds open to buff-colored, essentially formless flowers on a beautifully foliaged plant. 'Doubloons' produces one good,

long annual bloom and is hardier than most yellow climbers. I have heard reports of repeat bloom in the Pacific Northwest, but I have never seen it in Ohio. 'Doubloons' itself is now sold only by a few specialist nurseries, but its genes can be found in the ancestry of many yellow floribundas.

'NEW DAWN'
Dreer, USA, 1930

A sport of the climber 'Dr. W. van Fleet', this rose was originally sold as "Everblooming Dr. W. van Fleet." That it is not, but 'New Dawn' does produce a nice crop of blooms in the fall, after a massive show in the spring, and maintains the notably attractive foliage and all of the health and toughness of its parent. 'Dr. W. van Fleet' and 'New Dawn' are the two climbing roses you are most likely to find surviving on abandoned farmsteads in the Midwest. While 'Dr. W. van Fleet' typically grows to 20 feet in Ohio, 'New Dawn' grows to no more than about 12 feet. Like its parent's, 'New Dawn's blossoms are a pretty shade of apple blossom pink that fades to cream as they open, releasing a sweet scent.

'New Dawn' frames the front door at the residence of Dr. Charles and Mary Beutel in Rootstown, Ohio.

'PAUL'S LEMON PILLAR'
Paul, England, 1915

This strong grower produces large, bold, hybrid tea–shaped white blooms in abundance each June. The blooms achieve a nearly perfect, high-centered form when they are half-open and hold it for a good long time.

This climber is often described as lemon in color (and *Modern Roses*, the official stud book of roses published by the American Rose Society, goes so far as to describe the blooms as "pale sulfur-yellow"). In my garden, 'Paul's Lemon Pillar' is strictly white, and I side with those authorities who say that the name refers to this climber's scent, which is indeed lemony.

Introduced at a time when most climbers had small blooms, 'Paul's Lemon Pillar' was classified as a climbing hybrid tea even though it is not a mutation of a bush variety. This climber has the fault of flowering only on old wood while not being reliably winter hardy. Although a severe winter can rob you of a year of bloom, the plant is almost always strong enough to be back in full bloom the following year. It helps to plant 'Paul's Lemon Pillar' in a sheltered position. Mine has thrived up against, and wound its way through, a hedge of arbor vitae.

'Paul's Lemon Pillar', named for its scent rather than its color, was one of the first large-flowered climbers.

Rose Patents

Legislation providing for plant patents took effect in the United States in 1930, and 'New Dawn' was the first plant in the world to be so protected. In this country, plant patents protect a variety for seventeen years; during this period the rose cannot be propagated without payment of a royalty to the patent holder. This prohibition extends to the backyard gardener producing plants for his own enjoyment as well as the nurseryman propagating plants for resale. (Royalties currently range from about $.50 for most patented miniature roses to $1.50 for a AARS-winning hybrid tea. Some specialty roses, such as David Austin's English roses, may command an even greater royalty.)

In the era before rose varieties could be patented, a nurserymen had only two or three years to profit from a new introduction—nothing longer than the period of time it would take competing nurseries to secure budwood and propagate enough plants to sell. As we enter the era of genetic manipulation, biotechnology firms are seeking to have plant patent coverage extended beyond protection for one individual variety to include protection for specific genes.

In this way, the creator of the first blue rose, for example, could maintain control over any offspring hybridized from the prototypical, genetically engineered rose containing the blue gene.

But in protecting the investment of the genetic manipulator, how much diversity will be lost by discouraging the efforts of anyone else to improve upon his creation? This may be a particularly apt question when we consider that the firms making the greatest strides in genetic orchestration have no previous experience with roses. They may know what's blue, for example, without knowing anything else about roses.

A patent is no guarantee of quality, and patented roses are not automatically superior to nonpatented ones. To be patented, a rose needs only to be different from any other rose, not necessarily better. A patent indicates nothing more than that a nurseryman thinks he has developed a valuable, salable rose and has spent the time and money to give it legal protection. Many outstanding European roses enter American commerce without being patented; on the other hand, many patented American roses have turned out to be disappointments.

'PIERRE DE RONSARD' (MEIVIOLIN, 'EDEN ROSE '88')
Meilland, France, 1987

Here is a climber worth waiting for. It may not bloom until its second or even third year, and for a year or two after that may produce bloom only at the tips of its canes, which can grow to 12 feet in Ohio. After that, buds break out all over and smother 'Pierre de Ronsard' in bloom all summer long.

Healthy and hardy, 'Pierre de Ronsard' is cream blended with light pink, with large blooms perfectly cupped in the old garden rose style. Were it not for its modern-looking glossy leaves and lack

The classically formed 'Pierre de Ronsard' may be slow to start, but it is a climber worth waiting for.

of scent, this one could be an appropriate climbing companion to the Austin English roses.

In the sixteenth century, Pierre de Ronsard led the movement to develop French as a literary language. He is remembered as France's greatest patriotic poet.

'PIÑATA'
Suzuki, Japan, 1978

Yellow shaded with orange and red, 'Piñata' produces giant sprays of bloom and earns its garden keep with riot after riot of color. It does not grow as tall as some would want a climber to, reaching only 6 feet in the Midwest. A very tidy grower, it

is suitable for guiding around a modest pillar or as a free-standing specimen.

'Piñata' was one of the first Japanese roses to achieve success in the United States. Japan's climate is very similar to much of America's, and a rose that does well in one country should also do well in the other. Curiously, 'Piñata' has never been commercially introduced in its native land.

'WICHMOSS'
Barbier, France, 1911

For seventy-seven years, until Ralph Moore introduced 'Crested Sweetheart' in 1988, 'Wichmoss' was the only mossed climbing rose. As one might

The well-mannered 'Piñata' is a climber suitable for even the smallest garden.

deduce from the name, it resulted from a cross between *Rosa wichuraiana* and a moss rose ('Salet'). Its long, pointed buds show off the moss to good advantage. The small, blush, semi-double flowers appear in clusters of up to fifteen in midsummer; there is no repeat bloom. Like many older climbers, this one needs watching for powdery mildew.

Not the best behaved garden inhabitant, 'Wichmoss' wants to grow all over the place. Rosarians like me who want something different have made room for it. 'Crested Sweetheart' features deep pink blooms that are individually more spectacular than those on 'Wichmoss'. Unfortunately, it is shy with its bloom and does not produce very much of a show.

I have also grown and can recommend the following climbers and ramblers. All are repeat-blooming unless otherwise noted:

'America'
(JACclam; Warriner, USA, 1976)

Its coral-orange flowers of hybrid tea form often appear in spectacular sprays and have excellent repeat bloom. The plant is reluctant to climb in the North, where it can sometimes be mistaken for a floribunda. This rose has a pleasing fragrance, much like a milder version of the overpowering scent of its ancestor, 'Fragrant Cloud'.

'Aviateur Blériot'
(Fauque, France, 1910)

This wichuraiana rambler is noted for the refined form of its individual, apricot-yellow blooms. These fade to cream and appear in typically large wichuraiana clusters. It is nonrecurrent and grows somewhat modestly to 10 feet in Ohio. In 1909, Louis Blériot became the first aviator to cross the English channel.

'Clair Matin'
(MEImont; Meilland, France, 1960)

This climber produces symmetrical sprays of rather small, semi-double, sweetly fragrant, pale pink blooms with coral shadings. The dark green, leathery foliage enjoys excellent health. It grows to

For many years the sprawling 'Wichmoss' was the only mossed climbing rose. It remains the most profuse.

8 feet in Ohio and, for landscaping purposes, may be thought of as a large, free-standing shrub rather than as a climber.

'Dorothy Perkins'
(Jackson & Perkins, USA, 1901)

This quintessential rose pink rambler is outstandingly effective budded as a tall, weeping standard. It has one long annual bloom. Like most ramblers, 'Dorothy Perkins' is prone to mildew. (The German breeder Hetzel introduced a mildew-resistant form called 'Super Dorothy' in 1986.)

'Dublin Bay'
(MACdub; McGredy, Ireland, 1975)

This is a slow-growing climber that has never exceeded 7 feet in my garden. It produces clusters of small, hybrid tea–like, blood red flowers all season long and is valuable for its excellent health and ability to open its blooms even in cool, damp weather.

'Elegance'
(Brownell, USA, 1937)

One of the allegedly "sub-zero" roses bred by the Brownells of Rhode Island, 'Elegance' is notable not for its winter hardiness, which is unreliable north of Zone 6, but for its incredible profusion of perfectly formed hybrid tea-shaped (and -sized), pale yellow flowers. You may see a thousand blooms in June, but there is no repeat.

'Excelsa'
(Walsh, USA, 1909)

This cherry red version of 'Dorothy Perkins' grows rampageously to more than 20 feet. A once-bloomer in Ohio, it is reputed to offer modest autumn bloom in milder climates.

'Freisinger Morgenröte'
(KORmarter; Kordes, Germany, 1988)

This rose's forceful, coppery orange color with pink and yellow highlights requires considerate landscape placement. 'Freisinger Morgenröte' grows to 12 feet in Zone 6, producing gigantic sprays of blooms that boast rudimentary hybrid tea form. This is an excellent repeater that is healthy and incredibly hardy. It has everything a climber needs except for fragrance.

'Handel'
(MACha; McGredy, N. Ireland, 1965)

A traditional favorite, this is a great climber in a sheltered position, but it can look spindly after a severe winter. Although it may still be difficult to find, I believe that the super-hardy, larger-flowered 'Harlekin' (Kordes, Germany, 1986) represents an improvement over 'Handel' in the same color: cream edged with bright pink.

'Phyllis Bide'
(Bide, England, 1923)

This rose produces masses of fluffy, soft yellow with light pink flowers on a dainty-looking but vigorous plant. It grows to 8 feet in Ohio. 'Phyllis Bide' has good fragrance and outstanding repeat bloom. For many years this was the one reliable repeat-blooming rambler. It has recently been reclassified as a climbing polyantha.

'Pink Perpétué'
(Gregory, England, 1965)

A child of 'New Dawn', this rose is noteworthy for its ability to produce a great number of rose pink blooms while staying within bounds. Although it is perfectly hardy, it grows only 6 to 7 feet in Zone 6.

'Rhonda'
(Lissemore, USA, 1968)

This rose produces a lot of roughly hybrid tea–formed blooms in a boring, medium pink color. It is easy to grow in any climate.

'Rosarium Uetersen'
(KORtersen; Kordes, Germany, 1977)

This is the best climber I have found for growing up a wall. The fragrant, deep coral-pink blooms have approximately 142 petals, arranged in the rosette fashion of an old garden rose. 'Rosarium Uetersen' is both healthy and hardy.

'Royal Sunset'
(Morey, USA, 1960)

Most apricot climbers have a sparse, leggy growth habit, but 'Royal Sunset' is nice and bushy. It does, however, require generous winter protection north of Zone 7.

'Santana'
(TANklesant; Tantau, Germany, 1984)

Impervious to winter, this rose produces an impressive display of large, 20-petaled, rich red blooms against lush, glossy green foliage. It offers outstanding repeat bloom.

'Silver Moon'
(van Fleet, USA, 1910)

With 7 to 10 petals and about 10 to 15 small petaloids, the effect of this rose is that of a single-petaled rose. It makes very large blooms for a

---

Climbing on Walls

West walls are often too windy, and north walls seldom offer enough light, but climbers can be very effective when trained up a wall facing south or east. Because the soil near a foundation is often very dry, plant at least eighteen inches away from the wall and set the roots at an angle so that they will grow away from the wall and toward moister soil.

rambler, and the impact of stark white blooms against rich green foliage is startling. 'Silver Moon' is advertised as a rose that can cover a barn. That may be optimistic, but growing to about 15 feet it could definitely cover a shed. And it's fantastic on a fence. Expect mildew but not repeat bloom.

'Summer Wine'
(KORizont; Kordes, Germany, 1985)

This rose produces flat pink, five-petaled blooms with striking red filaments and golden stamens. Rather like a larger-flowered, climbing version of 'Dainty Bess', 'Summer Wine' has the added bonus of being fully outfitted with attractive foliage. It also has the fragrance of sweet apples.

'Swan Lake'
('Schwanensee'; McGredy, N. Ireland, 1968)

The best white climber for cut flower production, this rose can be prone to blackspot, which it is vigorous enough to overcome.

'Veilchenblau'
(Schmidt, Germany, 1909)

This rambler produces semi-double, magenta-purple blooms that open to violet streaked with white and fade to a bluish gray. Its growth is smooth and practically thornless. 'Veilchenblau' is happy to grow in semi-shade. The blooms are non-recurrent. It may sound worse, but *Veilchenblau* simply means "violet blue" in German.

Species Roses
(and a Few Near-Species)

In species roses we see the rose as it is found in nature, before intervention by man. These are roses made for forests, hillsides and meadows, but all can be grown and enjoyed in gardens. Most species roses require more room than we are used to providing for garden roses, but they demand less care.

It is often stated that species roses are, as a group, exceptionally winter hardy. This is coincidence masquerading as fact, the truth being that a species rose will be winter hardy for the place where it is native and, thus, in similar environments. Species roses are found naturally throughout the northern hemisphere, and those native to the icy Canadian North, such as *R. acicularis*, are inherently more winter hardy than those, such as *R. gigantea*, that grow wild in the frost-free regions of Burma. It is an anomaly of evolution that there are no roses native to the southern hemisphere.

Species roses are identified by the letter *R.* (an abbreviation for *Rosa*, the genus) followed by the individual species name. According to botanical convention, species names (such as *R. gallica*) appear in italics; the names of cultivated varieties, or cultivars (such as 'Double Delight'), do not. A species rose can best be defined as a rose that sets self-pollinated hips and will breed true from seed. If you sow seeds from a self-pollinated hip of any modern or old garden rose, you may get a bewildering variety of seedlings or many very similar ones. What you will never get, however, is an exact duplicate of the parent. With species roses you will, and for this reason they are the only roses that you can order from a seedsman as well as from a nurseryman.

In the five-petaled species roses are the building blocks for everything that roses have become over the centuries, and everything they can yet be. Of some 200 distinct species, fewer than a dozen have been hybridized extensively. The genes of some, such as *R. chinensis*, *R. multiflora* and *R. wichuraiana*, have been thoroughly integrated into the modern garden rose. The genetic possibilities of dozens of other species roses have yet to be seriously explored by the creators of new roses.

When I wrote in a magazine article that species roses are, in a way, a link with our ancestors who lived in caves, I got an indignant letter from a reader who wanted me to know that none of her ancestors ever lived in caves. Maybe so. But, wherever men were living when they first fell in love with roses, we can be certain that it was the simple, single-petaled species rose that caught their eye.

'AUSTRIAN COPPER' (*R. FOETIDA BICOLOR*)
Cultivated in Europe before 1590

In species roses we see today's genetically complex rose reduced to its most elemental components. Some components are naturally better than others; in 'Austrian Copper' we find both striking coppery orange color and a predisposition to blackspot.

This rose can be a spindly grower and is definitely a magnet for blackspot. For this reason it is best planted off by itself, perhaps in an undeveloped area of the garden. So isolated, it cannot draw disease to your other roses and may in time develop into an acceptable bush. If it does, you will

'Austrian Copper' revealing its origin. It is not unusual for one or more branches of 'Austrian Copper' to revert to the yellow blooms of R. foetida, *from which 'Austrian Copper' is a mutation.*

be well rewarded each spring. Unlike most other roses in this section, 'Austrian Copper' appreciates rich soil. It is not reliably hardy north of Zone 6 and is not a satisfactory garden rose in the Deep South.

This is a mutation from *R. foetida*, a mysterious rose that may not technically be a true species but is in any case the ancestor of all modern yellow roses. *Foetida* means "stinking," a reference to the pungent fragrance, which Bev Dobson has more kindly, and accurately, described as reminiscent of boiled linseed oil.

'HIGHDOWNENSIS'
Stern, England, 1928

One generation away from being a species rose, this rose possesses all of the best characteristics of the ideal "wild" rose. Its one annual flowering is extravagant; the single-petaled, light red blooms are pleasing in their simple elegance and are followed by distinctive, attractive rose hips. Rose hips come in many forms and textures and ripen to several autumn shades. Those on 'Highdownensis' happen to be bottled-shaped and bristly, finishing

Thriving in a variety of climates, R. hugonis *is the most adaptable of the yellow species roses.*

A generation away from being a species rose, 'Highdownensis' possesses all of the best characteristics of an ideal "wild" rose.

a brilliant red. The bush is clothed throughout the summer in healthy, somewhat dainty blue-green foliage. 'Highdownensis' needs room, growing eventually to 12 feet and spreading almost as wide.

Sir Frederick Stern raised 'Highdownensis' from *R. moyesii* and named it after Highdown, his garden. In America, it has gotten mixed up with 'Geranium', another *R. moyesii* seedling; if you order 'Geranium' from an American nursery you are likely to receive 'Highdownensis' instead.

R. HUGONIS ('FATHER HUGO'S ROSE', 'GOLDEN ROSE OF CHINA')
Discovered in China, 1899

This is one of several ferny-foliaged, early blooming, yellow species and near-species roses. While its blooms are not as elegant as some of the others, *R. hugonis* is probably the yellow species rose best suited for American conditions. It is disease free and winter hardy in Ohio, growing 5 feet tall and almost as wide. It was found in China by the Rev. Hugh Scallan, who lent this rose its botanical name. "Hugh" went into Latin as *hugonis*, and was taken out again by nurserymen as "Hugo."

R. PALUSTRIS ('THE SWAMP ROSE')
Discovered in the American colonies, 1726

This rose is native to North America from Nova Scotia west to Minnesota and south to Florida. While its papery pink flowers are rather ordinary, this species is remarkable for growing in wet, swampy soil. Where other roses die of wet feet,

R. palustris *is the only rose to thrive in wet, swampy soil.*

R. palustris thrives, and I have often wondered if this remarkable characteristic would make *R. palustris* valuable as an understock.

R. palustris makes big thickets of growth, which come into bloom after most other rose species. I remember watching big patches of it in bloom near the shores of Lake Erie each July and enjoying its sweet scent, long before I knew its name or that roses were not supposed to grow in marshes.

Its habitat alone should make *R. palustris* easy to identify. However, like all other species roses native to North America, it is armed with straight prickles. European and Asian species roses and all hybridized roses have prickles that are at least slightly curved. Knowing this makes it easy for amateur American plant explorers to distinguish a genuine native species from an escaped under-stock, such as *R. canina* or *R. multiflora*, or a hybridized rose.

R. PERSICA HYBRIDS
Developed in England by Jack Harkness, 1970s and 1980s

R. persica is more properly known as *Hulthemia persica*, the only species in the Hulthemia genus. Botanical authorities consider Hulthemia to be a sort of primitive version of the rose; it demon-strates its primal nature in its simple leaves (that is, leaves that are not split up into three or more leaflets) and lack of stipules. What *Hulthemia persica* has that roses don't offer is a bright red eye at the center of its yellow bloom. This makes for a spectacular contrast, which has been presented to the discerning rosarian in the form of four hulthemia/rose hybrids introduced by Jack Harkness.

Native to Iran, *Hulthemia persica* is a desert plant that is very difficult to grow in a garden sit-uation. It sends its roots to exceptional depths, but cannot abide an abundance of water. While in its rose hybrids we find much greater adaptability, a definite preference for dry conditions remains. In my experience, the *R. persica* hybrids are also unusually prone to phytotoxic reactions when exposed to modern garden chemicals, particularly fungicides. They are not reliably hardy in the North and should be grown in tubs (where water supplies can also be more closely regulated). All *R. persica* hybrids bloom in the spring, with no repeat bloom.

- 'Euphrates' (1986) has salmon pink, single-petaled blooms with a deep pink patch at the center. Although the eye is deep pink instead of red, the contrast with the salmon blooms is extremely effective, and this is the most striking of the three *R. persica* hybrids I have been able to grow.
- 'Nigel Hawthorne' (1989) resulted from a cross between *R. persica* and a hybrid rugosa and is the most vigorous and easy to grow of the hulthemia hybrids. It also has the largest flowers. The single-petaled blooms are a lighter shade of salmon pink than 'Euphrates' and pale quickly. Their eye-patch is a deep purplish red.
- 'Tigris' (1985) has yellow blooms with a red eye, like the original *R. persica* colors. Unfortunately, much of the drama of the single-petaled original is lost in the confusion of the many-petaled blooms of 'Tigris'. Its low, bushy growth makes 'Tigris' suitable for rock garden culture.

- 'Xerxes' (1989) is a single-petaled, yellow rose with a red eye. Unfortunately, my plant died over its first winter. Like all nonremontant roses, newly planted hulthemia hybrids do not bloom until their second year, so I never got to see 'Xerxes' bloom. It is no longer in commerce, which may mean that others had problems with it too.

'ST. JOHN'S ROSE' (R. × RICHARDII, R. SANCTA)
Known in the West since ca. 1900, but almost certainly ancient

Here we may have better reading than growing. 'St. John's Rose' is very similar to the roses depicted in the oldest pictures we have of roses (ancient wall paintings found on Crete) and is thought to be the same rose found in the chaplets on the heads of Egyptian mummies. It was definitely grown throughout the Middle Ages by Coptic Christians in Ethiopia. The Cambridge University geneticist Dr. C. C. Hurst (a geneticist who married his cousin) believed that 'St. John's Rose' was a natural hybrid between *R. gallica* and *R. phoenicea*. (*R. phoenicea* was a tender rose native to Turkey and now lost to commerce.)

'St. John's Rose' is a beautiful single-petaled bloom in pale pink shading to cream at its center. Its blooms appear to be scattered all over the low, spreading bush—one never gets the impression of profuse bloom, and there is no repeat. 'St. John's Rose' is quite prone to mildew.

Old Garden Roses

Old garden roses begin with the dawn of flower gardening. When early man started taking rose bushes out of the wild and bringing them home, the natural evolution of the species was effectively ended. Selection for the sake of survival alone was replaced with selection for any number of traits found pleasing to man. Most notable among these was the desire for extra petals; however, people also wanted fragrance, long-lasting blooms and extended periods of bloom. Roses found to possess such traits were increased by root divisions or slips.

As different rose species were gathered together in ancient gardens, cross-pollination was the inevitable and fortuitous result. This occurred in the same manner in which it had always done, on the wings of insects and in the wind. Development of new kinds of roses was hastened both by combinations of species that might not have had convenient or frequent opportunity to cross-pollinate in the wild and by observant gardeners standing by to supervise the resulting seedlings that would appear, as if by magic, in the garden.

And such was the genesis of the old garden roses, defined as all those classes of roses that existed prior to the introduction of 'La France', the putative first hybrid tea, in 1867. Under this classification system, all hybrid perpetuals, for example—a class of roses that existed prior to 1867—are considered to be old garden roses, even though the majority of hybrid perpetuals did not appear until after 1867, and one ('Waldfee') was introduced as recently as 1960.

It is customary for rose books to discuss mankind's long political and religious relationship with the rose, the wars that have been fought about roses, the heraldry of the rose, poems about roses and, if the book is published in the United States, anecdotes concerning Christopher Columbus and George Washington and their rose-related activities. But the anecdotes are rarely true, the poems are often very bad and the history is almost always rewritten to put roses, rather improbably, at the hub of all of mankind's endeavors. Suffice it to say that human beings have enjoyed a long and positive affiliation with roses, that various nations, religions and commercial enterprises have used the rose as a symbol, and that the rose is the official floral emblem of the United States.

We do not know for certain if rose hybridization was an art known, and then lost, in ancient China. We do know that Western man did not understand how to hybridize roses until the middle of the nineteenth century. Even when rose seeds were being sown on purpose, and seedlings selected for particular characteristics, little attention was paid to the choice of parents, and even after the mechanics of cross-pollination was understood there was fierce opposition to the revolutionary idea that the male parent, in the form of pollen, could play an equal role to the female. By the time the rose breeders got their science straight, several classes of roses—notably the albas and gallicas—had already fallen from favor. One wonders what could have been done with them—with the disease resistance of the albas, for example, or the crazy purple colors of the gallicas—if their breeders had understood what later rosarians knew.

Is it a conceit to think that out of the thousands of gallicas that were in commerce in the 1840s, the twenty that are easily found today are the very best? Or what of the thousands of hybrid perpetuals that have become extinct over the past hundred years? Have only the most vigorous or free-flowering roses survived at the expense of weaker plants that might have had flowers with particularly exquisite form or great fragrance or some other valuable characteristic?

In nearly every portion of the world, those who appreciate old garden roses have mobilized to search out and preserve forgotten varieties. From Texas to New Zealand, roses once given up for lost are being rediscovered, growing nameless and neglected in churchyards, cemeteries, abandoned homesteads and overgrown gardens. These roses are painstakingly identified, lovingly propagated and ultimately returned to commerce. The isolated islands of Bermuda and Mauritius have proven to be treasure troves of lost roses.

It is one of the minor ironies of the twentieth century that the mother lode of forgotten old garden roses is at Sangerhausen in the former East Germany. Founded by German rose growers in 1903, the rosarium at Sangerhausen remained in something like suspended animation under the benign neglect of both the Nazi and Communist regimes. Following the collapse of the Berlin Wall, Sangerhausen emerged, in Rip Van Winkle fashion, to a strange new world where all the roses are different. Now efforts are being made to preserve Sangerhausen as it is, a repository of a great deal of our rose past. One can only wonder if Sangerhausen were located in booming West Germany whether it would have been bulldozed and developed?

As many as 90 percent of the old garden roses once in commerce are now lost. And a number of old garden roses being sold today are undoubtedly mixed up or mistaken and not what we think they are. This creates opportunities for debate among old garden rose authorities and confusion for everyone else. With patient study and careful research, some rose mysteries have been gradually unraveled. It may be part of the appeal of old garden roses that the truth about the history and provenance of other varieties will remain forever beyond our reach, lost in the gardens of the past.

ALBAS

Here is a truly old group of old garden roses. Many of the varieties sold today have been in commerce for two hundred years or more. Albas reached their zenith at the end of the eighteenth century, and no significant introductions were made after the 1840s.

Alba means "white," but this group also includes pink and pink-tinted varieties. Whether white or pink, the color is always delicate and pleasing; there is usually a memorable scent. Albas are notably disease-proof with soft blue- or gray-green foliage on tall, shrubby plants. As a class they are extremely winter hardy and more tolerant of shade than most other groups of roses.

Their blooms, which appear in profusion in the spring, are small by modern standards. In the blooms of the albas we can see the development of the various forms of old garden roses: beginning with semi-double blooms not far removed from their species antecedents, progressing to double cupped form, moving on to double blooms with larger outer petals enclosing muddled central petals, and finally to very double quartered blooms with a button eye (a special point of beauty in old garden roses).

Albas do not repeat bloom and, like the other summer-flowering old garden roses, require a period of dormancy each winter. For this reason, they will not be successful in locations—such as southern California—where frost is not persistent.

'CELESTIAL' ('CELESTE')
Origin uncertain, probably much older than the first recorded appearance in eighteenth-century France

Balancing perfectly between the simplicity of species roses and the splendor of some later old garden roses, 'Celestial' boasts five rows of petals and the ability to display its golden stamens in the open flower too. The overall effect is one of ideal symmetry and perfect beauty.

The delicate pink blooms exude an extravagant, sweet scent. Not as well armed as the usual alba, 'Celestial' has few thorns. It grows bushy and fairly upright to about 5½ feet in Ohio.

'FÉLICITÉ PARMENTIER'

France; now recorded as an 1834 introduction, may be older

Massive quantities of small, ball-shaped, intricately formed, cream to flesh pink blooms appear each spring. 'Félicité Parmentier' does not grow as tall as the other albas and may want to lie down in

The alba 'Celestial' balances perfectly between the simplicity of species roses and the splendor of some later old garden roses.

your garden when it is weighted down with bloom. But there is nothing heavy about its clear, sweet fragrance.

'Félicité Parmentier' is hardy as a rock and impervious to blackspot and powdery mildew. This is the alba I recommend most often to suburban gardeners.

You may also want to try the following albas:

'Königin Von Dänemark'
('Queen of Denmark'; origin uncertain, 1816
and 1826 have been suggested as possible dates
of introduction)

The rose pink blooms—the richest color found in the albas—are a picture of button-eyed perfection. The plant has typically blue-green alba foliage, but thorns and slightly inelegant growth habit suggest some centifolia influence.

'Maiden's Blush'
('Great Maiden's Blush', 'Cuisse de Nymphe';
origin unknown, pre-1550)

This rose's pale pink, fragrant, flower form is usually confused by a muddled center. The bush is vigorous and upright. The French name commemorates the thighs of nymphs. A distinct variety, 'Small Maiden's Blush', is identical in every respect except for the size of the bush.

'Semi-Plena'
('Alba Semi-plena'; origin unknown, very old)

This semi-double, white rose is the strongest growing of all the albas, reaching 7 feet in Ohio. It has attractive red hips in the autumn.

GALLICAS

When the eighteenth-century Swedish taxonomist Linnaeus set out to put roses (along with all other plants) into a systematic botanical order, he named *Rosa gallica* after the Roman province of Gaul, only one of several places where the species grows wild. However, his choice of Gaul (roughly equivalent to present-day France) turned out to be neatly prescient, for nearly all of the significant hybrids

'Charles de Mills' produces the largest flowers of any of the gallicas.

of *R. gallica* were to be raised in France, years after Linnaeus's death.

Gallicas had their heyday in the first four decades of the nineteenth century, before the newly imported, repeat-blooming China roses mated with them and wiped them out. Very few gallicas were introduced after the 1840s, although one, 'Marcel Bourgouin', appeared as late as 1899.

Like the albas, gallicas bloom only once a year. Unlike the albas, they are as a class quite prone to mildew. Their pale foliage, even when disease free, can appear rather wanting. A gallica bloom does not typically last very long, but in its short life can display a dazzling progression of color changes, including many shades of purple, mauve, slate and gray not seen in other roses. For these bizarre colors, as well as numerous varieties that feature festive speckled or striped effects, the class has come to be known as the "mad gallicas." Not only are gallicas fragrant, but this fragrance actually increases when their petals are dried, making them ideal candidates for the production of potpourri.

While most make only modest growth (to 4 or 5 feet), gallicas reproduce very freely via underground suckers. This has helped ensure their survival in abandoned gardens, but may be an annoyance to the rosarian who has only limited space. For this reason, if it is important that your gallicas stay within bounds, you should avoid purchasing them as own-root plants and insist on specimens that have been bud-grafted onto an understock.

'CHARLES DE MILLS'
Origin unknown, but almost certainly nineteenth century

The largest of the gallicas, this rose has rich, velvety, wine red blooms turning purple as they mature. 'Charles de Mills' has as many as two hundred petals crammed into short buds, giving it an unusual sawed-off appearance that some find unsatisfying and incomplete. You may find that it can have a perfection all its own, possessing one of the more distinctive examples of the many forms we can associate with roses.

'Charles de Mills' grows with vigor to about 5 feet in the Midwest and is less troubled with mildew than the other gallicas. It has an excellent perfume. The canes and stems of 'Charles de Mills' have many small bristles that should not be mistaken for moss.

'LA BELLE SULTANE' ('MAHEKA', 'VIOLACEA')
France, ca. 1795

This tall gallica appears to have been at the end of the line when rose foliage was passed out. Out of

'La Belle Sultane' is a beautiful rose on a somewhat gaunt gallica plant.

flower, it has a distressingly gaunt appearance. However, the bloom makes up for all of that.

'La Belle Sultane' has wide, bold, almost single flowers of purplish red opening to reveal a white halo surrounding golden yellow stamens. When grown in full sun it can develop appealing blackish shadings at the edge of its petals. Writing in the 1932 *American Rose Annual*, the redoubtable Mrs. Frederick L. Keays describes this effect as "*échancrés en coeur.*" Today we might simply say, "Cool!"

'La Belle Sultane' is a beautiful and fun rose. Its narrow growth suggests it as a possibility for hedging, in combination with better-foliaged varieties. Colorful red hips persist well into winter.

I also recommend the following gallicas:

'Apothecary's Rose'
(*R. gallica officinalis*; before 1400)

This semi-double, light crimson rose has striking golden stamens. It is low growing, has a long bloom period and makes an excellent 3- to 4-foot-tall hedge. It has had at least a dozen names throughout its long history; the current name reflects its use as a medicinal rose throughout the Middle Ages. In early medicine, preparations made from rose petals were used to treat inflammation as well as for "purification of the mind" in the treatment of mental illness. As late as 1807, French growers of 'Apothecary's Rose' received an assurance from their government that their ointments would be used in all public and military hospitals.

In 1991, David Austin introduced a rose called 'The Herbalist', which is as close to a repeat-blooming twin of 'Apothecary's Rose' as we are ever likely to see. But even over five months of repeat bloom, 'The Herbalist' cannot match the number of blossoms that 'Apothecary's Rose' makes in one.

'Camaieux'
(Raiser uncertain, France, ca. 1830)

Small for a gallica, this rose is suitable for the most modest city garden. Its double flowers are purple splashed and striped with white, fading to gray and white.

'Cardinal de Richelieu'
(Laffay, France, 1840)

This rose's double blooms are fantastically purple. Although many of its characteristics are typically gallica, the smooth and shiny leaves suggest some China rose influence. It is named, incidentally, after a rather obscure Cardinal de Richelieu—not the one who is a character in *The Three Musketeers*.

'Président de Sèze'
(Hébert, France, 1836)

Perhaps the archetypal gallica, this rose has crazy colors and a slightly rumpled form on a plant that is eager to grow and spread. This rose's double blooms are plum, paling to lilac at the edges and eventually becoming a washed-out turtledove mauve.

'Rosa Mundi'
(*R. gallica versicolor*; original unknown, before 1581)

This boldly striped sport of 'Apothecary's Rose' duplicates all of its other qualities. Legend associates the name with Fair Rosamund, mistress of Henry II. While this is probably as dubious as most other rose lore, it nonetheless leaves the name 'Rosa Mundi' clearly out of the italics into which it is often incorrectly put.

DAMASKS

The original damask roses are supposed to have returned from Damascus, Syria, with the medieval crusaders. That crusaders—or their minions—brought rose plants back to Europe is fairly certain. Whether they got them in Damascus and whether the roses they brought back have any real connection with the roses we now call damasks is something we have no way of knowing.

Despite a beginning so rich in history (or legend), the damasks lack the kind of unmistakable characteristics we find in the crazy colors of the

The green-eyed damask 'Mme. Hardy' has an incomparable, matchless beauty.

gallicas or the many petals of the centifolias. Nevertheless, the damasks do have a distinct identity that may be best expressed in their long, tubular hips. Damasks are thornier than gallicas and much more rangy in growth; damasks have smaller blooms than do most centifolias.

Within the damask class we find 'Kazanlik' (*Rosa damascena trigintipetala*), grown as a cash crop to produce attar of roses for the perfume industry and generating an impressive percentage of the gross national product of Bulgaria, and 'Quatre Saisons' ('Autumn Damask', 'The Four Seasons Rose'), for centuries the only Western rose to offer repeat bloom. If you grow the extremely drab 'Quatre Saisons' today, you will see how desperate our ancestors must have been for any rose that offered bloom in the fall.

'MME. HARDY'
Hardy, France, 1832

With a famous green eye peering out from behind layer upon layer of creamy white petals, this is my favorite old garden rose. This rose invites comparison with modern imitators—several of the Austin English roses, for example—only to rebuff it with its incomparable, matchless beauty.

'Mme. Hardy' makes an upright bush, reaching about 5 feet in the Midwest. Its scent, while not strong, is pleasantly unique, reminiscent of Ponds cold cream.

The stock of 'Mme. Hardy' offered by at least two American nurseries has somehow become infected with rose mosaic virus. Because this is a variety that deserves to be grown in full health, you may want to specify virus-free plants and see if the nursery from which you are ordering will guarantee it. If they won't, there are others that will.

Here are two other damasks that I have enjoyed:

'Celsiana'
(Origin unknown, before 1750)

This rose's semi-double, light pink blooms fade to white and provide outstanding fragrance. Because it grows upright to about 4 feet, this is the best damask to choose for a smaller garden.

'Léda'
('Painted Damask'; origin unknown, before 1827)

Although not used in their breeding, 'Léda', with its very double, white blooms splashed with pink and red, anticipates the effect of the hand-painted roses. A great novelty, this sprawler must be trained to grow upright.

CENTIFOLIAS

These are the hundred-petaled roses, more or less. Centifolias are also called cabbage roses (for their folded-over form, rather than for their size). Early varieties appear as the opulent, many-petaled roses in the paintings of the old Dutch masters. The class achieved its greatest popularity between 1750 and 1840, but centifolias have always been an under-populated group of old garden roses. They are the youngest of the four classes of true old garden roses (albas, gallicas, damasks and centifolias) that existed in Europe before the influence of repeat-blooming roses from China.

Centifolias make thorny but not bushy shrubs, and most have stems that will bow to the weight of their opening blooms. Several grow as short as 3 feet and are suitable for planting in front of taller old garden roses. Most centifolias are richly fragrant; none offers repeat bloom.

'FANTIN-LATOUR'
Origin unknown

This rose was named in 1900 after the romantic/realist painter Henri Fantin-Latour, well known for his portraits of roses and other flowers. The origin of this variety is obscure and probably dates to the mid-nineteenth century. It cannot be identified in any of the pictures of Fantin-Latour (1836–1904).

While the soft pink blooms (which in this instance have about 200 petals) are classically centifolia, the foliage and growth shows pronounced China rose influence. So just as 'Cardinal de Richelieu' is not purely a gallica, 'Fantin-Latour' is not purely a centifolia. Still, it does not fit obviously into any other class. 'Fantin-Latour' grows virtually thornlessly to 6 feet and makes a graceful, healthy addition to any garden.

Here are a few other centifolias:

'Bullata'
('The Lettuce-leafed Rose'; origin unknown, before 1815)

Especially interesting as a leaf novelty, 'Bullata' is famous for its deeply crinkled foliage. It has double, deep pink, well-perfumed blooms.

'Petite de Holland'
(Holland, ca. 1800)

This modestly spreading bush has loads of small, double, medium pink blooms each spring. The blooms are close to being miniature (or as today's miniatures get bigger and bigger, perhaps they get closer in proportion to 'Petite de Hollande'). This is the ideal centifolia for small gardens.

'Village Maid'
('Belle des Jardins', 'Centifolia Variegata'; origin uncertain)

Each spring this tall grower makes a great display of ivory blooms striped and splashed with clear pink.

Although not a pure centifolia, the many-petaled blooms of 'Fantin-Latour' exemplify the ideal of the "hundred-petaled" rose.

MOSS ROSES

Ask almost anyone what he wants in a rose, and you are unlikely to hear, "stems, calyx and sepals embedded with downy glands that release a fragrant, resinous oil when touched." Despite these unlikely characteristics, the moss roses have ridden two waves of great popularity. The first followed their appearance as mutations in eighteenth-century Holland, where they generated much enthusiasm. The Dutch sought out new examples of moss mutation in roses and sent out specimens to the rest of the world. But, perhaps having learned their lesson from the tulip-mania chapter of their economic history, they did not become manic about the phenomenon. This was left to Victorian England and Second Empire France, where moss roses reached an apex of popularity and shifty nurserymen joined keen gardeners in scanning their stems and sepals for the slightest sign of bristliness that could be called moss.

That moss roses appeared as mutations in the first place is remarkable. That people did not reject them as bizarre anomalies is even more amazing.

Today, moss on roses is all wrapped up with Victorian sentiment, and when looking at a moss rose, we see more than a stem with lots of bristly little glands on it—we see a representation of a time in history that is appealing to many of us. I believe that moss roses are grown today as Victorian icons as much as for the pleasure their pine-scented moss actually provides. Moss is most attractive on a rose bud, and much of its effect is usually lost as the bloom opens and the moss disappears behind a bunch of petals.

As a class, moss roses are lanky growers, and most are prone to mildew. The mosses included here are mutations of centifolias, featuring heavy green moss, and of portlands, featuring sparse brown moss but with the added virtue of repeat bloom. Few moss roses were introduced after 1890, and twentieth-century efforts to improve the old garden mosses have been limited to famously failed efforts to introduce yellow and apricot shades. (Yellow and apricot mosses were introduced in the 1920s and 1930s and may still be found in a few specialist catalogues. However, I do not recommend that you buy them.) Moss has also attached itself to climbers (see 'Wichmoss') and,

thanks to the efforts of Ralph Moore, has been very successfully incorporated into modern miniatures (see 'Scarlet Moss').

'COMMON MOSS' ('COMMON MOSS', 'OLD PINK MOSS')
Origin believed to be Holland, 1696

The original moss rose, and still the best, 'Common Moss' is blessed with lavish helpings of both fragrance and moss. The clear pink color in the emerging buds is an excellent foil for the deep green moss.

'Common Moss' is winter-proof and easy to grow, but like almost all moss roses comes on a plant that is not particularly attractive when out of bloom. It will grow to a spindly 7 feet and soon forms a thicket from which rooted suckers can easily be separated.

'GÉNÉRAL KLÉBER'
Robert, France, 1856

This best-behaved moss rose maintains a dense, compact growth habit (to about 4½ feet in Ohio). At their best, the luminous pink blooms have classic quartered form, sealed with a button-eye in their center. Like 'Common Moss', 'Général Kléber' has an outstanding fragrance. Along with many other moss roses, 'Général Kléber' blooms late in the season. As a sport from a centifolia, it does not repeat bloom.

Although a member of the French nobility, Général Jean-Baptiste Kléber was sympathetic to the original goals of the French Revolution.

'Common Moss' is blessed with lavish helpings of both fragrance and moss.

You may also want to try the following moss roses:

'Mme. de la Roche-Lambert'
(Robert, France, 1851)

A gangly grower, this is one of the reddest of the old mosses. Its double blooms repeat once the plant is established. Unlike other red-purple old garden roses, 'Mme. de la Roche-Lambert' stands up reasonably well to hot sun.

As with any moss rose, the moss on 'Général Kléber' is most visible in the bud stage.

The portland 'Comte de Chambord' is one of the best repeat bloomers of all the old garden roses.

'Salet'
(Lacharme, France, 1854)

While not heavily mossed, this is the most reliable repeat-blooming moss rose. The blooms are double and medium pink; the plant can look quite spindly.

'White Bath'
(Origin uncertain, presumably England, ca. 1817)

A mutation of 'Common Moss', this rose shares its profuse summer bloom and excellent scent. The double, pure white blooms are particularly striking against a mossy background.

PORTLANDS

The portland roses mark the spot in rose history where the old roses began to give way to the modern. With the introduction of these repeat-blooming roses, the monopoly of the albas, damasks, gallicas and centifolias began to crumble. The portlands opened the door for the bourbons, the teas and the hybrid perpetuals, all classes that quickly surpassed the portlands in popularity. There may never have been more than one hundred portland roses in commerce; today there are less than a dozen.

Portlands may have originated in Italy and may have been imported to England by the second or third Duchess of Portland, who may or may not have been a keen rosarian. In any case, the original portland was called 'Duchess of Portland' and is apparently a cross between either a gallica or a damask and a repeat-blooming China. The damask characteristics are particularly obvious, and for many years portlands were also known as damask perpetuals.

Their growth is bushy and well mannered, with characteristically short-stemmed blooms nestled in shiny foliage. Most are suitable for smaller gardens, and almost all are quite fragrant. I doubt if all of the portlands were as good at repeat bloom as are those that survive today.

'COMTE DE CHAMBORD'
Moreau-Robert, France, 1860

Perhaps the best repeat bloomer of all old garden roses, 'Comte de Chambord' smothers itself in bloom several times each summer. The first bloom is sometimes a surprise because the buds can be hidden on their short stems in the large gray-green foliage. The blooms are warm pink, with some lilac undertones, and fabulously fragrant.

'Comte de Chambord' is disease resistant and winter hardy. For maximum repeat bloom, it is essential to deadhead blooms as they begin to spoil. It makes bushy, rounded growth to 4 feet in Ohio.

Nineteenth-century rose authorities are strangely unenthusiastic about 'Comte de Chambord', leading at least one present-day authority to suppose that the rose now known under that name is really a hybrid perpetual called 'Mme. Boll'. Arguing against this supposition is the typically compact, leafy, short-stemmed portland habit of 'Comte de Chambord'.

Here are two other portlands worth considering:

'Arthur de Sansal'
(Cochet, France, 1855)

The flat, intricately formed, very double, crimson-purple blooms often show a button eye. This rose repeats well. Its growth is short and may be troubled by mildew.

'Marbrée'
(Robert et Moreau, France, 1858)

Worth growing for its strange and pleasing color effects—double, deep pink to maroon blooms with paler pink mottling—this tall plant is prone to fungus diseases and disappointingly short of fragrance.

BOURBONS

A long time ago, on an island far, far away, farmers enclosed their fields with damask and China roses. Sometime around 1817 a natural hybrid arose from this damask-China combination. *Rosa* × *borboniana*, the first bourbon rose, was named after the island on which it was discovered. A property of imperial France, the Isle of Bourbon had upon its discovery been named for the French royal family. Republicans later renamed it Reunion Island, the name by which we know it today. Rosarians may not always be the best geographers, and information presented in a rose book published in 1991 incorrectly places Reunion Island in the Caribbean, not in the Indian Ocean as it should be.

Bourbons provide another push toward what we consider modern in roses. Their wide petals presage those required by today's rules for exhibiting roses. Their flowers are generally large and their fragrance is generous. Bourbons grow tall and may be faulted for an awkward growth habit and winter tenderness. Achieving their peak of popularity in the 1860s, bourbons were still being introduced in the twentieth century.

'MME. ERNEST CALVAT'
Schwartz, France, 1888

Tall to the point of being a semi-climber, 'Mme. Ernest Calvat' produces a bountiful crop of very large, loosely formed, very fragrant, light pink blooms. The foliage is a deep purplish green. This is a color sport from 'Mme. Isaac Pereire', a variety whose flowers are a magenta that seems harsh to me but is found in keeping with the true old garden rose character by others.

Mme. Ernest Calvat was the wife of Monsieur Ernest Calvat, a glove manufacturer. Even though she has a rose rated 8.3 (excellent) by the American Rose Society named in her honor, we do not know her first name.

In his brilliant book *Roses*, Jack Harkness—the British nurseryman, hybridizer and author—reports that as old garden roses were being revived in the 1930s, some veteran nursery hands who had experienced them in their original nineteenth-century incarnations expressed approval for the idea but wonder at the choice of varieties being revived. "The stars of [their] youth had been passed over," Harkness writes, "and the rejects put in their place." "Calvat was always rubbish," he recalls one nurseryman claiming. Could it be that those leading the old rose revival chose the wrong roses to revive? Of course. But a more likely explanation is that, while the roses have not

The bourbon rose 'Mme. Ernest Calvat' provides very fragrant blooms on a semi-climbing plant.

While not easy to grow, the bourbon 'Variegata di Bologna' can produce stunning blooms.

changed, tastes have. The ugly duckling of 1895 might have grown into a beautiful swan by the conventions of 1935, or 1995.

'VARIEGATA DI BOLOGNA'
Bonfiglioli, Italy, 1909

Not a typical bourbon or an easy rose to grow, 'Variegata di Bologna' demands rich soil and even when pampered may refuse to bloom, insist on mildewing, and grow aimlessly to eight feet or more. All of this can make the appearance of a perfect bloom even more rewarding. With wine red stripes on a creamy white background, 'Variegata di Bologna' has the potential to be absolutely stunning. If you have a lot of room and patience and the desire to see something really spectacular, this might be a rose for you. I wouldn't want to grow roses without it. This is believed to be a mutation from another Italian introduction, the purplish maroon bourbon 'Victor-Emmanuel'.

I also recommend the following bourbons:

'Mme. Pierre Oger'
(Oger, France, 1878)

A sport of the medium pink bourbon 'La Reine Victoria', this rose produces double, blush pink blooms that deepen in the sunlight. Are bourbons the only class of roses in which the mutations are more interesting than the originals?

'Souvenir de la Malmaison'
(Béluze, France, 1843)

This rose produces large, very double, exquisitely formed, pale pink blooms, but not very many of them. 'Souvenir de la Malmaison' may be more floriferous in a hotter climate and definitely requires hot weather to open properly. It was named for the Empress Josephine's famous rose garden outside Paris. There is a climbing sport, but the rose erroneously sold as "Climbing Souvenir de la Malmaison" in the United States is believed to be 'Garisenda', a rambler introduced in Italy in 1911.

'Zéphirine Drouhin'
(Bizot, France, 1868)

This bourbon produces semi-double, cerise blooms. The "thornless" rose, it is indeed almost free of prickles. This rose is ultra-vigorous and suitable for use as a climber or as a tall hedge. Should we be surprised that there is a sport? Called 'Kathleen Harrop', it is pale pink but identical to 'Zéphirine Drouhin' in all other respects.

HYBRID PERPETUALS

The hybrid perpetuals mark the triumph of the rose bloom over the bush. They were bred, selected and appreciated for the magnificence of their bloom rather than for their garden qualities. The emergence of hybrid perpetuals marked the beginning of the rose's long exile into "cutting gardens" safely hidden from public view. The idea that the rose is a wonderful flower on a poor plant began with the often coarse-growing, disease-prone hybrid perpetual. Even now that roses have been restored to good habit and health and make excellent garden subjects once again, this hundred-year-old idea persists. Of course, there are some hybrid perpetuals that are delightful in the garden, just as there are some contemporary roses that are not.

Most hybrid perpetuals are not anything close to perpetual in their bloom. Their name results from an overly enthusiastic translation of the French term *remontant*, which refers to roses that flower again, and does not indicate perpetual blooming. Most hybrid perpetuals are indeed remontant, flowering heavily in the spring with a good showing again in the fall and perhaps a few blooms in between. Some will rarely give any repeat bloom, but a select few of the later hybrid perpetuals, released after 1880, are indeed more or less perpetual, flowering in the regular cycles we are used to seeing in hybrid teas.

Bearing the largest blooms yet seen on roses and being able to last fairly well, the hybrid perpetuals ushered in the age of rose exhibiting. Ironically, it was the demands of exhibitors for high-centered form that eventually saw the hybrid perpetual class fall from favor and be replaced by the sleeker hybrid tea.

Pegging

To encourage the maximum amount of bloom from plants that sometimes want to put all of their efforts into making foliage and growing canes that reach toward the sky, one can revive the Victorian practice of "pegging" to encourage a flowering shoot to arise from every leaf internode. For a tidier landscape, and lots more autumn bloom, peg climberlike canes as they appear. Canes can be trained horizontally straight down the rose bed, right between their neighbors, as far as they will grow. Or, if you have spaced your rose bushes generously to begin with, try pegging in semi-circles for a mounded effect. Special rose pegs (sold by some specialist nurseries) are nice but not necessary. Croquet arches are ideal for pegging; short pieces of rope anchored by tent stakes work well, too. Pegging works for tall hybrid teas that are hesitant to repeat bloom (such as 'Die Welt' and 'Selfridges') as well as it does for hybrid perpetuals. In addition to encouraging repeat bloom, pegging is also a great way to get long stems for exhibition.

'ELISA BOËLLE'
Guillot père, France, 1869

Despite its somewhat enigmatic provenance, 'Elisa Boëlle' is a hybrid perpetual that's relatively easy to grow.

A favorite Victorian exhibition rose, the hybrid perpetual 'Her Majesty' is a rarity today. This may be the first color photo of 'Her Majesty' ever published.

In Search of the Perfect Bloom

How far would Victorians go in their quest for humongous, intricately formed exhibition blooms? Through nasty thorns and impossible mildew, around indifferent foliage and up nine-foot stems, if we are to be guided by the example of 'Her Majesty'. And exhibitors of that era would put up with almost any fault, so long as they were rewarded with a prize-winning bloom. With the sparse-blooming 'Her Majesty', they might be rewarded with *a* prize-winning bloom, but never two or three.

In the nineteenth century, rose show exhibitors did not have to worry about foliage because their blooms were exhibited and judged in specially constructed boxes, without any sign of leaves. The varieties that win trophies in the classes for old garden roses at rose shows today—often small-flowered but healthy specimens—wouldn't have had much of a chance in their own time.

A bit of a mystery rose, 'Elisa Boëlle' was reintroduced to commerce by the British nurseryman Peter Beales in the mid-1980s, only to be dropped a few years later. My plant from Beales matches contemporary descriptions of a white bloom, briefly tinted flesh pink when young, shapely formed with incurving petals, and light green foliage. Apparently identical to the rose pictured in Guillot catalogues, it has been a great bloomer in Ohio, giving autumn bloom as reliably as any hybrid perpetual. It does benefit from winter protection and appreciates the prompt removal of nonproductive canes. 'Elisa Boëlle' has a conspicuous scent, a rose fragrance that is rich without being cloying. Beware of any reference describing this rose as introduced by "Mr. Père." French for father, *père* is equivalent, of course, to "Sr." or "The Elder."

'HER MAJESTY'
Bennett, England, 1885

'Her Majesty' was bred by Henry Bennett, a Wiltshire cattle breeder who is credited as the first to approach rose hybridizing in a scientific manner. 'Her Majesty' is a stunning bloom on a horrible plant. Today it is a collector's item, a perfect example of what some of our ancestors sought in roses and what they put up with to get it.

'JUBILEE'
Walsh, USA, 1897

Sixty years into the hybrid perpetuals, 'Jubilee' represents something of a throwback. Its small, cup-shaped flowers are not opulent and do not appear on long stems. On the other hand, the bush, branching freely into a handsome shrub, is a joy to grow. 'Jubilee' is healthy in summer and very hardy over winter. It is reported to be remontant, but I have yet to see a repeat bloom over ten Ohio autumns. 'Jubilee' is a rich violet-red, appearing more purple when grown in some shade. Only moderately fragrant, its blooms do last well when cut.

Although first introduced in England, and named to commemorate the sixtieth anniversary of Queen Victoria's reign, 'Jubilee' is actually one of the few hybrid perpetuals raised by an American (in this instance Michael Walsh of Woods Hole, Massachusetts). While 'Jubilee'—perhaps the best of the American-raised hybrid perpetuals—has English connotations, the most famous of "American" hybrid perpetuals, the original 'American Beauty', was actually from France, where it was named 'Mme. Ferdinand Jamin'.

'ROGER LAMBELIN'
Schwartz, France, 1890

One of the oddest of all roses and, at its best, one of the most beautiful, 'Roger Lambelin' is an otherwise somber crimson red brought fantastically to life by a stark white outline, which sometimes extends into stripes shooting through the

The always odd and often amazing 'Roger Lambelin' is a hybrid perpetual that demands rich soil.

'Souvenir du Docteur Jamain' is a gloriously fragrant hybrid perpetual.

strangely fluted, carnation-shaped blooms. The effect is enhanced by 'Roger Lambelin''s habit of blooming in tightly packed clusters. 'Roger Lambelin' has a rich, honey-sweet fragrance. One authority has described it as "wine-like," to which I say, "Let's get our rose writers better wine!"

'Roger Lambelin' is a rose that responds especially well to a rich soil and will reward ample manuring with a good display of repeat bloom. In a good year, it can be coaxed to display three cycles of bloom in Ohio. Rosarians in the Southwest should be warned that this variety is naturally predisposed to rust, and extra feeding can make its foliage soft enough to succumb to powdery mildew.

The best evidence suggests that 'Roger Lambelin' is a mutation from the crimson-maroon hybrid perpetual 'Prince Camille de Rohan'. The Widow Schwartz must have had a talent for spotting sports; her nursery also introduced 'Mme. Ernest Calvat'.

'SOUVENIR DU DOCTEUR JAMAIN'
Lacharme, France, 1865

This magnificent rose has rich, plum red blooms with every petal folded into place just right. It is gloriously fragrant and responds superbly to pegging. Unpegged, its nearly thornless 10-foot canes can flap rather annoyingly in the wind.

'Souvenir du Docteur Jamain' will not last well as a cut flower, and its thin petals will fry to a crisp under the hot sun. Even in cloudy climates it will be happiest if planted in half-shade. More resistant to mildew than most red hybrid perpetuals, 'Souvenir du Docteur Jamain' picks up blackspot in my garden but does not seem to suffer for it.

The word *souvenir* has become overly associated with tourism and knick-knacks in America. When used in French rose names, it is meant as "in memory of" a person, such as Dr. Jamain, or a place, such as Malmaison.

Of the four dozen hybrid perpetuals I have grown, I can also recommend these:

'Baronne Prévost'
(Desprez, France, 1842)

In its flat blooms we see the earliest stage of hybrid perpetual development, with old garden rose form and a button center. (The middle stage hybrid perpetuals have globular form, and the last stage is very close to hybrid tea form.) 'Baronne Prévost' can be counted on to repeat its pink bloom. Its bush is rather compact and very tough.

'Ferdinand Pichard'
(Tanne, France, 1921)

The cup-shaped, carmine blooms, with the famous light pink and white stripes that later made their way into miniatures, are striking in spring, but rarely seen in the fall. This rose has good fragrance. The bush is tall and well clothed in foliage.

'Frau Karl Druschki'
(Lambert, Germany, 1901)

This snow white rose is high centered in the hybrid tea manner and has a strong-growing, 'Queen Elizabeth'–like habit. It is winter hardy, but not fragrant. Offered by more nurseries than any other hybrid perpetual today, this rose enjoyed worldwide popularity right from the start. However, in the same way that German toast became French toast in the wake of World War I, 'Frau Karl Druschki' became 'Reine des Neiges' in France, 'Snow Queen' in Britain and 'White American Beauty' in the United States. Gradually, it has reclaimed its rightful name in most places.

'General Jacqueminot'
(Roussel, France, ca. 1853)

The famous 'General Jack' rose, also known in some parts simply as the 'Jack Rose', makes a nice bush for a hybrid perpetual and is a good repeat bloomer. This clear red rose with a super scent is an important ancestor of red hybrid teas.

'Georg Arends'
(Hinner, Germany, 1910)

This rose produces very fragrant, pink blooms with subtle lilac undertones. It is a rampant grower and profuse bloomer; the flowers of 'Georg Arends' are just slightly less elegant than what we would expect from an early hybrid tea. It's at its best in cool weather.

'John Hopper'
(Ward, England, 1862)

This hybrid perpetual is a good grower and a great repeat bloomer. The bright pink blooms are large and fragrant; the plant could use some more foliage, but what it has is healthy.

'Mrs. John Laing'
(Bennett, England, 1887)

Silvery pink, its forty-five petals do not make as full a bloom as other hybrid perpetuals, but the flowers last well when cut. It offers excellent repeat bloom. An upright grower with handsome leaves, 'Mrs. John Laing' is unfortunately prone to blackspot.

'Paul Neyron'
(Levet, France, 1869)

The rose pink to lilac blooms can be immense, but its multi-petaled, muddled form could be described as abstract. Fortunately, the fragrance is good and the plant is healthy with very few thorns.

'Ulrich Brunner Fils'
(Levet, France, 1881)

Healthy, fragrant and well-behaved, this rose grows to 4 feet and is nearly thornless. Its deep rose red blooms are fully double. An excellent repeat bloomer, this is one of the best all-around hybrid perpetuals.

CHINA ROSES

No one knows for how long the Chinese enjoyed repeat-blooming roses. Was it for centuries, or millennia? In any case, Westerners discovered them in the late 1700s, to a general chorus of "Look what I found!" rather than "What hath China wrought?"

The repeat-blooming China roses were packed up and put on ships for Europe. Once there, they proved too tender for tough winters,

Alfred Parsons's painting of "R. chinensis" *from Ellen Willmot's* The Genus Rosa *(1910–1914). It is now generally agreed that there is no such rose as* R. chinensis. *Nevertheless, this illustration is valuable as a general representation of the earliest China roses.*

but were grown and enjoyed in greenhouses and conservatories. They were little plants, with loosely shaped, ephemeral blooms. In the early pink and red China roses, we see the genesis of all of the future "color changing" varieties—roses such as 'Double Delight' with pink or red tones that darken in the sun. In nearly all other modern roses, we can see China influence in smooth stems and leaves—and, of course, in repeat bloom. From a few original "stud" China roses sprang all of the capability for repeat bloom found in today's roses.

The present-day identity of the original China roses is the subject of spirited debate among enthusiasts. Do they persist under different names or are they extinct? The discussions continue on that count, but it is generally agreed that there is

no such thing as *Rosa chinensis*. The rose identified as such in Alfred Parsons's watercolor should be taken only as a general illustration of how the original China roses appeared.

'EUGÈNE DE BEAUHARNAIS'
Hardy, France, 1838

Wonderfully purple and pleasingly profuse, this is the one China I have grown with success outdoors in Ohio. It reaches no more than 20 inches in height for me, but is covered with clusters of 3-inch blooms most of the summer. It needs good winter protection in my sheltered corner of Zone 6 and does not seem to resent pruning in the spring.

The profuse 'Eugène de Beauharnais' is a China rose that can be grown outdoors as far north as Ohio.

Named for the Empress Josephine's son, who, thanks to his father-by-adoption, Napoleon, was not only Duke of Leuchtenberg, but Prince of Eichstädt as well.

TEA ROSES

With hybrid perpetuals, tea roses are the progenitors of the hybrid teas. Teas brought white and yellow shades, high-centered form and tremendous capability for repeat bloom into the equation. The origin of the teas themselves is somewhat controversial, but can with confidence be said to include both China hybrids and the Asian species *Rosa gigantea*.

Teas have a reputation for tenderness, which is deserved but not always understood. A typical tea rose will not survive a typical winter north of Zone 7, but close examination in February will reveal that it has not suffered winterkill any more severe than what many hybrid teas experience. What tea roses lack more than innate hardiness is an ability to remain dormant all winter long; they are killed by growing too much in the spring freezes and thaws. Where teas never suffer a check in growth, as in southern California, they can still be spectacular.

'Lady Hillingdon'
(Lowe & Shawyer, England, 1910)

Introduced just before teas were completely absorbed into the hybrid tea class, this apricot-yellow rose is one of only a few teas hardy enough to be grown outdoors in parts of the north. There is a reliable climbing form.

'Niphetos'
(Bougère, France, 1843)

A popular florist's rose in its century. I imported the 1889 climbing version of this rose from England. However, because it has never grown more than 3½ feet and blooms far too continuously for any climbing sport, I have taken it to be the original bush version. I grow it in a large tub, where it produces stark white blooms on drooping stems with admirable regularity from June into

The tea rose 'Safrano', from Henry Curtis's Beauties of the Rose, *first published in England 1850–1853.*

October. Moisture spoils the blooms on this one, so if it is going to rain when 'Niphetos' is going to bloom, I simply push 'Niphetos' into the garage.

'Safrano'
(Beauregard, France, 1839)

Its perfectly scrolled buds explode quickly into loosely formed, semi-double, saffron yellow blooms. This rose has a sharp but pleasant fragrance. 'Safrano' grows vigorously but without making very many leaves. A landmark yellow garden rose in warm climates, 'Safrano' is an important ancestor of the hybrid teas. It can be successfully grown in a pot in the North.

OTHER OLD GARDEN ROSES

Authorities have defined thirty-two classifications of old garden rose, many of which are only sparsely populated. In some cases, a category has been

When America's frontier was settled, 'Harison's Yellow' came along, traveling west with the wagon trains.

A Brief History of Noisettes

The original noisette was raised or discovered by John Champneys in South Carolina sometime before 1811 and is believed to be a cross between a China and the climbing *Rosa moschata*. He gave the resulting seedling, a pink climber called 'Champneys' Pink Cluster', to Philippe Noisette, a French nurseryman then in Charleston, who raised several seedlings from it. Noisette sent one of his seedlings to Paris, where it acquired his name, was painted by artists and improved by nurserymen.

created to define just a handful of rose varieties. A few categories, such as the boursaults, have experienced great popularity in the distant past, only to have faded into near total obscurity today. Winter tenderness has limited the appeal of other classifications, such as the noisettes, over much of North America.

'Alister Stella Gray'
(Gray, England, 1894)

This rose produces double, deep yellow blooms that pale at the edges. It is one of the noisettes, the only class of climbing old garden roses and the only class of old garden roses to originate in the United States. 'Alister Stella Gray' was hybridized by a Scotsman who moved to Bath, England, so that he could better grow his roses. He could never have raised 'Alister Stella Gray' in Scotland. It is not reliably hardy and requires extraordinary cosseting to survive north of Zone 7.

'Harison's Yellow'
('Harisonii'; Harison, USA, 1830)

Incredibly popular as the only yellow garden rose most Americans knew in the mid-nineteenth century, this double rose was descended in some obscure way from *Rosa foetida*. It is classed as a hybrid foetida, which makes it, according to the classification authorities, an old garden rose instead of a shrub. As a garden specimen it gives off a rather haggard appearance. However, it is tough, and one can map the routes of the wagon trains in plants of 'Harison's Yellow' found from New York to California. This rose does not repeat bloom.

'Lord Penzance'
(Penzance, England, 1894)

This single-petaled, soft rosy yellow specimen is one of sixteen hybrids of *Rosa eglanteria* introduced by Lord Penzance in 1894. Evidently, he had been saving them up for a while, and this is the one he chose to name for himself. 'Lord Penzance' has the same remarkable apple-scented foliage found in *R. eglanteria*. Usually, one needs to rub the leaves to get the full fragrance, but after a rain the apple scent will perfume the neighborhood. 'Lord Penzance' is very prickly and makes an 8-foot bush that spreads rapidly by underground suckers. For this reason, a budded specimen is to be preferred over one on its own roots. While I have not grown it, 'Lady Penzance' is said to offer more compact growth and a slightly deeper color.

'Stanwell Perpetual'
(Lee, England, 1838)

This rose produces double, blush pink flowers. Perhaps the best choice for anyone looking for a repeat-blooming old garden rose that looks really old. There is nothing modern about 'Stanwell Perpetual''s muddled, yet somehow charming blooms. Its growth is ferny and prickly, making a 4-foot mound in northern Ohio. This outstandingly fragrant rose is almost always the last rose of summer.

Shrubs

For many years, the shrub classification was used as a catchall class for any rose that did not conveniently fit into any other category and that had no commercial prospects. It was the rose world's dumping ground. Here one could find boorish cerise roses with unpronounceable Teutonic names, misbegotten children of ramblers from California and every other misfit of science that the world's hybridizers had created. There was a general understanding that shrub roses were winter hardy and perhaps more disease resistant than ordinary roses and that the rosarians who grew them were undoubtedly somewhat eccentric.

Today, with an increased emphasis on garden roses that can be grown with a minimum of chemical intervention and park and landscaping roses that require little care, shrub roses are suddenly popular. If 'Queen Elizabeth' were created for the first time today, it would be classed as a shrub, and the grandiflora classification would never have been necessary. However, had 'Queen Elizabeth' been called a shrub in 1954, very few people would have bought it.

In every aspect except two (cut flowers and roses for exhibition), shrub roses dominate recent rose developments. Within the shrub classification we find David Austin's English roses, the Meidilands and other exciting landscaping roses, and the emerging family of groundcover roses.

Who'd have thought it? In the 1990s, hybrid teas are getting smaller, floribundas are getting back to where they were thirty years ago and shrubs are where the rose action is.

'ANGELICA' (KORDAY, 'ANGELA')
Kordes, Germany, 1984

This rose has everything you could want in a shrub rose except fragrance. 'Angelica' is completely healthy, winter hardy and almost never off bloom. The smooth, nearly thornless canes are a joy to work around, and the huge corymbs of bloom lend themselves easily to flower arranging.

This shrub is the result of a cross between the polyantha 'Yesterday', whose influence one can

The vigorous, hardy shrub 'Angelica' can be grown as a climber in mild climates.

In 1986 'Bonica' was the first shrub to be named an All-America Rose Selection.

easily see, and the hybrid tea 'Peter Frankenfeld', whose contributions require an active imagination to picture. 'Angelica' is not patented in the United States, and anyone who wants one will find it remarkably easy to grow from cuttings and very happy on its own roots.

'Angelica' is rich, pure pink, shading to white at its center, with a lighter reverse. It grows 8 feet tall by 10 feet wide against an east-facing wall for me. In Japan, 'Angelica' is sold as a climber, and I think that anyone in a mild climate would want to consider using it as one.

'BONICA' (MEIdomonac)
Meilland, France, 1985

This is the shrub that broke down the doors in the American commercial marketplace. This break-through shrub produces an endless parade of clear, pink blooms on a bush that is the picture of health. It is hardy and tough, but its wide sprays of fluffy flowers give it a light and ethereal appearance in the garden—something one might usually expect only from a much more delicate rose. 'Bonica' is not a shrub that one must learn to like—you need only see it growing to appreciate its many qualities.

In 1986, 'Bonica' became the first shrub ever named as an All-America Rose Selection. At that time, its introducers blundered by not giving it an original name. The name 'Bonica' had already been assigned to a scarlet floribunda introduced in 1958, so 'Bonica' could not be exhibited or referred to in official rose society publications except under the awkward code name of MEIdomonac. Add to the clumsy naming some rather goofy publicity that stressed 'Bonica''s suitability as a habitat for birds, and many rosarians were left scratching their heads: "Let me see, they didn't bother to give it a name of its own, and they say birds will like it." But many who took a pass that first year have since been converted.

I have grown 'Bonica' since before its commercial introduction without ever having seen any

birds living in it. Of course, a rose that thrives without chemical spraying helps to encourage bird populations in the wider sphere of nature beyond its narrow, slightly spreading branches.

'HEIDELBERG' ('GRUß AN HEIDELBERG')
Kordes, Germany, 1959

The kordesii climbing shrubs originated by Wilhelm Kordes in the 1950s are noted for their shiny foliage, disease resistance and winter hardiness. 'Heidelberg' is more elegantly formed than many of them and provides a consistent second crop of its 4½-inch blooms each fall. The flowers are bright crimson with a rose red reverse; orange shadings appearing in cool weather. 'Heidelberg' is not very fragrant, a failing it shares with most of the kordesiis. 'Heidelberg' grows with vigor to about 6 feet, making an excellent free-standing shrub or pillar-type climbing rose.

Exhibiting Kordesiis

Because the kordesiis are classified with the shrubs, that is where kordesii specimens must be exhibited in rose shows conducted under the rules of the American Rose Society. Nurseries are not diligent about differentiating the kordesiis they offer from their climbers, and many a novice exhibitor has seen his entry of 'Dortmund', 'Heidelberg' or 'Parkdirektor Riggers' disqualified on account of being entered as a climber instead of a shrub. Two important rules for new exhibitors: First, it doesn't matter what the catalogue sells a rose as; second, just because it climbs, doesn't necessarily mean it's a climber. Official classifications can be found in the *Combined Rose List* and the publications of the American Rose Society.

'Heidelberg' is one of the landmark kordesii climbing shrubs originated by Wilhelm Kordes in the 1950s.

'LAVENDER DREAM' (INTERLAV)
Ilsink, The Netherlands, 1985

'Lavender Dream' is a versatile, effective landscaping rose that appreciates some shade.

'Lavender Dream' makes great masses of semi-double blooms. These begin as bright lavender and fade quickly to lilac. Growing to a compact, bushy 3½ feet and covered with huge sprays of small blooms all summer long, this rose is rather like a smaller version of a hybrid musk. 'Lavender Dream' is a rose that complements its neighbors rather than demanding attention for itself, and it is very easy to include in the perennial border. It does appreciate some shade and may not be at its best in southern California and other areas of unrelenting heat.

'LILLIAN GIBSON'
Hansen, USA, 1938

Rosa blanda grows wild across much of the northern United States and in many parts of Canada, where it is known as the Hudson's Bay Rose and the Labrador Rose. As one would expect, it is very hardy and also notable for the size of its flowers (3 inches is large for a species) and its lack of thorns. 'Lillian Gibson' is one of its few hybrids.

Growing 5 feet high and almost as wide, 'Lillian Gibson' produces a cascade of nonfading,

The extraordinarily hardy 'Lillian Gibson' is one of the few hybrids of R. blanda.

salmon pink flowers every summer. Although not elegant, they are nicely double and richly fragrant. There is no repeat bloom.

'Lillian Gibson' is extraordinarily winter hardy, and by virtue of canes that turn brilliant red provides uncommon garden interest during the winter. If you are ever possessed with the desire to plant a spirea, stop before it's too late and plant 'Lillian Gibson' instead.

'PEARL DRIFT' (LEGGAB)
LeGrice, England, 1980

'Pearl Drift' is an innovative cross between 'Mermaid', a beautiful but notoriously tender,

slow-growing and tough-to-breed-with, single-petaled yellow climber, and the hardy 'New Dawn'. 'Pearl Drift' is 'Mermaid''s first recorded descendant and one of only a few hybrids related to 'Mermaid''s mother, the species *Rosa bracteata*. (Ralph Moore's recently introduced shrub 'Muriel' and climber 'Pink Powderpuff' are the only other two I am familiar with.)

'Pearl Drift' is covered with shiny, narrow leaves on willowy canes. It grows wider than it does tall, which to some nurseries qualifies it as a groundcover (by this same method of reckoning, however, 'Crimson Glory' would also be a ground-cover). 'Pearl Drift' finishes the summer 3½ feet tall by 5 feet wide for me. Its pearl-colored, semi-double blooms appear in profusion in spring and

An innovative breeding success, the glowing 'Pearl Drift' makes a fine, wide shrub.

The simple beauty of 'Pink Meidiland''s single-petaled blooms make it the most striking of any of the Meidilands.

continue steadily until frost. It has occasionally mildewed in my garden, but has demonstrated perfect winter hardiness in an exposed position.

'Pearl Drift' is a shrub that would be excellent even if its background weren't so unusual; I recommend it highly. It is one of the last legacies of the great English rosarian Edward LeGrice.

'PINK MEIDILAND' (MEIPOQUE, 'SCHLOSS HEIDEGG')
Meilland, France, 1985

Of the dozen Meidilands introduced so far, 'Pink Meidiland' is still the most striking, and none of the others can match the simple beauty of its single-petaled, pink blooms with a conspicuous white eye. A rose looking very much like 'Pink Meidiland' appeared on a commemorative stamp issued by the United States Postal Service in 1994.

Some Meidilands are semi-groundcovers, but 'Pink Meidiland' grows upright to about floribunda proportions. Like many Meidilands, 'Pink Meidiland' produces attractive rose hips that persist well into winter. Unlike many, it is not a constant bloomer, and you may find its spring and fall

What's a Meidiland?

The breeder of Meidilands defines them as everblooming, low-maintenance, disease-tolerant, hardy, vigorous shrubs and suggests using them for quick ground coverage, erosion control and mass plantings. That some of them are exceptionally beautiful may be taken as a bonus.

bloom explosions separated by a distressingly long fuse.

The difference between disease tolerance and disease resistance may be seen in 'Pink Meidiland' growing happily despite some blackspot. This rose shows no mildew and gives no fragrance.

'RACHEL BOWES LYON' (HARlacal)
Harkness, England, 1981

Bred in Britain from the native American species *Rosa californica*, 'Rachel Bowes Lyon' demonstrates several characteristics of its species antecedent, namely small, round leaves, big clusters of bloom and prominent stamens. Toss in a full measure of remontancy and semi-double, pink blooms that marble—that is, display color variegations—in the manner of the spinosissima (or Scotch briar) roses, and you have a very interesting shrub indeed.

'Rachel Bowes Lyon' grows by many small branches into a 5-foot thicket of bloom. The sprays that appear in spring are more spectacular than those that follow, but 'Rachel Bowes Lyon' never sits idle, remaining in bloom well into autumn. This shrub must be one of the most winter-hardy roses ever bred in England. As to disease, 'Rachel

'Rachel Bowes Lyon' was bred in Britain from the native American species R. californica.

Bowes Lyon' follows the crowd. Plant it next to healthy roses, and it will remain healthy. Plant it next to a blackspotter, and it will blackspot. It was named for the Queen Mother's sister-in-law, reported to be an enthusiastic gardener.

'SALLY HOLMES'
Holmes, England, 1976

'Sally Holmes' is a breathtaking rose that is often sold as a climber and best grown as one in all but the most severe climates. Gigantic trusses of perfectly arranged buds and blooms appear all up and down the disease-resistant, narrow-leaved plant throughout the summer. While growing with extreme vigor, 'Sally Holmes' makes foliage that is lighter green than most other roses. This should not be mistaken as a sign of disease or nutritional deficiency.

The pale apricot buds open to pure white, single-petaled blooms. These make excellent cut flower sprays if taken just before opening. 'Sally Holmes' shows affinity to the hybrid musks, but has a character all its own. Its breeder, Robert Holmes, is also responsible for the stalwart floribunda-climber 'Fred Loads' and the new 'Fairy Snow', a white version of 'The Fairy' about which I am very enthusiastic after only one season of growth. Unlike many breeders who introduce three or four often indifferent roses each year, Holmes has limited himself to introducing one outstanding rose every ten years or so.

There are many other worthwhile shrub roses. In addition to those detailed in the sections that follow, I also heartily recommend the following:

'Cardinal Hume'
(HARregale; Harkness, England, 1984)

One spray of the small, double, purple blooms makes a complete bouquet. This rose is always in bloom and always richly fragrant (its cinnamony scent has been compared to that of the candy Red Hots). Vigorous and tremendously hardy, its only fault is a tendency to blackspot. 'Cardinal Hume' grows wider than tall and is sometimes catalogued

The rampageous, beautiful 'Sally Holmes' is a shrub rose that is most effective when used as a climber.

as a groundcover, which it is not. David Austin includes this one with his English Roses.

'Carefree Wonder'
(MEIpitac; Meilland, France, 1991)

This upright, bushy plant is the ideal hedging rose. It combines the toughness of Dr. Buck's prairie roses with some of the color interest of the hand-painted roses in its bright pink and cream blooms. Constant deadheading is required for best performance.

'Esprit'
(KORholst, 'City of Birmingham', 'Holstein '87', 'Petit Marquis'; Kordes, Germany, 1989)

This well-mannered shrub rose grows to healthy floribunda proportions and covers itself with disease-free leaves and lots of semi-double, red bloom. Because 'Esprit' is sterile, it is able to put all of its energy into bloom production. Its long list of synonyms proclaims the commercial success it has enjoyed around the world.

'Morgenrot'
(KORheim; Kordes, Germany, 1985)

The bright clear red, single-petaled flowers open to reveal a modest white eye and an immodest boss of bright gold stamens. Abundant light green foliage makes a fine backdrop for this stunning display. Always healthy and always in bloom, this is a rose that makes people smile. A shrub that every garden has room for, this rose grows compactly and vigorously to about 3 feet.

'Nevada'
(Dot, Spain, 1927)

This rose produces single-petaled, white blooms that show pink tints in the fall. An outstanding shrub, 'Nevada' is not just always in bloom but almost always covered in bloom. It grows to 5 feet and just as wide in the Midwest. The foliage is pale green but quite healthy.

'Romanze'
(TANezamor; Tantau, Germany, 1985)

One of the healthiest of all roses, 'Romanze' produces masses of large, fuchsia pink blooms.

Although double, the flowers open so quickly that one gets the effect of a semi-double rose. This is a rose you can plant and forget, unless you are a hybridizer, in which case you may want to breed with its incredibly healthy, floriferous genes.

'Simplicity'
(JACink; Warriner, USA, 1978)

Notable for its health and extraordinary floriferousness, the individual, semi-double, pink blooms have a lively, fresh appearance but lack the charm we usually seek in roses. Marketed by Jackson & Perkins as a living fence, 'Simplicity' has achieved great, and deserved, commercial success. From the time it was introduced, Jackson & Perkins sold this rose only in lots of ten. This has made it economical to use for hedging, but frustrating for those who have for some reason (usually a severe winter) lost one link of their living fence. Now 'Simplicity''s patent has expired, and replacement plants should be available individually from several nurseries. The recent introductions 'Red Simplicity' and 'White Simplicity' are not sports of the original 'Simplicity'.

'Tall Story'
(DICkooky; Dickson, N. Ireland, 1984)

With graceful, arching growth to 6 feet, this rose makes beautiful sprays of semi-double, very pale yellow to cream blooms. In many respects this is like a modern, remontant version of the alba 'Semi-plena'. With a code name like DICkooky, one might expect it to be strange in some way, but 'Tall Story' is the picture of easygoing elegance. It deserves to be much more widely grown.

'Windrush'
(AUSrush; Austin, England, 1984)

This shrub rose produces semi-double, light lemon yellow blooms that fade to white in hot weather. It is intensely vigorous and always in bloom. Every blossom sets a hip, but seed-setting does not seem to slow flower production. It grows to 8 feet in northern Ohio. 'Windrush' is a better-growing, healthier—but paler—version of the popular 1950s shrub 'Golden Wings'. It was bred by David Austin but not considered one of his English roses.

Hybrid Musks

Here's a quick multiple-choice quiz. Joseph Pemberton

  a. was an Anglican curate
  b. originated the hybrid musk roses
  c. lived all his life in a round house with his sister
  d. all of the above

If you answered "d" you are correct, and if you have ever grown 'Moonlight', 'Penelope' or 'Robin Hood' you have been rewarded with the enduring genius of this somewhat curious man.

Although a few hybrid musks, including 'Robin Hood', display a compact habit, most are limber growers bearing huge clusters of small blooms. Their combination of persistent, relatively free-form growth and delicate-looking, fragrant blossoms associates perfectly with the idea of a cottage garden. Hybrid musks are ideal for planting in a border of tall perennials or around small trees; most hybrid musks are content in dappled shade. They are all repeat bloomers, and as a group have an excellent health record.

Pemberton introduced his first hybrid musks in 1913. He interpreted the phrase "hybrid tea" literally and classified his new roses according to the teas and hybrid teas in their ancestry. Upon realizing that these hybrid teas were completely different from the hybrid teas people were accustomed to, British rose society officials soon persuaded Pemberton to rename them hybrid musks. They are, in fact, only very distantly related to *Rosa moschata*, the musk rose, and bear a closer resemblance and family connection to the ramblers bred from *R. multiflora*.

Seventy years after his death, the hybrid musks and the Rev. Pemberton are still inseparable, despite some often excellent later introductions by his successors, J. A. and Ann Bentall, by Kordes in Germany and by American amateurs. Recently, Belgian rose breeder Louis Lens (the creator of the great hybrid tea 'Pascali') has devoted much of his attention to hybrid musks. Unfortunately, the new Lens hybrid musks are not yet available in the United States.

'Clytemnestra'
(Pemberton, England, 1915)

Ruffled, double, salmon chamois blooms reminiscent of noisettes appear all over this 5-foot bush covered in the typical dark green, narrow hybrid musk foliage. This rose offers excellent repeat bloom in sun or in half shade. In the world of mythology, Clytemnestra murdered her husband, the king, and was in turn slain by her son. One wonders what an Anglican clergyman saw in her.

'Cornelia'
(Pemberton, England, 1925)

Double, strawberry blooms flushed yellow—the overall effect being peach-pink—open quickly to reveal particularly attractive golden stamens. This rose produces impressive sprays all summer and has a notably strong autumn bloom. It has a strong, sweet, somewhat glutinous fragrance.

'Moonlight'
(Pemberton, England, 1913)

This creamy white, semi-double rose is well named. It combines rampant growth with unflagging repeat bloom. An outstanding shrub and one of my favorite hybrid musks, 'Moonlight', like many of the hybrid musks, was raised from the seminal German rambler 'Trier'.

'Penelope'
(Pemberton, England, 1924)

This rose produces semi-double, very palest pink blooms that fade to white and have lemon centers. The most elegant of the hybrid musks, it is the least industrious (of the ones I have grown) at repeat bloom. Recurrence can be encouraged by diligent deadheading of spent blooms. If you do not deadhead, you may not see autumn flowers, but you will get surprisingly attractive orange hips.

'Robin Hood'
(Pemberton, England, 1927)

'Robin Hood' grows to 4 feet in height and nearly as wide, making a neat hedge. This rose blooms in awesome abundance. Appearing as pink from a distance, the blooms are actually bright cherry red

One of the most compact of Joseph Pemberton's hybrid musk roses, 'Robin Hood' makes an excellent hedge.

with a white eye, an exception to the Pemberton preference for soft colors.

One of the greatest stud roses of all time, 'Robin Hood' is an ancestor of 'Queen Elizabeth' and, through a separate line, of nearly all modern floribundas as well as many of David Austin's English roses. This rose was introduced by Florence Pemberton after her brother's death in 1926.

HYBRID RUGOSAS

Most modern shrub roses have such a complicated lineage that it would be impossible (or, as in the case of hybrid musks, misleading) to associate them with any particular species roses. The hybrid rugosas stand alone as a class that has increased in number and variety while still maintaining some of the essential character of its species progenitor. Some modern rugosas, of course, show more of these characteristics than others.

The essential rugosa characteristics are winter hardiness, disease resistance and wrinkled leaves (which is what *rugose* means). To these ingredients, *Rosa rugosa* adds a dash of remontancy, and one can expect repeat bloom from almost all of its offspring.

If you visit coastal Maine today, you might find it hard to believe that rugosas are not native Americans. While indigenous to Manchuria, Korea and Japan, they are quick to naturalize and are especially noted for their suitability in seaside gardens. While rugosas may be tough enough to stand up to the salt in sea spray, they cannot take modern chemicals. To avoid defoliation, I am always careful to skip the rugosas whenever I am spraying synthetic fungicides in the garden.

Fortunately, few rugosas attract disease, and those that do are strong enough to grow despite it.

The rugosas' stocky habit and thorny growth makes them a logical choice wherever an impenetrable hedge is required. Rugosas produce large, attractive, tomatolike rose hips that are commonly used in the production of vitamin C.

'AGNES'
Saunders, Canada, 1900

A cross between *Rosa rugosa* × *R. foetida* 'Persiana', this was the first yellow rugosa and is still the most satisfying. While not a strong yellow color—it can vary with the weather from muddy apricot to ivory—'Agnes' makes a sturdy, healthy, very hardy bush. This very thorny rose has exceptionally crinkled foliage and a rich, raspberrylike fragrance. On the minus side, 'Agnes' does not offer repeat bloom with any reliability, and its papery petals do not match the toughness of the rest of the bush.

'JENS MUNK'
Svejda, Canada, 1974

Working for Agriculture Canada's research department, Dr. Felicitas Svejda used rugosas extensively in the breeding of her series of super-hardy roses named after Canadian explorers. Like all other members of the Canadian explorer series, 'Jens Munk' is very hardy. Many of the explorer roses, however, are several generations removed from their rugosa roots and lack essential

'Agnes' was the first yellow rugosa. Sometimes it is more yellow than at others.

One of the finest modern rugosas, 'Jens Munk' is one of the Canadian Explorer series of super-hardy roses.

characteristics of the class. Not only is 'Jens Munk' an exception, it's one of the most excellent modern rugosas.

'Jens Munk' has semi-double, clear pink blooms that range slightly toward rugosa mauve and enclose an attractive boss of stamens. It's a constant bloomer, releasing a refreshing, spicy scent. While quite vigorous (reaching 5½ feet in Ohio), it forms a shapely bush that deflects any of the usual criticism about rugosas being coarse growers.

You may also want to try these rugosas:

'Hansa'
(Schaum & Von Tol, The Netherlands, 1905)

This rose is the same purple that crimson roses are criticized for fading to, but the double blooms are fresh looking and effective against 'Hansa''s rich green, rugose foliage. It makes an excellent trouble-free hedge, growing to 6 feet and almost as wide. With strong spring and fall bloom, it offers only scattered flowering in between. 'Hansa' has a

Rose Names vs. Bureaucracy

Rose Names vs. Bureaucracy

Rosarians should be grateful Mrs. Munk didn't name her explorer son John, as the Canadian explorer series also includes 'John Cabot', 'John Davis' and 'John Franklin'. Perhaps in consideration of the multitude of other Johns, explorer John Connell's rose was registered as 'J. P. Connell'. That marked quite a concession on the part of the registration authorities, whose complex and sometimes baffling code of rose name etiquette severely discourages the use of initials at the beginning of a name. (Because of this, the Harkness nursery was forced to register its floribunda named for a man known to all of his neighbors as E. E. Greenwell as 'Mr. E. E. Greenwell', and 'L. D. Braithwaite', the rose David Austin named for his father-in-law, could only be registered as 'Leonard Dudley Braithwaite'.)

rich clove scent. Its only weakness is in the stems, which are short and too flimsy for cutting.

'Linda Campbell'
(MORten; Moore, USA, 1990)

An important introduction, 'Linda Campbell' is clearly the best pure red double-petaled rugosa, showing none of the mauve and purple tones common to the class. It makes a bushy shrub, growing to 4½ feet in northern Ohio. The nonfragrant blooms are often borne in wonderfully large sprays.

'Robusta'
(KORgosa; Kordes, Germany, 1979)

This hybrid rugosa provides constant bloom from a thorny bush that grows bolt upright past 7 feet in Ohio. The bright cherry red, single-petaled blooms appear all up and down the bush. This is perhaps the best rugosa for a season-long garden display. (Note that the Kordes rose called 'Pink Robusta' is not a sport and not as impressive.)

Rosa rugosa alba
(Ancient)

This great rose is also a great garden ornament. Its fragile, single-petaled, snow white blooms enclose cream-colored stamens and are spectacular against glossy green foliage.

R. rugosa rubra
(Ancient)

A variation of the species *R. rugosa*, this rose itself is variable, and you may notice subtle differences in plants procured from different nurseries. Like the other species rugosas it offers repeat bloom on new shoots that arise in the summer, rather than true remontancy from the same canes that carried the first flush of summer bloom. The single-petaled blooms are purplish red.

'Vanguard'
(Stevens, USA, 1932)

This orange-pink rose is a most unusually colored rugosa. A tremendous grower, 'Vanguard' has perfectly formed, glossy foliage and good fragrance. Repeat bloom is spotty, and this variety is not as hardy as other rugosa hybrids.

Dr. Buck's Roses

If rose breeders are guided by the proverb "Seek and ye shall find," perhaps the truest definition of the hybridizer's art is in the ability to find things not being sought. Dr. Griffith J. Buck had that gift. He wanted to breed shrub roses that would be winter hardy in the Midwest, and he succeeded. Along the way he also took a step toward blue in roses and developed numerous varieties whose amazing colors are unmatched in modern roses.

Buck's first mission at Iowa State University, where he was a professor of horticulture, was to study and improve rose understocks, the "wild" roses onto which garden roses are bud-grafted. Later, he set out to breed shrub roses that would be healthy in the summer and hardy enough to survive a winter on the Iowa prairie. He found hardiness and health, and freckles too.

Growing Roses from Seeds

Both *R. rugosa alba* and *R. rugosa rubra* are relatively easy to grow from seeds. There are a dozen different ways to grow roses from seeds, and rather than argue the merits or demerits of various schemes, I will simply explain what I do. Other methods may prove equally effective.

First, harvest rose hips in the fall after there have been several light frosts, but no killing frost. Shell the hips and remove the seeds, washing all hip flesh from them. If you are not organic, you will want to soak your rose seeds in a weak Captan solution to avoid rotting. After soaking for 6 to 12 hours, remove the seeds and plant in a tray of moist ProMix or similar soilless mixture. Enclose the tray in a plastic bag and place in the refrigerator. When the seeds start to sprout—this will usually happen in about six weeks—remove the tray from the refrigerator and place it under fluorescent lights in a basement, garage or some other cool place. Keep moist.

As the seedlings develop their true rose leaves, remove them from the tray and plant in deep, 2- to 4-inch pots (the kind in which many nurseries sell their own-root miniature roses), again using a soilless mixture. Watering with a weak Captan solution will guard against damp-ing off, a fungus disease that kills young seedlings. Important: Do not feed your rose seedlings—even weak solutions of fertilizer will prove fatal. I never feed rose seedlings until they have four sets of leaflets and appear to be growing well. If a seedling appears to be struggling, food will not save it.

Although there is no predicting what you might get, it is also fun to grow seeds harvested from hips of modern roses. Seedlings of repeat blooming roses will offer their first flowers indoors on tiny plants when just three to four months old, and it is always a great surprise to see the incredible variety of shapes and colors that can result from a self-pollinated rose hip. You will get to see true colors and petal shapes in the tiny first seedling blooms, but double varieties will put on more petals as the seedling grows or when it is budded onto an understock. You may notice that many of your seedlings have narrow petals (usually considered a fault) and that a seemingly disproportionate number of them will be pink, even if their parent isn't. If you find a really interesting seedling, bud-grafting it onto an understock will enable you to observe its full potential in a relatively short period of time.

'Freckle Face', with dark red blotches on a paler background, was registered in 1976. Its sister seedling, 'Sevilliana', does not show any freckling, except in very cool weather, but is able to pass freckles on to its offspring.

In 1983, Buck developed 'Blue Skies', a hybrid tea that was claimed to be the first modern rose to match "lobelia blue" on the Royal Horticultural Society color chart. This it did, but unfortunately lobelia blue was not as blue as the introducing nursery led customers to believe, and 'Blue Skies' did not grow with very much vigor. For these reasons, 'Blue Skies' soon fell from favor, perhaps the last attempt at a blue rose by someone breeding roses the old-fashioned way, in a greenhouse instead of a laboratory.

Of the more than fifty Griffith Buck hybrids that have been registered, only about twenty are readily available. Even more remain nameless, grown only under test numbers. Iowa State University is establishing a new display garden at Ames, Iowa, that will preserve all of the roses that Dr. Buck developed. For anyone deeply interested in roses, it will be a necessary—and rewarding—pilgrimage.

The crazy colors of 'Distant Drums' appear on a vigorous, free-blooming plant.

'DISTANT DRUMS'
Buck, USA, 1984

A descendant of the gallica 'Belle Isis', this is the closest thing we have to the crazy colors of the gallicas brought up to date. 'Distant Drums' is an incredible mixture of mauve, slate, purple and tan, changing according to the season and as the flower develops. At times you may see slate gray and brownish tan flowers on the bush at the same time.

The flowers have forty wide petals that open quickly to an attractive, shallow cup shape. They have the same intense, aniselike fragrance found in several of David Austin's English roses. 'Distant Drums' makes a bushy, well-branched shrub, growing upright to 4 feet in Ohio. It is always eager to bloom, not always waiting to make long stems under its buds.

'DORCAS'
Buck, USA, 1984

My favorite of the freckled roses, this rose is beautifully unique without having that aura of weirdness that sometimes can settle over a novelty rose. Quite apart from the freckles, 'Dorcas' has all of the qualities required of a great garden rose, blooming early in the season and straight on until frost. The autumn blooms are often the most spectacular. 'Dorcas' comes in sprays of up to ten of its freckled pink blooms. These are great for cutting and appear on a tall, healthy bush.

I also recommend the following Griffith Buck roses:

'Carefree Beauty'
('Audace'; Buck, USA, 1977)

This rose produces semi-double, light rose pink blooms. Growing to 5 feet in Zone 6, it is a picture of health. It could be said that the path to 'Bonica''s commercial success is strewn with 'Carefree Beauty''s petals. Legend has it that this rose scored high enough in the AARS trials to be declared a winner, but that the organization wasn't ready to reward a shrub. America's backyards were ready, however, and the commercial success of 'Carefree Beauty' may have sent a wake-up call to America's nurserymen.

'Honeysweet'
(Buck, USA, 1984)

This is one of the most floriferous of all modern roses; in my garden it is rarely without bloom from Memorial Day to Thanksgiving. Growing as a compact, bushy shrub, it could just as easily have been called a vigorous floribunda. Most of the orange-apricot blooms appear in tightly packed, attractive clusters.

'Pearlie Mae'
(Buck, USA, 1981)

Registered as a grandiflora, 'Pearlie Mae' bears cup-shaped, yellow blended with pink blooms with a pink reverse. These appeal singly and in sprays of up to eight. The bush is healthy, vigorous and slightly sprawling. It was named for Pearl Bailey.

Perhaps the most refined of Dr. Buck's freckled roses, 'Dorcas' has all the qualities of a great garden rose.

'Queen Bee'
(Buck, USA, 1984)

High-centered buds open to cup-shaped, dark red blooms that release a rich, damask fragrance. This rose looks like a small, 1930s hybrid tea on an ultra-vigorous bush. Not as profuse a bloomer as some of the Buck roses, the tall bush is healthy and very winter hardy. After his retirement, Dr. Buck recommended that others use 'Queen Bee' in their hybridizing.

ENGLISH ROSES

David Austin's English roses combine the rich fragrance and multi-faceted, many-petaled bloom form of the best of the old garden roses with the practical habit and repeat bloom of the second-best of the modern roses. It's an unequal marriage—so far we have seen much more of the charm of the old roses than we have the repeat bloom of the modern—but a very successful one nonetheless.

Austin has named almost one hundred varieties of English roses to date, with plans to introduce five or six new ones each year. Many are quite similar to one another, and rosarians will eventually settle on a dozen or so that will endure. After they are all sorted out, English roses will probably be seen as a phenomenon similar to that of the less well-named hybrid musk. Just as perceptive plantsmen treasure Joseph Pemberton's 'Moonlight' and 'Penelope' today and have forgotten all about his 'I Zingari' and 'Princess Nagaka', rosarians in the next century may well still grow Austin's 'Heritage' and 'Mary Rose' but probably will not deed space to his 'Glastonbury' or 'Proud Titania'.

Many of the early English roses, introduced twenty-five years ago, were named for travelers in Chaucer's *Canterbury Tales*. Most of the more mellifluously named, better-educated pilgrims, such as 'The Squire' and 'The Wife of Bath', were so honored. The Clerk, The Cook and The Manciple were not. Characters from Shakespeare provide names for many of the English roses introduced in the early 1980s (such as 'Fair Bianca' and 'Wise Portia'). Since the mid-1980s, Austin has accepted commissions—often associated with various charities—to name roses for individuals and museums, castles and causes, as well as purveyors of throat lozenges ('Fisherman's Friend') and expensive soap ('Evelyn'—for Crabtree & Evelyn).

The English roses have struck a responsive chord in gardeners who are bored with the stereotypical harshly colored, scarcely fragrant modern rose. As such, they are a reaction against the roses of the 1960s more than those of the 1990s. The popularity of the English roses runs at odds with an insistence for disease resistance in roses, and with the exceptions of a few particularly healthy varieties that I have noted below, no one should buy an Austin introduction believing that it offers any special immunity to either blackspot or mildew. Most English roses, however, suffer their diseases gladly, and with no apparent diminution of bloom. If you are willing to suffer their diseases gladly too, English roses can indeed be grown without resort to fungicide sprays.

Many of the English roses grow too large for the small garden. However, there is anecdotal evidence, corroborated in my own garden, that growing them on their own roots will help to encourage more compact growth.

Other rose breeders are following Austin's success right into their hybridizing houses and are emerging with their own versions of new-old roses. Poulsens of Denmark calls them "cottage roses," and the world's most powerful rose breeders, Meillands of France, have settled on the "romantica" label. From California, rose breeder Harvey Davidson has introduced a line of "olde" roses described as hybrid teas with old garden rose form. The official rose classification–making bodies have yet to sanction a distinct class for these roses, which are still lumped together with all of the other modern shrubs. However, the rose world could not possibly find better criteria for English roses than that provided by David Austin himself: beautiful form, based upon the rosette model; soft, rich, pure colors; pleasing natural growth; attractive foliage; and, as an absolute requirement, good fragrance.

'Fair Bianca' is the perfect English rose for smaller gardens, consuming no more space than a floribunda.

'EMANUEL' (AUSUEL)
Austin, England, 1985

'Emanuel''s rosette-shaped, nicely fragrant flowers are pink with gold, for an overall effect of apricot. This is a strong growing, thorny, upright bush whose modern-looking foliage needs protection from blackspot. Its stems are not strong enough to hold the blooms upright, but the height of the bush makes this drooping effect rather charming, as the blooms of 'Emanuel' can look you right in the eye. 'Emanuel' offers excellent repeat bloom. This rose was named for the British dress designers David and Elizabeth Emanuel.

'FAIR BIANCA' (AUSCA)
Austin, England, 1982

'Fair Bianca' is an English rose for every garden, taking up no more room than a floribunda. It makes a twiggy bush, growing upright to about three feet. 'Fair Bianca' looks exactly like an old rose, only a small and well-behaved one. If it has a fault, it is in the pale green, sparse foliage.

The blooms have creamy white petals arranged in perfect rosette form, ending in a button eye. They appear in large, perfectly arranged sprays that have an excellent vase life when cut. In northern Ohio, I get a plantful of sprays in June and another in September. For any bloom in between, I must depend on the appearance of basal breaks.

This is one of the English roses that David Austin describes as having a "myrrh" fragrance. Léonie Bell, an old garden rose authority and co-author and illustrator of *The Fragrant Year*, reported 'Fair Bianca''s scent as that of "strong anise." Most of us are more familiar with anise than with myrrh, and Léonie Bell's impression seems exactly right to me.

'THE COUNTRYMAN' (AUSMAN)
Austin, England, 1987

This is one of two English roses (the other is 'Gertrude Jekyll') that David Austin says could just as easily be called a portland. 'The Countryman' is worth growing for its massive spring bloom and excellent health, but otherwise offers few improvements over authentic old garden roses.

The strongly fragrant, deep pink blooms are made of many narrow petals formed into an elegant rosette. The bush might best be described as free-form, but when its branches are full of bloom, the weight will force them into an attractive mound shape. This mound may display several hundred blooms in spring. Unfortunately, repeat bloom is very poor, and when you cut off the dead blooms to encourage recurrence, the bush will start flopping around again. ('The Countryman' might not be organized, but it is healthy.) Named for the British magazine published for men who have Range Rovers, hounds and perhaps a title,

'The Countryman' is an English rose that offers massive bloom in the spring.

'The Squire' produces spectacular, richly fragrant blooms.

this rose should not be confused with the pink American shrub rose called 'Countryman', which does not have old garden rose form.

'THE SQUIRE'
Austin, England, 1977

Purest crimson formed to perfection, this is still the most spectacular flower of all the Austin reds. It has a rich damask fragrance similar to but—to my nose—more refined than that found in 'Crimson Glory'.

The plant is three feet of gauntness, with many more thorns than leaves. It is best to put it in a bed around something bushy, spray it with fungicides and wait for it to bloom. If you can ignore the bush and remember only the blooms, 'The Squire' will not disappoint you.

'THE YEOMAN'
Austin, England, 1979

One of the original *Canterbury Tales* roses. While David Austin has dropped it from his catalogue, it is still available from numerous other nurseries. (Many nurseries are notorious for stocking their own introductions long after every other grower has abandoned them. Despite listing more than 600 roses in his catalogue, Austin has shown no reluctance to abandon his own varieties when they do not live up to his expectations.) I have a sense that 'The Yeoman' may do better in the United States than it has at home in England.

Despite lacking vigor and attracting mildew, 'The Yeoman' flowers well enough throughout the summer. Its color is a blend of warm pink and yellow that has not appeared in any of the later Austin introductions. Dr. Griffith Buck used 'The Yeoman' in his breeding program, and it is a parent of the remarkable 'Distant Drums'.

'THE WIFE OF BATH'
Austin, England, 1969

'The Wife of Bath' is a tough little rose, making wiry, upright growth to about 2½ feet. This rose

One of the original Canterbury Tales *roses, 'The Yeoman' is a blend of warm pink and yellow not found in any of the later Austin introductions.*

Although short growing, 'The Wife of Bath' is one of the toughest of the English roses, thriving under a wide variety of conditions.

blooms and blooms; while it is a plain pink and ends up with a looser form than some of the later Austins, it could embarrass them with its productivity.

'The Wife of Bath' is another one of the English roses described by David Austin as having a myrrh fragrance. In this case, however, the fragrance is quite distinct from the scent of 'Fair Bianca' and not anything like anise. I cannot recollect this scent in any other rose. While not at all displeasing, the perfume of 'The Wife of Bath' could fairly be described as unusual.

I also have grown the following English roses:

'Abraham Darby'
(AUScot; Austin, England, 1985)

An English rose resulting from a cross of two modern roses (the floribunda 'Yellow Cushion' and the climber 'Aloha'), this rose produces coppery apricot blooms with pink and yellow undertones. It is the most disease-resistant of the English roses I have grown. Its long, arching canes make it suitable for use as a modest climber. Warning: The prickles are enormous (up to 1 inch long!) and dangerous. 'Abraham Darby' was named for an industrial revolutionary who was famous for building iron bridges in nineteenth-century Britain.

'Belle Story'
(AUSelle; Austin, England, 1984)

With clear pink blooms highlighted in peach that fade slightly, this rose has the charm of a semi-double peony with excellent rose fragrance. It is very resistant to powdery mildew and was named for one of the first nurses in the British Royal Navy.

'Bibi Maizoon'
(AUSdimindo; Austin, England, 1989)

This graceful bush, small by English rose standards, has elongated centifolialike leaflets. While its rich pink blooms are individually more elegant, 'Bibi Maizoon' lacks the free-blooming nature of 'Mary Rose'.

'Bredon'
(AUSbred; Austin, England, 1984)

This short, tough bush grows and blooms like a floribunda on steroids. Rosette-shaped blooms of buff yellow blended with cream and pink appear in immense clusters and have a pleasing, raspberrylike fragrance. This rose needs watching for mildew.

'Canterbury'
(Austin, England, 1969)

This English rose produces lovely, semi-double, pearlescent pink blooms on a sparse, low bush. 'Canterbury' needs to be planted amid bushier varieties for best garden appearance.

'Constance Spry'
(Austin, England, 1961)

The exquisitely formed, cup-shaped, soft pink flowers are extremely large, but never vulgar. This is the original English rose, and it does not repeat bloom. 'Constance Spry' grows 12 to 15 feet and can, with some difficulty, be trained as a climber. However, it will be most spectacular where it is given room to sprawl. It was named for the renowned English flower arranger.

'Dove'
(AUSdove, 'Dovedale'; Austin, England, 1984)

This rose's pink buds open to blush-colored blooms that appear in large sprays on a modest, somewhat loose-growing bush. 'Dove' has much of the character of a tea rose, but is perfectly hardy in the northern United States. It makes good cutting stems. David Austin has condemned this one for a tendency to blackspot, but it has proven perfectly healthy in Ohio.

'English Garden'
(AUSbuff, 'Schloß Glücksburg'; Austin, England, 1990)

This rose's buff yellow blooms fade to white in hot weather, and intensify to apricot in cool weather. A short plant without much vigor, it has disturbingly pale green leaves. This is still the best of the low-growing yellow English roses.

'Fisherman's Friend'
(AUSchild; Austin, England, 1987)

Blooms of deepest crimson, fading to purple, are immense but not as elegantly formed as other red English roses. This variety gives good repeat bloom for so large a rose. Very fragrant and very prickly, it is still the best rose ever named for a cough drop.

'Graham Thomas'
(AUSmas; Austin, England, 1983)

Everything good about this rose, named for the famous British plantsman, is in the neatly formed, fragrant, golden yellow blooms. After a decent spring display, the tall, lanky plant is disappointingly sparse for me. This rose needs extra winter protection north of Zone 6.

'Heritage'
(AUSblush; Austin, England, 1984)

This, David Austin's personal favorite among his introductions, produces soft pink, perfectly cupped, rosette-shaped blooms. The most elegant of all of the English roses, it has a commanding scent that could be described as a refreshing blend of lemon and honey. Its blooms appear in clusters throughout the summer. The plant—which grows to 4 feet and is unusually thornless for an English rose—could be faulted only for insufficient foliage. It is extremely winter hardy.

'Lucetta'
(AUSemi; Austin, England, 1983)

'Lucetta' produces soft, clear pink, semi-double blooms. The long canes (to 8 feet) offer little in the way of repeat bloom; you must depend on basal breaks that appear throughout the season for that.

The modern-looking, glossy foliage is quite disease resistant. This is one of the many English roses bred from the floribunda 'Iceberg'.

'Mary Rose'
(AUSmary; Austin, England, 1983)

The best grower and bloomer of all the English roses, this variety is rarely out of rich pink flowers from Memorial Day into October in my Zone 6 garden. It forms a dense, twiggy bush, growing vigorously and somewhat unevenly to 5 feet. Not as elegantly formed or as fragrant as other English roses, 'Mary Rose' is very valuable for its floriferousness and vigor. There are numerous sports, of which the most notable are the white 'Winchester Cathedral', the pale pink 'Redouté' and the medium pink and white 'Striped Mary Rose'. Apart from bloom color, these sports are identical to 'Mary Rose' in every way.

'Othello'
(AUSlo; Austin, England, 1990)

'Othello' blooms in red shades fighting with purple, the purple eventually winning. The large, rather cabbagelike flowers can appear in surprisingly large clusters. It has excellent fragrance and no shortage of vigor. At 8 feet tall by 6 feet wide after just two years in my garden it is growing, one might say, not wisely but too well.

'Sharifa Asma'
(AUSreef; Austin, England, 1989)

This rose has soft pink, perfect rosette blooms on a modest, well-behaved plant (to 3 feet for me) that will fit into any garden. With great fragrance, this is an overall excellent English rose except for sickly looking foliage.

'Sir Walter Raleigh'
(AUSspry; Austin, England, 1985)

The large, bright pink, fragrant blooms have a rather shaggy appearance. Planted effectively as a hedge at the Elizabethan Gardens, Manteo, North Carolina, this plant is disappointingly spotty in my garden.

'Swan'
(AUSwhite; Austin, England, 1987)

This rose produces white blooms with buff-cream interiors. The buds may be tinged green in the manner of many modern roses. Blooms of 'Swan' can be breathtakingly beautiful when they open wide; they are, however, easily ruined by damp weather. This is one of the best English roses to cut, having a vase life of up to ten days.

'Sweet Juliet'
(AUSleap; Austin, England, 1989)

The small, apricot yellow blooms are neatly formed and appear in well-arranged clusters. 'Sweet Juliet' has excellent fragrance. Bred from 'Graham Thomas', it is a much better rebloomer.

'The Dark Lady'
(AUSbloom; Austin, England, 1981)

This strong, bushy grower has adequate repeat bloom and a rich, pure rose fragrance. Except for what he wrote in his sonnets, we don't know what Shakespeare thought about his Dark Lady, and nowhere in those poems does he compare her to wallpaper or even the finest fabrics. However, it is with these domestic comparisons that this dusky red rose is being sold.

'The Pilgrim'
(AUSwalker; Austin, England, 1991)

Well-scented and beautifully formed as classic rosettes, the soft yellow flowers pale disappointingly to white. This tall grower bears its blooms only at the top of long canes, rather than all up and down the bush. Therefore, 'The Pilgrim''s garden appearance will be improved if it is planted behind a shorter, well-foliaged rose.

'Warwick Castle'
(AUSlian; Austin, England, 1986)

The large (4½-inch), luminous pink blooms last very well and are among the most effective English roses to use in arrangements. The bush grows wider than it does tall and does not bloom as much as I would like it to.

'William Shakespeare'
(AUSroyal; Austin, England, 1987)

This rose produces intense red blooms that fade to a purplish black. It has a luxuriant, unforgettable fragrance. This tall, narrow, stiff-looking plant can ill afford to lose any leaves to disease (but, alas, it almost certainly will). 'William Shakespeare' blooms well in the spring, and again in the fall, with no blooms to be seen in between. Its narrow, practically naked growth habit calls for careful garden placement.

GROUNDCOVER ROSES

Many roses make creeping, procumbent growth. But using roses as groundcovers involves a series of tradeoffs. First, and most importantly, a groundcover rose will not smother weeds. If you have weeds where you want to plant groundcover roses, believe me that it will be easier to deal with the weeds before you plant the roses. Thorns are an integral part of roses, and running into thorns is part of growing roses. However, trying to weed under a thicket of groundcovers can become an impossible task. Rather than concentrating on breeding thornless hybrid teas for their novelty value, hybridizers could perform a real service by creating thornless groundcovers.

Most groundcover roses are not dual-purpose roses. They do not recommend themselves as cut flowers and are generally impractical to cut for exhibition purposes. Today's prototypical groundcover produces a mass of tiny blooms, much like an old rambler growing sideways instead of upright. (Groundcovers do, however, have a much better overall health record than the ramblers.) There is no reason why groundcover roses could not cover themselves in full-size blooms and be just as attractive—if not even more so—but so far they do not. Groundcovers are marketed for sale to large-scale purchasers—such as highway commissions, park boards and zoos—who want low-maintenance roses and are intrigued by the idea of buying one rose that can be planted on a six-foot center instead twenty-five roses planted two feet apart.

Because most groundcovers are planted in public places, it is disappointing that, as a class, they are not more fragrant. But the class does enjoy an excellent and well-deserved reputation for good health, and most groundcovers are classic low-maintenance roses, thriving without any extraordinary attention. Most will grow quite happily even when their fading blooms are not deadheaded because they are sterile and produce no hips, because they can continue to bloom even while setting hips or because they have one long, annual flowering followed by the appearance of rose hips.

In the home garden setting, groundcover roses are ideal for embankments and other sunny but hard-to-access areas. Many of the bushier growers can also make superb specimen plants, planted by themselves or in small clumps at the edge of a lawn or around a landscape feature, such as a lightpost.

'FERDY' (KEItoly, 'HANAMI-GAWA')
Suzuki, Japan, 1984

'Ferdy' is a spectacular rose, well worth growing despite its lack of repeat bloom. The coral-pink flowers appear in large sprays strewn all up and

'Ferdy' is a spectacular cascading rose, providing massive color impact for over a month each summer.

One of the bushiest groundcovers, 'Fleurette' comes close to the thornlessness that will make groundcovers especially valuable.

down its long, arching canes. Individually, the small 20-petaled blooms are pretty but not particularly memorable. Observed en masse, they are incredible.

The plant has tiny leaves, many thorns and no health problems. While winter hardy, it appreciates a sheltered position in Zone 6 northward. 'Ferdy' will trail along the ground for 7 to 10 feet or produce a valuable, cascading effect if allowed to grow on a tripod or trail over a retaining wall. An established plant of 'Ferdy' in full bloom is one of the unforgettable highlights of spring.

'FLEURETTE' (INTERETTE, 'FLAVIA')
Ilsink, The Netherlands, 1977

An underrated groundcover, this rose bursts forth twice each summer with a massive display of single-petaled, light pink blooms. These appear to sparkle against the rich green foliage. One can usually find a healthy scattering of bloom in between the two main flushes.

While its habit is more upright than some other groundcovers, 'Fleurette' does make the very dense growth that we expect from this class. Its growth is very uniform, meaning that you can plant three of them, or three hundred, and not worry about a hodgepodge result. It grows 3 to 4 feet high by 5 to 6 feet wide. The bush is healthy and comes close to the thornlessness we need in groundcovers.

'ROSY CARPET' (INTERCARP)
Ilsink, The Netherlands, 1984

As near to perfection as one can expect from a groundcover, 'Rosy Carpet' makes a dense mound of leafy growth that is covered in spring and again in fall with masses of small, single-petaled, deep pink blooms. 'Rosy Carpet' does have prickles, but

'Rosy Carpet' comes as near to perfection as one can presently expect from a groundcover rose.

they are not large. It has a light, clean fragrance and combines outstanding disease resistance with polar hardiness. It grows 6 to 7 feet wide in northern Ohio.

BACK TO THE FUTURE

There is more to the story of the development of roses than a progression from the simple, single-petaled species rose to the sophisticated hybrid tea and the creation of popular new classes such as English roses and groundcovers. To their credit, many hybridizers have done more than merely pile on petals and reach for the high-pointed form now considered ideal. Along the way, many rose breeders have taken detours off the progress highway, reaching into the rich gene pool of roses to create quirky yet valuable varieties that have proven to be more charming than commercially successful. The following portraits describe two of my favorites.

'BLUE BOY'
Kordes, Germany, 1958

What do you call the result of a cross between the nineteenth-century pink moss rose 'Louis Gimard'

The centifolia-shrub 'Blue Boy' can be startlingly blue when the weather cooperates.

and the 1951 floribunda 'Independence' (the rose that ushered pelargonidum, the pigment responsible for geranium orange-red coloration, into the large-flowered roses)? Because it lacks moss, Kordes classified it as a centifolia, and he called it 'Blue Boy' because, despite its rather unlikely parentage, it can be startlingly blue.

'Blue Boy' produces large, scrolled, reddish purple buds that will mature in cool weather to the most amazing blue flowers you could imagine in a rose. 'Blue Boy' is a once-bloomer and is of little value in areas that never see cool weather with the first flush of rose bloom. In much of the North, however, it can be dazzling.

Many rose classifications were rationalized upon the American Rose Society's publication of the ninth edition of *Modern Roses* in 1986. At that time 'Blue Boy' was reclassified from centifolia to shrub.

'JAMES MASON'
Beales, England, 1982

As a result of a cross between the gallica 'Tuscany Superb' and the 1952 shrub 'Scharlachglut' (itself half gallica), 'James Mason' is three-quarters gallica, yet a rose that could not exist until modern times.

It grows taller than most gallicas (to 7 feet in Ohio) and produces a brilliant display of nearly single-petaled, bright red blooms (that fade in just

'James Mason' is a gallica-shrub producing a memorable display of bloom each spring.

a few hours to deep pink). 'James Mason' forms a tough plant, reproducing freely via suckers and growing very easily from cuttings.

The actor James Mason and his wife Clarissa were both keen rosarians, and Clarissa Mason arranged for Peter Beales to name this seedling for her husband. At the same time, Mason was sponsoring the introduction of a fascinating apricot miniature from Harkness called 'Clarissa'. I have always kept 'Clarissa' and 'James Mason' in the same bed. It makes a good story.

'Clarissa' was originally registered as a China, a classification that reflects many of its characteristics, but was converted to a miniature in the same rationalization that turned 'Blue Boy' from a centifolia into a shrub.

Tree Roses

Tree roses, more properly called standard roses, are manufactured by bud-grafting a rose variety on top of a straight, leafless rootstock stem. Most standards are budded at between 3 feet and 3 feet, 3 inches. Half (or patio) standards are usually budded at between 20 and 24 inches. Nurseries offer miniature standards at heights ranging from 12 to 18 inches. Weeping standards, which consist of climbing or groundcover roses budded onto a 5-foot stem, are very popular in Europe and can create spectacular displays. Unfortunately, no American nursery offers weeping standards anymore; the excuse offered for this is that their size makes it impossible to ship them via the postal service or UPS, and truck freight is too expensive.

There is no such thing as a classification of "tree rose." Any rose can be budded as a standard and become a tree rose. But not every rose should be. Varieties that have a bushy, mounded, compact pattern of growth, that grow wider than they do tall or that have a trailing or cascading habit make the most striking standards. Roses that grow bolt upright make the least effective standards.

Tree roses are focal points, and any fault a rose possesses is likely to be magnified when the variety is elevated on a standard stem. Because no standard can be expected to remain in bloom constantly, poor foliage and disease become even more unacceptable for roses budded as standards.

In addition to elevating particularly prized, low-growing rose varieties to eye and nose level, standards add the element of height to the rose landscape in places where climbing roses might not be appropriate (in the middle of a lawn, for example). They are most effective when used sparingly. Planting one standard on each side of your front steps can be dramatic. But planting a dozen standards along the walkway leading to your front steps will almost certainly be melodramatic. It is best to think of standard roses as accent trees, not as something to plant in groves.

Standards are very effective planted in tubs (the seven-gallon size works best) and lend themselves to underplanting (in the tub) with miniature roses or annual flowers such as alyssum. Tubs can be carted into an unheated garage or shed for the winter, thus solving the greatest dilemma of tree rose culture: winter tenderness. With a bud union some three feet above the ground, standards are prone to winterkill anywhere that sees temperatures falling below 10° F. The usual remedy is to tip them over, bury them and then resurrect them in the spring. This is completely effective, but not always practical, and always a lot of work. I recommend planting standard roses in tubs even if you want to integrate them into your garden landscape. In such cases, the tub can be sunk into the ground and removed late each autumn.

It is essential that standard roses be staked for support. Those with bushy heads should be pruned rather severely to maintain their compact habit. Trailing types can be shortened according to your taste.

The following tables list my favorite rose varieties for use as standards, half standards and miniature standards. I include pale colored and highly fragrant varieties among my choices for standards, even though they may act as lightning rods for Japanese beetles where that pest is a problem.

The bushy growth and free-flowering nature of the miniature 'Orange Sunblaze' recommend it as a particularly fine mini standard rose.

Recommended Standards

Class	Rose	Color
Hybrid teas	'Cary Grant'	Orange
	'Fragrant Cloud'	Coral-red
	'Helmut Schmidt'	Yellow
	'Just Joey'	Apricot
	'Lady Rose'	Orange-red
	'Madras'	Cerise
	'Mikado'	Red blend
	'Mon Cheri'	Red and pink
	'Olympiad'	Red
	'Paul Shirville'	Pink
	'Peace'	Yellow with pink
	'Président Leopold Senghor'	Deep red
	'Pristine'	Blush
	'Savoy Hotel'	Light pink
	'Sheer Elegance'	Orange-pink
	'Silver Jubilee'	Coral-orange and pink
	'Tequila Sunrise'	Yellow with orange-red
	'The McCartney Rose'	Rich pink
	'White Masterpiece'	White
Grandifloras	'Sonia'	Pink
	'Tournament of Roses'	Pink
	'White Lightnin''	White
Floribundas	'Amber Queen'	Apricot
	'Anabell'	Orange
	'Anisley Dickson'	Reddish salmon
	'Escapade'	Pink with white
	'Glad Tidings'	Deep red
	'Iceberg'	White
	'Margaret Merril'	White
	'Matilda'	White with pink
	'Pleasure'	Pink
	'Sexy Rexy'	Pink
	'Showbiz'	Scarlet

Class	Rose	Color
Polyanthas	'The Fairy'	Pink
	'Yesterday'	Pink
Climbing miniatures	'Nozomi'	White
English roses	'Heritage'	Blush pink
	'Mary Rose'	Pink
	'The Countryman'	Deep pink

Recommended Half Standards

Class	Rose	Color
Grandifloras	'New Year'	Apricot orange
Floribundas	'Amber Queen'	Apricot
	'Hakuun'	White
	'Regensberg'	Pink and white
	'Showbiz'	Scarlet
	'Sun Flare'	Yellow
	'Trumpeter'	Orange-red
Polyanthas	'The Fairy'	Pink
Miniatures	'Robin Redbreast'	Red
Patio roses	'Brass Ring'	Apricot
	'Hakuun'	White
	'Laura Ashley'	Purple
	'Sweet Chariot'	Purple
English roses	'Fair Bianca'	White

Recommended Miniature Standards

Class	Rose	Color
Miniatures	'Acey Deucy'	Red
	'Autumn Fire'	Orange-red
	'Debut'	Red and white
	'Dee Bennett'	Orange
	'Magic Carrousel'	White with pink
	'Minnie Pearl'	Pastel pink
	'Orange Sunblaze'	Orange
	'Rise 'n' Shine'	Yellow
	'Starina'	Orange-red
	'Winsome'	Mauve-pink

Cultural Notes

In short, plant your roses in the sun, give them water and keep all the healthy leaves you can. Beyond that, you can make rose growing as easy or as complicated as you want. These notes are based on my experiences growing roses in USDA Zone 6b (roughly the mid-zone of the country). Your experience may differ, and I urge you to trust your experience more than anything you read in a book.

In *Old Garden Roses*, Edward Bunyard said, "The nursery foreman who knows his apples by the leaves alone, the shepherd who recognizes all his sheep, do so not by superior brains, but by careful observation stimulated by some measure of interest, or it may even be love." If you care about your roses, have a desire to learn more about them and have time to give them, they're going to do fine.

PLANNING AND PREPARATION

Choosing a Site

Roses like sunshine and fresh air, so avoid any location that does not get at least a half day of sunshine (morning sun being preferred to afternoon) or that is so crowded (by buildings or by other plants) that air cannot move around freely. On the other hand, if you plant your roses in an open field,

you may encounter wind damage during the growing season and increased losses over the winter. Thus, the ideal, open site for roses would include some kind of windbreak.

When choosing a site for your rose garden, try to anticipate the future growth of any trees or large shrubs. If forced to compete with the roots of larger plants, roses will lose. If you are not certain whether a possible site has enough sunlight for roses, put potted roses there for a summer to see how they do.

Good drainage is essential. To test this, you can dig a hole (at least 15 inches deep), fill it with water and see if it drains away within 12 hours. If it doesn't, you will have to install drainage, build raised beds or find another site.

It is often said that roses like clay soil, and so they do. But they like sandy soils too, when improved by organic soil amendments. Clay soil is not always a blessing, being heavy to work with and more subject to poor drainage. Roses will grow in any soil that grows good vegetables, annual flowers, a lawn or vigorous weeds.

New Beds

To allow for settling, prepare new rose beds in the summer for fall planting or in the fall for spring planting. Beds should be prepared to a depth of 15 to 18 inches. Building raised beds can improve drainage, but will also require more frequent

The home garden of Paul E. Jerabek in Kirtland, Ohio.

watering and, possibly, more diligent winter protection. If you use timber or railroad ties to construct raised beds, make sure that this wood has not been treated with deadly creosote.

A good recipe for a 100-square-foot rose bed is:

- 18 cubic feet organic matter (half peat moss, the remainder compost, leaves, ground bark, rotted sawdust, well-rotted manure or any similar organic material)
- 5 cubic feet perlite or builder's sand
- 20 pounds gypsum
- 15 pounds 0-46-0 fertilizer (see page 177) or equivalent phosphorous source (such as triple superphosphate). Bone meal can also be used, but a much greater quantity would be needed.
- 2 pounds Epsom salts (magnesium sulfate)
- Dolomitic limestone (as indicated by soil test). Unless your soil is quite alkaline, you will need to add at least 10 pounds of limestone to balance the very acidic peat moss.

I really believe in perlite for making soil lighter and less compactable. When my wife added perlite (at just 2 cubic feet per 100 square feet) to a nonachieving bed, the roses performed better than they had in seven years.

In addition to being an important ingredient in new rose beds, gypsum is also a valuable addition to established beds. Gypsum acts as a "soil flush," purging the salts that can build up with prolonged applications of chemical fertilizers. When applied annually, gypsum will eventually act to loosen clay soils.

PLANTING

Before planting, prune away all twiggy and broken stems. Also trim off any broken roots. It is better to dig a hole to fit the roots than to shorten the roots to fit the hole. However, if because of some special circumstance you are faced with a choice of pruning the roots or twisting them around the bottom of the planting hole, then it is better to prune

them. Years ago, the eccentric Oregon rose grower and anti-tax crusader Roy Hennessey commanded all of his customers "Don't prune the roots!" while at the same time sending roots that often exceeded 24 inches in length. Mr. Hennessey caused a lot of backache, but he grew good roses, and it is extremely unlikely that you will receive 24-inch roots from any nursery today. Almost all roses are mechanically harvested, with both the stems and roots being pruned severely to accommodate contemporary storage and shipping requirements.

Planting the bud union above ground will stimulate basal breaks but provides real winter protection problems in the North. Planting the bud union below ground level discourages basal breaks but encourages the plant to own-root itself (something many gardeners find advantageous). Planting in Zone 6, I have settled on a middle course, setting bud unions exactly at soil level. However you set the bush at planting, it is likely to sink an inch or so over its first year.

If you want to build one of those little mounds in the bottom of your rose planting hole, as is so often recommended to secure the height of the bud union, and spread all the roots around it, I am not going to stop you. But I believe it is unnecessary and ill-suited to the way most rose roots are shaped. What I recommend—and do—instead is to study the plant. Almost invariably, one side will have made less growth than another. If you plant this side where it will receive the most sun possible, you will have your best chance for a more perfectly balanced plant.

Many nurseries will send a "How to Plant" guide with their roses, and most of these picture a pair of feet tramping down the soil around the newly planted rose. The idea—to eliminate air pockets—is commendable and necessary, and foot trampling will present no problem on sandy soil. However, roses need to breathe too, and if you have heavy soil—not to mention heavy feet—it might be kinder to your rose plants to use your hands instead of your feet.

Complete the planting process by mounding the plant with soil to a height of 8 to 10 inches. If you are planting in the fall, this mound will see

Planting a rose:

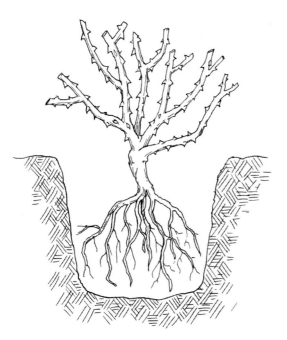

1. Prepare hole big enough to accommodate all roots.

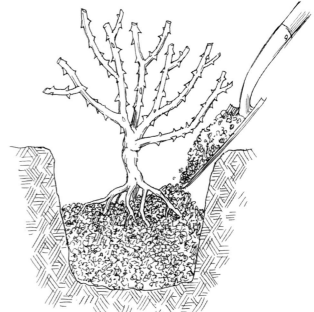

2. Fill in hole with fine soil.

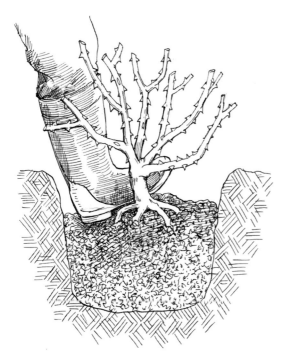

3. Firm down soil as you go.

4. Final soil level 1 inch above graft.

your rose through winter. If you are planting in the spring, it only has to keep the canes from drying out until new growth can begin. To this end, be sure to keep the mound moist. After you see new growth in the spring, gently wash the mound away with water. To avoid shock to the plant, it is best to remove the mound on a cloudy day. Watch your mounded roses carefully; new shoots that grow for too long inside the mound will become white instead of red or green and are subject to sun scald.

How quickly a newly planted bare root rose springs into growth depends on the condition of the plant and on your climate. New growth should appear in 10 to 14 days under ideal conditions. In the North, a perfectly healthy plant can take as long as five to six weeks to display new sprouts after planting in the spring.

Potted roses should be planted in a hole somewhat deeper than their pot. Make sure that the soil has been broken up at the bottom of the planting hole, so that rose roots will have no trouble entering it. Slide the rose out of its pot by gently grasping at the shank just below its bud union or, for own-root plants, by tapping all four sides of the pot, setting it on its side and gently easing the plant out.

Apart from a source of phosphorous, such as triple superphosphate or bone meal, don't apply any fertilizer at planting time. I generally don't start feeding my new roses until after their first bloom.

In general, hybrid teas can be planted 20 to 24 inches apart in the North, 30 to 36 inches apart in the South, and up to 48 inches apart in gardens that stay frost-free. Floribundas can be planted much closer together, especially if you are growing them primarily for garden effect rather than individual cut stems. Even though I am mindful of the necessity of good air circulation, I have had good luck planting most floribundas just 12 inches apart in Zone 6. Miniatures can be planted from 8 inches apart in the North to 18 inches apart in the South. Shrubs, climbers and old garden roses are so variable in size that no attempt can be made to recommend a uniform garden spacing. It all

depends on your climate, the size of the variety you're planting and the size of what you've planted next to it. As a very general guideline, allow a planting distance of two-thirds of the expected height of the variety you are planting. Don't forget to leave ample room between the rose and the edge of the bed: For this, half the expected height of the rose is usually satisfactory. It always makes sense to save more room around a particularly prickly variety.

If you are planting many roses, it is a good idea to stake out where each one will go ahead of time. Even though I have done it myself, I recommend against planting roses three deep in a bed. When this is done, the middle row is bound to suffer. If you never plant roses more than two deep, your roses will be happy, you will be happy (because you do not have to struggle to get to your roses) and your soil will be happy (because you will not be compacting it by walking around on it). Name tags in front of each rose variety can be removed by children and dogs, so keeping a rose garden plan on paper or in your computer is also a good idea. Garden visitors do appreciate rose name tags, and some will inevitably become more interested in the names than the roses. After spending more than an hour in my garden, one visitor told me that she thought she could grow roses as well as I do, but she could never think up names for all of them!

Wrong-Time Roses

In my experience the French do it, the Canadians do it and one year even a California nursery did it. Occasionally, bare-root roses are shipped to customers at inappropriate times. What do you do if roses arrive on your doorstep before spring reaches your garden?

First, bring them indoors. Keep the unopened parcel in a cool cellar or breezeway or in a frost-free garage. The plants may not have been freeze-damaged in transit. There is hope, but you do not want the roses sprouting forth now. Your aim is to keep the roses in a dormant state.

Next, register your dissatisfaction with the nursery. It may already be too late to reserve replacements for delivery at the proper time that same spring, but in any case it is important to go on record right away with your complaint. You may have received dead roses; if they are alive, you have received a substantial measure of inconvenience. A reputable nursery will want to put things right.

To bridge the time until you can plant them properly, the wrong-time roses will need to be buried outdoors or potted indoors. Immediately before you do either, remove them from the box and soak the entire plants in (preferably muddy) water for 12 to 24 hours.

Is your garden frozen solid? If it is not, and you have a spot where you can bury your roses until proper planting time, start digging. A site with perfect drainage is essential. This can often be found right up against the house, where the ground can remain unfrozen most of the winter. Dig a trench as deep as the box the roses came in is wide and long enough to accommodate each bundle of roses. There is no need to separate roses that the nursery has tied together. You may want to add a length of plastic clothesline to help you find your buried bundles in the spring. Set the bundles lengthwise in the trench (or if the roses are not bound, set the plants lengthwise, canes of one on top of roots of the next, all the way down your trench). Cover with soil.

When you dig the plants up in a month or two, you will have a better idea if they are dead or alive. Live plants will almost always plump up and show swelling at the bud-eyes (the bumpy nodes on the canes) after being buried. (Burial is also excellent treatment for rose plants that have dried out in shipment.)

If the garden is frozen solid when bare-root roses are received, your best course of action will be to pot them and keep them indoors until kinder weather arrives. Once again, find the coolest, frost-free place you can to keep these containers. Roomy, 12-inch pots are best—each one will take a 20-pound bag of potting soil. When you cut the tops of the canes back to about 8 inches at potting,

brown or black pith will warn you of frozen plants. Prune away any obviously dead wood. But even white-pithed plants could be doomed by roots recently frozen in transit. (Rose roots freeze and die at 14° F.) Time will tell. Sometimes the most hopeless-looking plant will grow and even prosper. Roses can surprise you. So can nurseries.

Transplanting

Depending on how hard you want to work at it, roses can be transplanted at any time. But the only really sensible time is when they are dormant, and I have had much better luck with spring transplanting than with fall. Transplant roses after light pruning but before they start growing in the spring. Save as much root structure as possible and do everything possible to minimize the time the plant spends out of ground. (Treatment with a vitamin B-1 solution couldn't hurt and might help.) Water thoroughly and keep the canes covered until they start to break dormancy—dirt, sawdust and beige plastic bags all work well.

GROWING

Water

Water makes everything happen. The old rule of 1 inch of rain per week may be applicable in some areas, but so long as your rose beds are well drained they will be happy with two or three times that amount of water. (Incidentally, 1 inch of water over a 1,000-square-foot garden means 600 gallons of water.) Two or three light waterings can never equal the value of one good soaking.

Mulch

The purpose of mulch is to keep the soil temperature steady, conserve water, prevent weeds and, in some cases, enrich the soil. Organic mulches will provide extra humus as they break down. Bacteria feed on this humus, creating nitrogen in a form plants can use. Mulches should not, however, be confused with fertilizers and are not a substitute for them.

Architectural mulch (such as bark or pebbles) may or may not look attractive in your garden. These types of mulch will definitely make it more time-consuming to incorporate organic soil amendments, and the inconvenience of pushing mulch aside and then having to pull it back may force you into a dependence on liquid and foliar fertilizers. Architectural mulches make convenient hiding places for spider mites. All mulches consume nitrogen as they break down, but wood chips consume massive quantities of it. To keep your roses growing evenly, give them about a handful of nitrogen fertilizer (such as urea 45-0-0) for each bushel of mulch.

Organic mulches may host fungus spores or, in the case of manures, contain weed seeds. Additionally, manure mulches seem to offer an ideal staging ground for the devastating rose midge. As soon as it has been spread, drench rotted manure with liquid diazinon to prevent midge. An organic mulch should start becoming part of your soil as soon as it is applied. I have been very satisfied with leaf mold, in the form of a composted leaf humus prepared and sold by a county recycling agency. Leaf mold is a superb soil conditioner and holds water extremely well. Whatever mulch you use, do not spread it so deeply that water cannot quickly penetrate to your rose roots. Coverage of 3 to 4 inches works well with most mulches.

Some rosarians claim to be cultivators instead of mulchers, controlling weeds and aerating their soil with frequent hoeing. But whether they know it or not, cultivators are mulchers too, and their mulch is called "dust." If you cultivate your roses, be sure to do so as shallowly as possible. Rose roots can grow very near to the soil surface and can easily be damaged. It is also essential to avoid injuries to rose canes because these make perfect entryways for crown gall and downy mildew disease.

Blind Shoots

Sometimes a repeat-blooming rose will throw a shoot that does not produce a bloom. There are numerous possible explanations for this:

1. rose midge (see page 184)
2. cold weather (when the bud should have formed, the weather may have been too cold for it to do so)
3. too much nitrogen fertilizer
4. nonproductive growth (Numerous varieties—including the otherwise excellent floribunda 'Georgette', several hand-painted roses and many orange and yellow hybrid teas raised in Germany—produce tall, climberlike canes that do not bloom. These canes usually appear in the autumn and represent a genetic rather than cultural defect.)
5. It could be a sucker (see page 190).

Disbudding

If you are interested in producing especially large blooms to use as cut flowers or for exhibiting, watch for small clusters of buds to appear at the top of a stem and remove all of the buds except for the center one. These baby buds can be very easily broken off with your fingers as soon as they are large enough to handle. Removing sidebuds at this early stage will minimize any scarring. The one remaining bud should then grow into a larger bloom than it would have otherwise.

If you want to exhibit a spray of roses, you will need to disbud in reverse, removing only the center bud from what should be a fairly large cluster of buds. If not removed, the center bud will open before the rest, spoiling the display. Many floribundas and shrubs, and most polyanthas, throw sprays that are composed of several distinct clusters of buds. In these cases, an exhibitor will disbud the terminal bud from each of the individual clusters.

Weeds

A thick mulch is the most effective way to stifle weeds among your roses. Although time-consuming, cultivation is an effective method of control as long as care is taken to avoid deep hoeing and injuries to the canes. Some pelletized pre-emergent weed killers are safe to apply around roses first thing in the spring: Be sure to read the label to make sure you are using a product labeled for use with roses. The only liquid weed killer that can be used around roses is Roundup (also sold as Kleenup). Even with Roundup, extreme care must be taken to avoid injury to roses. Never use this product when the wind is blowing or when humidity exceeds 75 percent.

A separate sprayer must be dedicated for weed killer use because it is impossible to wash away all traces of weed killer. Never use a sprayer that has contained weed killers to spray anything but weed killer. Most weed killers kill weeds by causing them to grow themselves to death. Weed killer affects roses by causing weird, stringy, elongated growth with tiny leaves. Cut all such damaged growth out and water as well as your drainage allows. In most cases, the rose will recover and grow normally after a month or two.

If you employ a lawn service contractor, be certain that they do not spray any liquid weed killers on the lawn around your roses. It is bound to drift, and your roses are guaranteed to be damaged. Insist that they use granular weed killer only, if they use any weed killer at all, and that they keep it well out of the rose bed.

FEEDING

Those Three Numbers

The three numbers on bags of fertilizer refer to nitrogen, phosphorous and potassium in that order. For example, a fertilizer labeled 10-15-12 would contain 10 percent nitrogen, 15 percent phosphorous and 12 percent potassium (the remaining balance being inert ingredients).

- Nitrogen makes plants grow. Too much nitrogen will leave you with stems and leaves (often elongated stems and leaves) at the expense of blooms. Too much nitrogen later in the season will encourage new, soft growth that reduces a plant's winter hardiness. With too little nitrogen, a plant will grow poorly, producing smaller flowers and weak, thin stems. I like to start out after pruning with a high-nitrogen organic, such as blood meal or fish emulsion, applied according to the label's instructions.

- Phosphorous promotes healthy root systems and good bloom production and size. With too little phosphorous, bloom production will drop, and leaves at the bottom of the plant will turn purplish red. I always add phosphorous, usually in the form of triple superphosphate, when planting roses.

- Potassium works much like motor oil, smoothing the way for all of the other nutrients and micro-nutrients. A lack of potassium can be indicated by poor blossom color and leaves with yellow tips. Potassium is often lacking in sandy and red clay soils and in areas that are poorly drained. Potassium nitrate provides the perfect boost for those looking for perfect autumn blooms. Scratch no more than a scant tablespoon around each bush six to eight weeks before your peak autumn bloom and water in well.

In addition to nitrogen, phosphorous and potassium, roses also require calcium, magnesium and sulfur, all of which should be present under most conditions. There are also seven necessary micro-nutrients, of which the most essential are iron and magnesium.

A deficiency of iron can be diagnosed from chlorosis (leaves turning yellow while their veins remain green). Chelated iron is sold at garden supply stores, but you may want to have your soil tested first. An improper pH level can make iron unavailable to your plants. Roses are said to grow best with a soil pH of between 6.0 and 7.0. (7.0 being neutral on the pH scale of acidity and alkalinity). You do not have to become a soil scientist to grow good roses, but checking to make sure that your soil pH is somewhere in this slightly acidic range is not a bad idea. Applications of chemical fertilizers drive the pH down into the acidic range; applications of lime push it back up toward alkalinity. Lime can take a long time to act; it is most effective to apply it in the fall and let it work over winter.

Magnesium activates many valuable enzymes already present in your soil and is easy to add to your rose bed in the form of Epsom salts. Epsom salts have a reputation for promoting basal breaks in roses. I use a small handful around each bush in the spring and again in early July.

The easiest way to feed roses is with a water-soluble, well-balanced fertilizer (such as 20-20-20). Apply fertilizer according to the label's directions once a month throughout the growing season, stopping six weeks before the first expected frost.

A time-released fertilizer (such as Osmocote) can provide your roses with a steady supply of food for up to three months. While time-released fertilizers cost much more than ordinary kinds, they can be invaluable time-savers. Soil tests in northern Ohio have shown that rosarians who have depended on these products exclusively for several years may accumulate so much potassium in their soil that it becomes unusable. Like every food, Osmocote is best as part of a larger diet, rather than as something fed all by itself. When used as part of a larger menu of rose foods, Osmocote provides a constant source of "background" food, helping to level out any peaks and valleys in your feeding program. Moisture is necessary for the plant food in Osmocote to be released.

The best time to feed the roses is when it is raining. The second best time is just after it has stopped.

Organics

Organics are generally more bulky than synthetic foods. Therefore, they take more time to apply. While taking longer than synthetics to act, they also provide benefits over a longer stretch of time. Organics generally require warm soil to work their wonders. They can be applied when the soil is cool, but won't do much until it heats up.

- Alfalfa meal (sold as rabbit food) contains triconatol, a growth stimulant valuable to roses. Applied liberally each spring, alfalfa meal does double duty as a soil conditioner. Alfalfa must be thoroughly mixed into the soil and is not an effective mulch.

- Whether whole fish, fish meal or fish emulsion, a dose of fish can add a real boost to your rose feeding program. Fish emulsion is sold "deodorized," but whole fish and fish meal will probably attract cats, dogs, raccoons and other beasts to your garden.

- Seaweed is not a complete fertilizer, but it is incredibly rich in the trace minerals that roses need. Nothing works better than seaweed to improve rose foliage. It is most economical when applied as a foliar spray. (I use an inexpensive hose end sprayer to apply seaweed because it can clog the finer mechanisms of more expensive sprayers.)

- Cottonseed meal is an excellent high-nitrogen organic, but its acidic pH makes it more effective in alkaline gardens.

Rural feed stores are often a cornucopia of products that rosarians need, often offered at savings over what suburban garden centers charge. In addition to the usual chemicals, look to feed stores for all of your bulk organics, such as alfalfa meal, cottonseed meal, fish emulsion and meal and many kinds of mulches.

Easy Compost

There is no better soil conditioner for roses than compost. I use it as a top-dressing for roses grown in pots and tubs and spread as much around the garden as I am able to make. Instead of the traditional compost pile, or one of the newer compost tumblers, I make my compost in trash bags. This is not a new idea. I got it years ago out of *Organic Gardening*, back when it was an odd-size little publication with stories about people who ate weeds and hellfire and brimstone advertisements from Mr. Ben J. Quisenberry, the famed Ohio River tomato seedsman and Prohibitionist. Anyway, organic gardeners who did not have room for a compost heap were urged to rake all of their autumn leaves into plastic trash bags, stash them behind the garage or in some similar out-of-the-way spot and forget about them for a few years. And so I did.

The process works all by itself—the leaves become black, crumbly compost in about three years with no turning, rotating or forking. One can accelerate the process and gain up to a year by adding some finished compost, manure or, especially, earthworms to each bag. For the ultra-organized, color coding can save prying into unfinished compost a year or two down the line: white bags in year 1, followed by green the next year and finally brown or black is a sequence that has worked well for me. For the ultra-lazy, prebagged leaves can usually be found around the neighborhood each autumn. While hardwood leaves such as oak are preferred over the gooey maple for winter protection, within the confines of a plastic bag all leaves seem to compost equally.

Ironically, the new more environmentally correct lawn and garden bags made with biodegradable cornstarch are not a good choice for trash bag composting. We want the leaves to decompose within the bag, not have the bags decompose around the leaves. However, if you are stuck with cornstarched plastic for your composting, keep the bags out of the sun (this will keep them together longer) and keep them in a place where you can easily maneuver (because in three years' time you will probably have to shovel your compost). The old, less destructible plastic enables you simply to carry bags of finished compost—black gold—over to the rose beds. Whichever way it gets there, trash bag leaf compost is unrivaled as a high-quality, no-fuss, no-muss, practically free soil amendment.

PESTS AND DISEASES

None of these potential problems should discourage you from growing roses. It is unlikely that you will see more than a few of them at any one time, and the amount of effort that you devote to controlling them depends on how close to absolute perfection you want your roses to grow. If you are not already a perfectionist or planning to become a rose exhibitor, complicated measures of pest and disease control are seldom necessary. With adequate food and plenty of water, many roses will be quite pleasing even when far from perfect.

Diseases

Blackspot

Rose blackspot is easy to identify because the spots have a frilly edge. Blackspot is usually seen first on mature leaves. Eventually, leaves with blackspot turn yellow and drop off. In a severe infestation, which is most likely to take place during or immediately following a period of wet weather, a plant can be defoliated in a short time. It can be difficult for a plant to refoliate in the same growing season and to survive a tough winter after defoliation. Blackspot kills more roses in the winter than it does in the summer.

Roses that are described as resistant to blackspot will still show the spots, but have leaves that will live a long time with them. No rose has been shown to be completely immune to blackspot, and after a leaf gets blackspot it is doomed.

Blackspot can be prevented but not cured. Fungicides can protect new foliage from blackspot, but do nothing to help leaves that are already showing symptoms. If you choose to apply a fungicide, begin immediately after spring pruning and continue according to the label's directions throughout the growing season. If you use a nonsystemic fungicide (read the label; most, but not all, powders are nonsystemic), you will need to reapply it after every rain or heavy dew.

Blackspot needs water to spread and is seldom a problem in the Southwest and in other dry climates. In other parts of the country, it is wise to limit overhead watering to the morning. If you are battling blackspot, eliminating overhead watering altogether may be a good idea.

Blackspot spores are so common, and so tiny (more than 30,000 fit on one blackspot), that the old advice to vigorously sanitize the garden of all fallen leaves is sometimes seen as overly fussy. However, I still think it is a good idea, especially as it can help to eliminate the much less plentiful downy mildew fungus (see page 181).

Blackspot was not as serious a problem in the days before factory smokestack scrubbers and other anti-pollution devices. In the 1940s and 1950s, rosarians living near industrial complexes rarely had to worry about blackspot because all the sulphur in the air acted as an incidental fungicide.

A dormant spray of lime sulphur is often recommended as an environmentally superior method of blackspot control. However, dormant oil and lime sulphur are two of the most toxic things we can use in the rose garden, and there is little real evidence that they are effective in preventing blackspot. If you feel a desire to spray your roses when they are still dormant, you would do better to spray them with the same fungicide that you use in the summer.

Poorly pithed and weak twiggy growth left on roses is an open invitation for blackspot to attack. Severe spring pruning is the most effective, "natural" way of blackspot control.

Anthracnose

Most often found on descendants of *Rosa multiflora* and *R. wichuraiana* (including many ramblers, climbers and polyanthas), anthracnose is characterized by dark, purplish, brownish black spots on the foliage. As they mature, these spots develop grayish white centers. Eventually, the centers of the spots will die and drop out, leaving small holes in the leaves. Like blackspot and downy mildew, anthracnose spores are spread via moisture, but unlike in those more deadly diseases, the leaves rarely turn yellow and defoliation is uncommon.

Anthracnose was once easily controlled by metallic-based fungicides. More recent rose fungicides, developed to control blackspot and powdery mildew, have little effect on anthracnose. Fortunately, anthracnose spreads very slowly compared with other rose fungus diseases and is rarely fatal.

Powdery Mildew

Powdery mildew appears as a fine white growth covering the upper, youngest part of the plant: Stems, leaves and buds can all be coated in white, and in a severe attack buds will become distorted and unable to open.

Powdery mildew is most common in areas of high humidity and whenever warm days are followed by cool nights. Its spread is encouraged by poor air circulation. Keeping your roses well fed can generally help them fend off powdery mildew, but giving them too much nitrogen will only encourage the soft top growth that powdery mildew likes best.

Overhead watering between the hours of 11:00 A.M. and 3:00 P.M. can break the cycle of mildew spores. The most effective fungicides against powdery mildew are systemic, meaning that within 6 to 8 hours after application they have entered the plant tissue and cannot be washed off. For this reason, a combination of spraying fungicides and overhead watering can be quite effective. Because powdery mildew appears first at the top of the plant, severe examples of it can be easily pruned away, with no harm and much good done to the rest of the plant.

Baking soda is an effective natural means of controlling powdery mildew. While a baking soda spray will kill powdery mildew, it also kills the leaf surface on which mildew is growing. For this reason, it is not an ideal method of control for rose exhibitors or anyone who demands perfect foliage.

Downy Mildew

Once confined to greenhouses where roses are grown, downy mildew swept across the nation in the early 1990s, devastating rose gardens and surprising many rosarians. The name can be confusing because the downy part of downy mildew can only be observed under a microscope. What you will see in an infected garden are leaves that display irregular purple spots, turn yellow and drop off. An infected leaf will usually drop off the plant at the slightest touch. Rose plants under attack by downy mildew can be defoliated very quickly, and some may not be vigorous enough to recover.

Downy mildew will not spread when the temperature is lower than 41° F. and will be killed when temperatures stay above 81° F. for twenty-four hours. Because of this, greenhouse rose growers can simply turn up the thermostat to kill downy mildew. While few of us live in a climate where temperatures can be expected to remain over 81° F. for twenty-four hours at a stretch, downy mildew can be effectively held dormant whenever daytime temperatures are consistently above 80° F., with nighttime lows staying above 60° F.

Like blackspot, downy mildew spreads in moisture. Overhead watering will facilitate the spread of downy mildew, as can poor soil drainage.

Spores of downy mildew can continue to live on dead plant material, so all infected leaves and other plant parts should be removed from the garden and destroyed.

Downy mildew can be prevented by application of a fungicide containing copper, manganese or zinc. Note that the newest, systemic fungicides do not contain these elements, and many older fungicides that do contain them have been removed from the market, or had their uses restricted, either because of direct environmental concerns or because of the cost of complying with Environmental Protection Agency product reregistration procedures.

In a severe infestation, downy mildew will spread throughout a plant and down into its roots. For this reason, a soil drench fungicide recommended for control of root rot diseases can also be applied as a supplementary method of control.

Rust

Rust appears as small orange spots on rose foliage. The spots begin with a narrow green or black border; eventually the entire spot becomes almost black. Rust-infected leaves will defoliate, sometimes quite rapidly.

Rust is most common in regions with mild winters; I have seen it in my Ohio garden only once. While many of the newest fungicides designed to combat blackspot and powdery mildew have proven to be unsuccessful in controlling other rose fungus diseases (such as anthracnose and downy mildew), most of them will provide adequate control against rust.

Botrytis

This fungus is prevalent only during cool, rainy spells. It appears as a gray mold on rose buds; in a severe case buds will be prevented from opening. The best remedy is to cut off infected buds, seal them in a plastic bag to prevent the botrytis spores from spreading, and discard.

Crown Gall

Crown gall is a tumorlike growth caused by the bacteria *Agrobacterium tumefaciens.* In its appearance and its rapid, uncontrolled growth, it is similar to cancer in mammals. The galls, or tumors, are usually found at or just below the soil surface around the crown of the plant (the "knob" where the cultivar has been bud-grafted onto an understock). But crown gall can appear on own-root plants as easily as on budded ones, and galls can also appear on the roots and on the upper branches.

There is anecdotal evidence that roses may live a very long time with tiny galls, demonstrating no noticeable ill effects. Large galls resemble bumpy potatoes (and whenever I get a call from someone who says they have a potato growing on their rose bush, I know it is crown gall). Plants with galls approaching potato size usually show a marked decline in vigor. The best remedy is surgical: Cut the galls away (and be sure to sterilize your pruning saw afterward). Many rosarians treat the wound with a disinfectant such as liquid bleach or Lysol. I used to do this too, but stopped after I noticed no difference in recovery rates between roses that were disinfected and those that weren't. I am always careful to leave the spot where the gall has been removed exposed to sunlight.

Some plant pathologists believe that the crown gall bacteria spreads systemically through the rose plant, meaning that excising the gall is doing nothing more than addressing the most obvious symptom of a larger problem. This may or may not be true. I do know that I have had numerous rose plants grow on quite happily for many years after the removal of large crown galls while other roses have died despite a complete excision of their gall. Cuttings taken from plants infected with crown gall will almost always become infected too, even if there was absolutely no visible evidence of gall on the cutting.

How can you avoid crown gall? First, and most obviously, never introduce a plant that has it into your garden. Second, avoid injuries to your roses. The crown gall bacterium needs a wound (such as a nick from a hoe) to enter a rose plant. Weather may also play a part: I almost always find crown gall after an exceptionally wet fall and winter and almost never after dry ones.

You may read advice about fumigating your soil if you have had crown gall. I believe this is written by the same fussy people who wash their hands dozens of times a day. Whenever a rose bush has succumbed to crown gall, I do remove the soil where it grew and replace it with fresh soil from a place where roses have not grown. This may or may not be necessary, but requires just a small amount of effort compared with the peace of mind it returns.

Pests

Aphids

Aphids, tiny winged insects that are usually green (but can also be pink or white), are a rose problem primarily in the spring when roses have a high nitrogen level and are producing lots of succulent growth. Aphids drain the sap from growing shoots and can, in a severe infestation, cause misshapen leaves and buds. They have incredible reproductive powers (females are born already pregnant, thus eliminating the need for males), and it is best to wipe out colonies as they appear early in the growing season. I have never needed chemicals to control aphids nor have I purchased extra quantities of beneficial insects such as ladybug beetles, green lacewings or praying mantises. Any observant gardener can easily control aphids by finding colonies on the newest shoots of each plant and squashing them between his forefinger and thumb. If you are squeamish, a strong jet of water directed at the aphid colony will do the same job.

Aphids produce a sticky substance called honeydew, which is a favorite of ants. Ants will actually "farm" aphids for their honeydew, and if you see ants marching up and down your rose plants, you almost certainly have aphids. With a flavor described as similar to that of maple sugar candy, honeydew is a favorite confection in parts of the Middle East.

Leaf-Cutter Bees

Leaf-cutter bees cut small, perfectly circular holes in rose foliage. They use this material to feather their nests, and because they do not ingest it, the usual chemical controls will not work. Leaf-cutter bees are rarely more than a minor problem, and most gardeners find their precision work a wonder of nature and a thing of beauty. If you don't, you can follow them back to their nests, which are made in wood or soil, and exterminate them there. These bees are traditionalists and prefer the dull matte foliage of old garden roses to the glossy modern kind.

Japanese Beetles

Japanese beetles have a ravenous appetite for rose blooms, preferring lightly colored and strongly scented varieties. During severe infestations, or when there is a lack of bloom, Japanese beetles will eat rose foliage too (reducing it to a lacelike appearance). The beetle season lasts about two months—one month of more beetles every day, followed by one month of decreasing beetles. In northern Ohio I usually see the first Japanese beetle around the 4th of July and expect them to be all gone by Labor Day. So, as bad a pest as Japanese beetles are, they have no real effect on the flowers of once-blooming roses nor do they affect the peak spring and fall blooms of the repeat-blooming roses.

Beetles will lay eggs in lawn areas around your roses and return year after year. There will be fewer beetles after a severe winter and more after a mild one. In my experience, there is some kind of symbiosis-in-reverse between Japanese beetles and rose midge. If you have a lot of rose midge, you will not see many Japanese beetles, and vice versa.

I rely on hand-picking, heading for the garden each evening with a large disposable cup half-filled with soapy water. It is not necessary to use gasoline or kerosene—dish soap kills them just as well. Japanese beetles reflexively tumble downward to escape danger. So position the cup just under the bloom and tap slightly; most will fall right into the soapy water (and they won't fly out). When your cup is full, seal it in a plastic bag and place it in the

Japanese Beetle Control

Method of Control	Pros	Cons
Sevin	Kills beetles on contact.	Kills bees too; must be reapplied every 3 days for effective control.
Milky spore disease	Safe to use; a bacteria and not a chemical. Kills beetles where they breed. Apply just once, and it will multiply on its own.	Takes 3 to 5 years for full effectiveness. Not effective if you have a small garden and neighbors do not also apply milky spore.
Neem-based products	Natural insecticide derived from the neem tree. Spray kills beetles on contact as well as later-arriving beetles that ingest neem residue on petals and leaves.	Residual effect is limited. Must be reapplied every 3 to 5 days. Demand for product has caused economic and social disruptions in India, where neem trees grow.
Hand-picking	Squashing beetles can be quite satisfying.	It's messy, time-consuming and ultimately impractical.
Beetle traps	Lures beetles from adjoining properties, pleasing neighbors.	You end up with more beetles than you started with.
Beetle bonnets	Covering a special bloom with lightweight netting is virtually foolproof protection.	Impractical; can look silly to those who do not love roses as much as you do.

garbage or bury deep. Hand-picking is most effective at dawn or dusk, when the beetles are quiescent, or after a rainfall, when the beetles are waterlogged.

Cane Borers

Cane borers drill holes into the end of rose canes, causing them to become nonproductive and eventually die. Rosarians in many parts of the country may never see damage from cane borers or may lose only a few canes a year from their activities. If, however, you live in an area where borers are a real problem, you may want to seal all your cane ends as you prune. Elmer's glue is a much cleaner sealant than plant tar; because it dries clear, adding food coloring to the glue will let you see where you've sealed.

Earwigs

Earwigs are large, soft-bodied insects that climb into rose blooms at night and chew their way out in the morning. During times of drought, they may keep cool in rose blooms during the day as well. Our ancestors found earwigs in their ears after sleeping on the ground so, by comparison, finding them in our roses is really not too bad. Songbirds love earwigs, and if you see birds apparently attacking your rose blooms, you are witnessing the best method of control. Alternatively, a chemical soil drench can be used to break the earwigs' breeding cycle.

Inchworms

Inchworms may descend from deciduous trees and into your rose beds in the spring. Rose buds are a special treat for these tiny caterpillars, which can only be controlled by diligent hand-picking or the somewhat less practical method of spraying the oak and maple trees from which they fall. If you have one inchworm, you have a hundred, and if inchworms are a problem in your garden, you may want to add a hat to your spring wardrobe or keep track of what is in your hair.

Rose Midge

Proponents of integrated pest management, a philosophy of pest control based upon respect for the environment and an underlying conviction that nature can take care of itself better than humans can, advise against ever spraying insecticides before insect pests have actually been spotted. In almost all cases, this is excellent advice. In the case of rose midge, however, it is exactly wrong.

The microscopic rose midge devastates a rose garden by robbing it of bloom. Growing tips of succulent new shoots appear to have been burned to a crisp by feeding action from this insect's larvae. Shoots that should end in a bloom don't, and the rosarian finds himself with a garden full of foliage. For those seeking an environmentally sound approach to culture, there is unfortunately no such thing as integrated midge management. Literally a fly-by-night pest, rose midge has no known predators, and there is no effective means of natural control. The rosarian who waits to see midge damage before acting against it will find himself out of luck and out of bloom.

Rose midge is controlled in the soil by diazinon. Young midge will be killed as they hatch in diazinon-laced soil. It's never too early to broadcast diazinon granules for prevention of rose midge. Rose midge is most common in the East and Midwest, and rosarians interested in preventing midge attacks should apply diazinon immediately after pruning.

As chemical companies promote the use of the soil insecticide dursban, diazinon is becoming more difficult to find. The Environmental Protection Agency has banned diazinon from golf courses and turf farms, and several states have taken it out of the hands of private citizens altogether. Dursban is not necessarily a more efficacious or even safer substance (and I am aware of no controlled study of its value in fighting rose midge). If you want to experiment, buy dursban.

If you want to prevent midge, buy diazinon—and use it.

Recently, soil scientists have discovered that, in certain instances, soils treated with the insecticide oftanol were found to promote "enhanced degradation" of soil insecticides such as diazinon. Oftanol-active soils contain microbes that actually feed on that insecticide; in some cases, they have turned to diazinon when oftanol is no longer available. In this manner the normal diazinon residual period of 21 to 15 days can be cut to less than 7 days. Obviously, rosarians who are using diazinon to control midge should not employ oftanol anywhere on their lawn or garden.

Scale

Rose scale can be dull white, gray or light brown. It looks like a crust forming on rose stems and will look like a lot of little clam shells up close. What you are seeing is the cast-off skeletons of the scale insect—the insect itself is likely to be inside this skeleton house. I have always controlled this pest by simply cutting off the stem where the scale insect has chosen to nest. Insecticides may prove effective in a severe attack.

Thrips

Thrips are tiny, sucking insects that make buds turn brown and cause brown spotting on open blooms. Sometimes thrip damage can be so severe that buds will not open. Thrips can be controlled by misting buds with a systemic insecticide. Thrips are not a rose-specific pest, so planting roses away from host plants such as iris can cut down on thrip incidence in the first place.

Acorn Weevils

Acorn weevils can arrive in force with the first flush of rose blooms, puncturing and in some cases severing green buds. When I first noticed this damage in 1989, I suspected raids of cardinals, my state bird, picking on our national flower once again. (Cardinals will sometimes eat green rose buds.) The discovery of brown, long-snouted weevils (just larger than Japanese beetles) marching up rose stems was a surprise. I surprised them back with a popular insecticide and wasn't troubled again. Of course, hand-picking works too (the best harvests are in the evening when weevils are active). Acorn weevils could be a particular problem if you garden near oak trees, especially in years following a bumper crop of acorns. While almost completely absent from recent rose literature, acorn weevils (*Curculio rectus* Say.) are not a new pest, being pictured and described on page 167 of the 1945 *American Rose Annual.*

Spider Mites

Spider mites thrive in hot, dry weather. They usually feast first on a plant's lowest leaves, which become bronzed, yellow and sickly. You will notice sandlike grains on the underside of a mite-infested leaf. Direct a strong stream of water to the underside of leaves to help break webs and wash mites away. Persistent water washing can control but not conquer mites. For faster action, follow water washing with a miticide. (Mites are not insects and will not be killed by insecticides. Many insecticides kill mite predators along with rose pests.) Keeping weak, twiggy growth pruned away from the bottom and lower interior of rose bushes can help discourage spider mites, as can thorough irrigation of rose beds.

Spider mites can be a major problem on miniature roses grown under lights indoors. Don't even think about using a miticide indoors. If water washing fails to give adequate control, you can subdue mites on indoor miniatures by dabbing the underside of each leaflet with a cotton swab dipped in rubbing alcohol.

Better Roses Through Chemistry

- If you decide to spray toxic chemicals, protect yourself by wearing rubber gloves, protective clothing, a respirator face mask and head covering. Remember that chemicals are most dangerous in their undiluted form; never mix your spray solution without wearing rubber gloves. Wash thoroughly afterward and launder your spraying apparel separately from other clothes.

- Always read product labels carefully. Never exceed recommended dosages. Take all safety warnings seriously.

- The best time to spray is first thing in the morning or last thing in the evening, that is, not in the heat of the day. Never spray your roses if they have not been well watered or are under stress for any other reason. Obviously, it is neither safe nor effective to spray in windy conditions (another argument for evening, when atmospheric conditions are usually calm).

- Hand-held, trigger-type spray bottles are economical only for very small gardens. Hose end sprayers are inexpensive and make sense for gardens of up to about 100 roses. Because hose end sprayers are not particularly efficient in their use of spray materials, anyone growing more than about 100 roses will easily recoup the cost of a more expensive pump-type sprayer through savings on spray materials. Electric, atomizing sprayers are the most efficient sprayers of all, but before investing in one, be sure to determine how convenient it will be to have a power cord winding through your garden.

- Clean leaves are happy leaves. Make it a habit to give your roses a thorough water washing before spraying pesticides. I try to do this first thing on Saturday morning, before spraying the roses that evening.

- Chemical fungicides work best in an acidic solution. If your tap or well water is alkaline, add 1 tablespoon of white vinegar per gallon of spray mixture.

- Powdered chemicals need hot water to dissolve completely. Because you don't want to be spraying your roses with hot liquid, use a small mixing container of hot water to dissolve your chemical powders.

- Spreader-stickers, agents that help your spray material adhere to the foliage, are not necessary with most modern pesticides. (For example, all of the products marketed by Ortho already contain a spreader-sticker as part of their "inert" ingredients.) However, a spreader-sticker (such as Dawn or Palmolive dish soap) can be very helpful if you are spraying baking soda or some other home-made solution.

- A systemic pesticide (such as Funginex) will be safely inside your plant six to eight hours after application; at that point, rain cannot wash it off. Rain will, of course, wash away all nonsystemic products. For complete protection, these will need to be reapplied after each rainfall.

- Mixing 1 tablespoon of liquid plant food (such as 20-20-20) with each gallon of spray solution may help carry systemic fungicides into the leaves more thoroughly.

- Always mix a fresh batch of spray solution each time you spray. Never try to save leftover solution.

- Don't buy out-of-date chemicals and never buy more than you can use in 18 months. Never store garden chemicals where they could freeze over winter.

Becoming Organic

- It is not easy to suddenly become organic by going out and buying ladybugs or other beneficial insects to release into your garden. The most likely thing they will do is fly away (although, if you are lucky, they will lay some eggs before they leave). It is better to encourage beneficial insects to come into your garden of their own accord, and the best way to do this is to stop spraying pesticides.

- Even some "organic" remedies can be harmful to people, pets, birds and especially fish. Always read and follow all safety precautions as noted on the product label.

- Mono-cropping encourages pests specific to that crop. If your garden contains a wide variety of plants, it is less likely to encounter a plague of any one pest.

- Don't blame your chosen protection program if you did not implement it properly. No product—organic or synthetic—will do any good sitting on the shelf.

PRUNING

No Secrets

The pruning of roses is often described as a "ritual" and made to sound so mysterious that the novice can feel lost before he begins, as if everyone but him knows the secret handshake. But there are no secrets to rose pruning; only common sense. Roses are pruned for three reasons:

1. to remove dead wood
2. to eliminate all weak, useless or diseased growth
3. to shape the plant

In shaping most modern roses, you will decide whether you want to prune relatively high, leaving 12 to 18 inches on a hybrid tea, for example, to get the maximum bloom possible, or relatively low, leaving just 4 to 6 inches on a hybrid tea, to get fewer blooms, but of the highest quality. This is not entirely a matter of personal preference: The winter usually decides how severely canes need to be cut back in the North.

Keep a Rose Calendar

Keeping a special rose calendar of everything you do in the garden will pay big dividends. Not only will you see at a glance when you last sprayed or fed your roses, you can get a head start on next year by studying this year's completed calendar. If your roses were disappointing in September, what did you do (or not do) in August? A rose calendar makes answering such questions easy.

To promote season-long health and the strongest canes, it is vital to keep pruning until you reach good healthy white pith. Brown-pithed canes will often flower, but rarely prosper, and usually die after a weak spring bloom. The only time I settle for imperfect pith is with once-flowering roses (the climber 'Elegance' is my favorite example) where hard pruning would mean sacrificing this year's bloom.

For any rose grown strictly for garden display, relatively high pruning is usually advisable. An exception to this rule should be made for older, leggy hybrid teas. Bushiness can be encouraged to a certain extent by severe pruning. For any rose from which you intend to harvest cut flowers, cut back at least to where the cane is equal to the thickness you want in a stem.

Regardless of how lightly or severely you prune, be sure to remove all weak, twiggy growth from the bottom and interior of the plant and aim to keep the center of the plant as open and free from crossing branches as practicable.

When old canes (usually identified as having the most weathered-looking bark) start to become unproductive, they should always be removed flush with the crown of the plant. If your rose bush has many canes, you can afford to be ruthless in removing them. If your rose bush has only a few canes, you must be more selective (and more charitable). Prune roses that have only one or two canes back to 6 inches to encourage lateral breaks.

Pruning a Rose

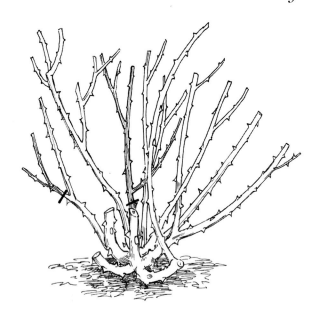

1. Remove old or dead wood.

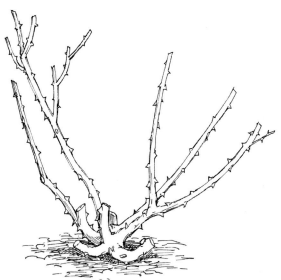

2. Open up center.

3. Hard prune for large blooms.

4. Lighter pruning for good display of flowers.

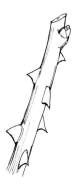

5. Pruning cut above outward-facing bud-eye.

What's the Worst That Could Happen?

Many new rosarians express concern that they will hurt their roses during the pruning process. But what's the worst that could happen? Once-blooming varieties could be inadvertently cut back to the ground, and their flowers would be lost for a year. If all of your roses are repeat-blooming, the worst thing that could happen is that you do nothing, and your unpruned rose garden becomes a straggly mess.

Equipment

The anvil type of pruner is bad for roses because it cannot cut without crushing the part of the cane that you want to leave on the bush. Use the curved, scissors-type of pruner and don't waste your time on a cheap one. You will also need long-handled lopping pruners and a small pruning saw—and thorn-proof gloves! (Goatskin is a traditional favorite, but several new synthetic materials are equally impervious and kinder to goats.)

You may have read that you can save time by pruning miniature roses with hedge shears or a lawn mower. Yes, these roses can be pruned with these devices (just as hybrid teas can be pruned with a chain saw or a machete), but if you have taken the time during the growing season to learn the growth habits of your miniatures, there will be no substitute for the studied approach of cutting back minis inch by inch, eye to eye.

When to Prune

Pruning into live wood is your signal for the roses to grow, and much can be lost by getting roses to grow too early, before the threat of killing frosts is past. Northerners can look to the forsythia: When it blooms, it is safe to prune your roses. Southerners will usually find the best time to prune between the blooming of the dogwood and the redbud trees. Obviously, it makes sense to look at the weather forecast in addition to the bushes and trees. If a return to subfreezing temperatures is expected, pruning should be delayed.

Prepruning, taking the blackened dead tops off of roses, can be done during any favorable weather. Because you are cutting only into dead wood it won't matter to the plant and will make the critical pruning time more efficient. The more roses you have, the more time this will save.

I prune in two cycles. First, I go around and cut everything back to live, white-pithed wood. Then, after a couple of weeks, I return to prune each cane to just above a bud-eye (the red swelling on the cane). Here is where one can really shape the bush, which will grow in the direction that the bud-eye is pointing. In most instances, pruning to an outside eye is advisable, to help produce an open, vase-shaped plant. Keeping the middle of a rose bush open will promote healthy air circulation and help prevent fungus diseases and spider mites. But if you want to dissuade a rose from growing too wide, simply prune it back to inside-pointing eyes.

Emergency Backups

If you've waited until the proper time to prune, you should not worry too much about your garden being frosted after pruning. Fully developed rose leaves will take six degrees of frost (to 26° F.), and immature leaves and new shoots are even hardier. If a new shoot is killed by frost, the cane is standing by with two emergency eyes at the base of the shoot that has died. As these auxiliary eyes start growing, thumbnail prune the one that does not offer the best direction for the plant.

Thumbnail pruning means eliminating potential branches before the rose has invested anything in them. Scrape off bud-eyes wherever their growth would be undesirable (such as in the center of a bush) or duplicative.

Old Garden Roses and Climbers

When I began growing once-flowering old garden roses, I followed the advice that they should be cut back by about one-third after their annual bloom. I have since rejected this advice because pruning old garden roses after they bloomed eliminated their hips, which are in many cases extremely attractive, and because it was really hard to maneuver around (and especially inside) the old garden roses when they had all their leaves on. So now I prune the once-bloomers first thing in the spring, the only time when I can really see the bones of the plant. I cut out any wood that is obviously dead, shorten twiggy branches, reach into the center of the plant to remove any clutter and shape the bush.

Ramblers should be pruned just as if they were really tall old garden roses. Remove all obviously dead wood, along with any weak, twiggy growth, first thing in the spring. When an old cane shows signs of slowing down, remove it entirely to encourage new basal breaks. The modern continuous-blooming climbers, such as 'America' and 'Compassion', which produce basal breaks that bloom their first year, should be pruned to live wood in the North and to shape the bush in the South. Older repeat-blooming climbers, such as 'New Dawn', offer repeat bloom only from wood that is two to three years old. For these climbers (which also include the recent introduction 'Pierre de Ronsard'), concentrate your efforts on the lateral stems that branch off from the main canes. Shortening them will improve the quality of bloom and the profile of the plant.

Practice Makes Perfect

As you get to know your roses, you will observe how each variety reacts to pruning. Winters can help rosarians in this regard: If an unusually severe winter cuts your roses back more severely than your pruners would have, pay special attention to how each variety reacts. You will undoubtedly notice some that benefit from a more severe treatment and others that suffer from it. In time, you will be able to picture how your roses look in summer when you are pruning them in the spring, and this mental image will prove an invaluable aid to your pruning.

Suckers

Suckers are growths that arise from the rootstock onto which a rose cultivar has been bud-grafted. Any growth appearing from beneath the bud union (the knob where the graft occurred) is a sucker and must be removed. Suckers usually grow with great vigor, but one cannot count on the old folk wisdom that you can tell a sucker because it has seven leaflets per leaf instead of the usual five. Many modern roses can have seven leaflets, particularly when they are well fed, and some varieties used as understocks have only five leaflets. Sucker growth will usually look different in some way—color, shape of leaflets, thorns or lack of them—from the rest of the plant. But the only way to tell for sure is to see where a cane is growing from. All growth from beneath the bud union must be rooted out from where it starts. Pruning it off at soil level will only encourage it to grow back twice as fast.

When people say they have a rose that has "reverted" or "gone wild," they have a grafted rose that has suckered successfully. Most understocks are once-bloomers, so by the time a sucker flowers for the first time, in its second year, it may have completely swamped and killed the variety that was bud-grafted onto it. Suckers are never a problem, of course, on own-root plants.

A Never Ending Process

Pruning continues throughout the growing season. Every time you deadhead (that is, remove) a bloom you are pruning the bush. I try to keep as much productive foliage on the bush as possible. If I am not interested in exhibiting from a particular stem, I no longer follow the traditional advice about cutting stems back to a five-leaflet leaf. Instead, I simply remove the faded flower. While I prune rather heavily in the spring, I believe that my roses are happier and more productive with this lighter approach during the growing season. It takes sun and leaves to make rose food, and, in a sense, cutting off rose leaves is the same as putting the plant in the shade.

Exception: I prune any miniature rose with a tendency to leggy growth (and that includes most of the miniatures with hybrid tea form) severely throughout the growing season. In most cases, this makes them smaller but much better plants.

Weak, nonproductive, twiggy-type growth should always be removed, especially when it accumulates at the bottom center of the plant.

WINTER PROTECTION

Winter Protection Begins in the Summer

Don't apply any nitrogen fertilizer during the last six weeks of the growing season. Nitrogen will encourage soft, sappy growth that is easily killed in the winter. At the same time as you stop feeding nitrogen, stop deadheading spent blooms. Allowing them to set seeds and form hips sends a signal to the plant to slow down.

Maintain protection from insects and disease and never stop watering. A rose that comes through summer healthy is much more likely to survive a tough winter than one that has had to struggle.

Do You Need Winter Protection?

Do you need winter protection? If you grow modern roses and live north of Zone 6, or wherever temperatures are expected to either fall below 0° F. at any time or remain below 20° F. for extended periods, yes. Rosarians in sheltered locations will generally need less winter protection than those who grow their roses out in the open. Every garden is different, and it is important to know your microclimate. Do your neighbors grow roses? If so, what do they do about winter protection? If they do nothing, what happens?

Why, What and When

Winter protection of roses is not designed to keep the plant warmer. Rather, when properly applied, it will slow desiccation. Plants cannot take up much water at low temperatures but continue to lose moisture through tissues. Well-placed winter protection shields the rose plants from fluctuating temperatures and keeps them from heaving out of the ground.

What to use for winter protection?

- Sawdust is an excellent choice. It's light. It conforms easily to make a tight mound around the bush. And it's easy to remove in the spring, when it can simply be spread throughout the rose bed.

- Soil is hard work and not that much better, if at all, than sawdust. Soil for winter protection must be brought to the rose beds from another part of the garden. Digging soil up from around the bushes for winter protection will either damage the roots or expose them to winter injury and is worse than providing no winter protection at all.

- Styrofoam rose cones are effective under many conditions but have several serious drawbacks. First, roses must be cut back severely enough to fit under the cones. Second, if you have a lot of roses to protect, cones for them present a substantial storage problem during the nonwinter months. Third, to avoid stimulating excessive winter growth, cones must be removed whenever the weather warms. Finally, rose cones make attractive dwellings for mice, which will eat the bark off of your roses. If you do use rose cones, be certain to secure them so that they don't blow away.

- Newspaper, wire or preformed plastic rings (available at most garden supply stores) can be placed around each rose bush and filled with hardwood leaves or mulch. These rings make much higher mounding possible but don't add much else.

- Snow, and lots of it, makes for excellent winter protection. But you can't always count on it.

When to apply protection? Protection should be applied after a hard freeze, before temperatures plummet to single digits (Fahrenheit) and after culling varieties you no longer want. There is no point spending extra effort by winter protecting expendable varieties. Maintain winter protection until it's time to prune in the spring and never let your rose beds dry out, even when the plants are dormant.

CONTAINER CULTURE

When I lived on a tiny lot in the city, I grew several hundred roses in 5-gallon pots. My main reason for growing roses in pots was to save space and to turn paved areas into rose beds. Today, even though I no longer have to worry about saving space and have no paved areas, I still use pots to grow especially tender varieties and new varieties that I want to evaluate. I use black plastic pots, and what these lack in aesthetic appeal they make up for in good moisture retention, heat absorption and relatively light weight. New roses will get off to a quicker start in the warmth of a heat-absorbing black plastic pot than they will in the ground. Mature roses are also very happy in these pots, and from the perspective of exhibiting success, as a city rosarian I won as many trophies from my 300 roses in pots as I did from my 300 in the ground.

The minimum size I recommend for growing full-size roses is a 5-gallon pot (or about 12 inches). If you have the room for them and the muscle to lift them when they are full, 7-gallon pots work even better. If you choose an irregular size of pot and are not interested in bonsai roses, remember that depth is more important than width.

Whether you choose plastic or some other material, such as wood or clay, drainage holes are essential. My potting mixture consists of one-third commercial potting soil (I am not picky about this and use whatever is on sale), one-third compost and one-third vermiculite laced with Osmocote time-release fertilizer. Constant watering is critical for success in container roses, and one must be prepared to water every pot every day, if necessary.

Pest and disease control methods are the same as for roses grown in the ground, with the added benefit that any severely infested plant can be picked up and carted off to a "hospital" or some other location where it will not contaminate its neighbors.

I winter my container-grown roses with perfect success in a detached, unheated garage, watering them very lightly once a month. And I winter my car outside, thus eliminating exhaust fumes, often a cause of failure in garage storage. If you have an attached garage, you may find that it is not cold enough to keep the roses dormant throughout the winter, something that is essential. In this case, and if you cannot find a barn or a shed to keep them in, the surest way to winter your roses is to remove them from their pots and bury them.

PROPAGATION

Nurseries propagate most roses by budding—grafting a bud-eye of the desired cultivar onto a host understock. (A bud-eye can be found at every junction of leaf and stem, and these are the same eyes to which we prune in the spring.) Some roses are grown commercially from cuttings on their own roots. These include virtually all miniatures, many of the Meidiland-type landscaping shrubs and some old garden roses. Nurseries specializing in old garden roses are about equally divided between those who offer budded plants and those who sell plants on their own roots. A further division occurs between those who sell mature,

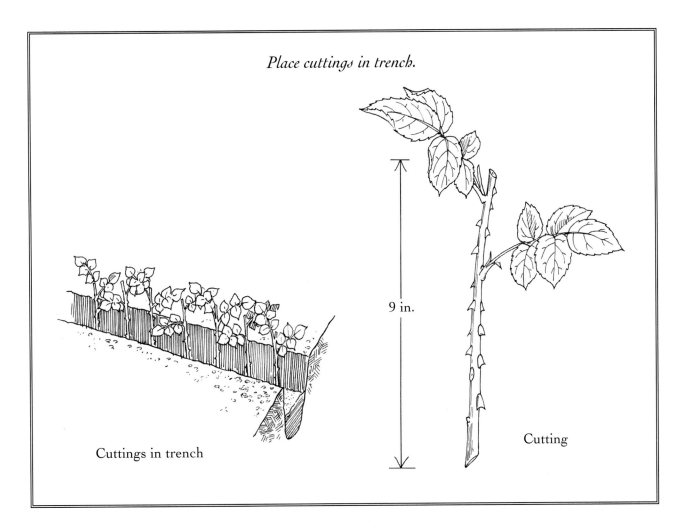

Place cuttings in trench.

9 in.

Cuttings in trench

Cutting

field-grown, own-root roses and those who offer much smaller, greenhouse-grown, own-root roses in 2- to 4-inch pots. The greenhouse-grown old garden roses will usually take one year of good growth to catch up to the field-grown ones.

While some varieties will root much easier than others, in general it is easy, almost instinctive, to grow roses from cuttings. Anyone can learn to bud roses, but he will learn much more quickly by actually seeing it done. Propagating becomes a hobby in itself for many rosarians and is a way to preserve family heirloom roses, foundling roses, sports and roses that are no longer in commerce. Some rosarians insist on budding their own roses as a way of avoiding plants infected with rose mosaic virus. From a practical point of view, however, if the rose variety you are looking for is offered in commerce, it will be much more economical simply to buy it. It is illegal to propagate any rose whose 17-year patent has not yet expired, whether or not that rose remains in commerce.

Cuttings

Softwood cuttings are taken during the growing season. Cuttings can be rooted in the ground or in pots (which makes transplanting much easier). Select a 6- to 9-inch length of stem from underneath a mature bloom on the plant you want to reproduce and remove all but the top one or two sets of leaflets. Make an angle cut just below a bud-eye at the bottom of the stem, dip in rooting hormone (if desired) and plant half-deep in loamy soil or sand. If you are striking (starting) a lot of cuttings at once, it makes sense to dig a narrow trench and fill it with sand. Cover each cutting with a fruit jar. (The old, large pickle jars are

Budding a Rose

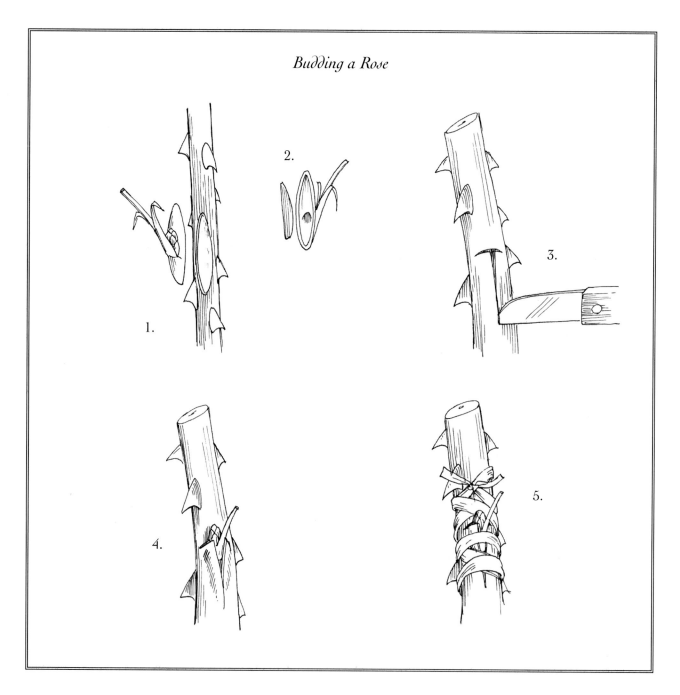

excellent for this purpose. Today I save glass cider jugs and have the bottoms burned out. This way I can use the cap to ventilate the cutting.) Provide shade and keep moist. As new shoots appear, remove the jar for a few hours each day. After 7 to 10 days, remove the jar entirely.

Hardwood cuttings are taken after the growing season, but before either the rose or the ground is frozen. Make sure that the source plant is completely dormant and the wood well ripened.

Six-inch sections of dormant wood can be planted outside, in a place where they can remain throughout the next growing season. Hardwood cuttings should be buried so that only about one-quarter of their length remains above the soil. They should not be expected to establish themselves over the winter and should be covered with a glass jar first thing in the spring and handled in the same way as softwood cuttings.

Budding

To bud-graft a rose, you will need:

- Budwood from the cultivar you want to reproduce (i.e., a section of stem from beneath a mature bloom containing bud-eyes. Bud-eyes occur at each leaf axil. Save a section of leaf behind each eye to act as a handle.)
- Understock (i.e., the "wild" rose onto which you will bud your variety). Usually this is *Rosa multiflora* or *R. canina*, but in Florida the variety 'Fortuniana' is preferred as an understock. To obtain understocks, you can grow *R. multiflora* or *R. canina* yourself from seed harvested in late fall, purchase understocks in quantity from a nursery or make cuttings from understock suckers that appear in your garden.
- Budding knife or a very sharp pocket knife
- Cut rubber band (at least ¼-inch wide) or a commercially produced budding patch to secure the bud-eye to the understock
- A great deal of patience

The time to bud is when your understock is growing freely, so that the bark will separate easily from the wood. This means August in Ohio, but could be much earlier or a little later in other parts of the country.

Assuming that your understock is already growing in full sun, at a spot where you can provide it with ample water, the first step is to select an understock with a main stem of ⅜ inch in diameter (or less if you are budding particularly small bud-eyes) with at least 1 inch between its lowest branch and roots. Of course, you can remove lower branches until you have at least 1 inch of room.

Make a horizontal cut about ¼ inch long just beneath the lowest branch on one side of the understock. From the center of this incision, cut downward for about 1 inch, so that you have carved the letter *T* into the bark, but not into the wood. Next, check to see if you can easily pry the bark away on both sides of the vertical cut. If so, you're in business. If not, the understock is not ready for budding onto. (You can try again later, on the other side of the understock's stem.)

To prepare budwood, remove a bud shield from your stick of budwood by slicing downward from about ⅔ inch above the bud to about ⅓ inch below it (the idea being, of course, to match the size of the incision you have made in the understock). Pinch out the wood from inside the eye, being careful to avoid tearing out the eye itself.

To bud, push the bud shield into the cross of the T-cut and downward until it reaches the bottom of the vertical cut. It should end up resting flush against the white wood of the understock and being enclosed snugly by its bark, the eye looking out at you. Next, snap on the bud patch; or if you tie with a cut rubber band do so from bottom to top, covering the entire incision, but not the bud itself.

It is essential to keep the understock well watered following budding. Any check in growth will result in failure of the bud to take.

If the eye is still green after four weeks, you have been successful and are on your way to a new plant. Protect well over winter. Next spring remove the rubber band or budding patch and "top off" the understock by removing all growth to within about 1 inch of the bud-eye. In its maiden year, before it has time to solidify from a mere eye to a bud union, the shoots that arise from this eye will be very susceptible to wind damage. Unless you are in a very sheltered location, it will be necessary to stake the new shoots to avoid blowouts. Pinching the first shoot or shoots back will encourage more basal growth and give you a better plant.

That fall, fifteen months or so after you bud-grafted your rose, your new plant will be at the same stage as the budded plants that are sold by nurseries and will be ready to transplant. If you are able to maintain budded plants in the same place where they were budded, with no transplanting, you may find them to be superior to any other roses you have ever grown.

Annotated Bibliography

American Rose Society, *American Rose Annual*. Published annually in book form 1916–1990, in magazine format since 1991. During the long editorship of J. Horace McFarland (1916–1944) the ARS *Annual* served as a clearinghouse for information about roses introduced throughout the world. More recent emphasis has been on rose exhibiting. Editions from all eras contain cultural advice that remains valid today.

Austin, David, *David Austin's English Roses*, 1993. A firsthand account of the development of the English roses.

Bales, Suzanne Frutig, *Burpee American Gardening Series: Roses*, 1994. An excellent, environmentally sound guide to the basics of rose growing.

Beales, Peter, *Classic Roses*, 1985. The first comprehensive photographic guide to old garden roses.

Bunyard, Edward A., *Old Garden Roses*, 1936 (reprinted 1978). A graceful, almost poetic study of mainly pre-1840 roses. This landmark book represented the first step out of the dark ages of neglect for old garden roses.

Dickerson, Brent C., *The Old Rose Advisor*, 1992. An encyclopedic compilation of contemporary evaluations of the repeat-blooming old garden roses. Not an "advisor," but an invaluable research tool. Contains hundreds of color plates from the French *Journal des Roses* (1877–1914).

Ellwanger, H. B., *The Rose*, 1901. An important critical catalogue of roses in commerce at the turn of the century, written by a New York nurseryman. Ellwanger had more opinions than diplomacy and included a list of all of the world's rose breeders ranked in order of the quality of their roses. (Poor M. Oger of France came in 32nd, with Ellwanger's comment "Last and least, is one of the oldest raisers who has sent out a large number of sorts, but the rose public, perhaps being prejudiced, have never seen merit in anything he has produced.") A valuable reference that is uncommonly fun to read.

Fagan, Gwen, *Roses at the Cape of Good Hope*, 1988. Many nineteenth-century roses lost to the rest of the world have survived in South Africa and in Mauritius, and Gwen Fagan tells their story in a lavishly produced, oversize book featuring photos of rose blooms, stems, leaves and hips reproduced in actual size.

Fisher, John, *The Companion to Roses*, 1986. An encyclopedia of rose-related topics; good for reference and browsing.

Genders, Roy, *The Rose: A Complete Handbook*, 1965. The most comprehensive rose guide of the 1960s and already an important source of information about vanishing varieties.

Gibson, Michael, *The Rose Gardens of England*, 1988. The essential tour guide for any rosarian traveling to England and an interesting reading for everyone else.

Harkness, Jack, *Roses*, 1978. Comprehensive, accurate and beautifully written. The best rose book ever.

——— , *The Makers of Heavenly Roses*, 1985. The real-life stories of the individuals and families who created the roses we grow. Reads like a novel that you can't put down.

Druitt, Liz, and G. Michael Shoup, *Landscaping with Antique Roses*, 1992. Although written from a southern perspective, much of the landscaping and variety information will be useful to rosarians in the North as well.

Hennessey, Roy, *Hennessey on Roses*, 1943. Opinionated, combative, and at times bizarre, but always completely original. Some of Hennessey's scientific opinions (particularly his notions about "ions" affecting roses grown in high altitudes) have since been discredited, but much of his cultural advice remains to the point.

Hole, Dean S. Reynolds, *A Book About Roses*, 1901 (there are several reprints). Not entirely politically correct, perhaps, but Dean Hole was a true rose lover who wrote about rose growing as he knew it. His book contains both valuable information about roses and rose growing as well as (unconscious) insights into the Victorian mind.

Krüssmann, Gerd, *Rosen, Rosen, Rosen (The Complete Book of Roses)*, 1974. The German author, who had previously written *The Complete Book of Trees*, died before this massive book was completed. It is, therefore, somewhat uneven. Nevertheless, it contains much rose and rose-related information—and trivia—that remains unavailable elsewhere.

LeGrice, E. B., *Rose Growing Complete*, 1976. The most thorough book on rose culture, it is written in a style that is both simple and profound.

LeRougetel, Hazel, *A Heritage of Roses*, 1988. A beautiful book from an authority on old garden roses. Fascinating and valuable, with much original research.

McCann, Sean, *Miniature Roses: Their Care and Cultivation*, 1991. The most up-to-date guide to miniature roses, written in an engaging and easy-to-read style.

McGredy, Sam, *Look to the Rose: A View from New Zealand*, 1986. A breezy yet information-packed read from one of the world's greatest rose breeders, it is illustrated with watercolors by Joyce Blake.

Osborne, Robert, *Hardy Roses*, 1991. Relevant information for northern gardeners.

Paul, William, *The Rose Garden*, 1848 (reprinted 1978). A comprehensive look at the rose world in the mid-1800s. British nurseryman William Paul wrote this book when he was 26 and produced regular updates until his death in 1902. He was probably the last man living to know everything there was to know about roses.

Phillips, Roger, and Martyn Rix, *The Random House Guide to Roses*, 1988. With over 1,400 photos, the best contemporary photo guide to roses.

Royal National Rose Society (Great Britain), *The Rose Annual*, 1907–1984. An invaluable resource for rosarians on either side of the Atlantic and always full of fascinating sidelights for Anglophiles. (The 1959 edition, for example, features the rosarian Lord Grenfell wondering if England's rainy weather has been caused by "sputniks and that kind of thing.") The RNRS *Annuals* edited by Jack Harkness (1979–1984) are particularly noteworthy. Since 1985 the RNRS has published a quarterly journal instead of an annual.

Thomas, Graham Stuart, *The Old Shrub Roses*, 1955 (revised 1978).

———— , *Shrub Roses of Today*, 1980.

———— , *Climbing Roses Old & New*, 1983. These three classic volumes about classic roses are written by the rosarian largely responsible for their resurrection in England.

Verrier, Suzanne, *Rosa Rugosa*, 1991. A complete examination of the rugosa roses.

Welch, William C., *Antique Roses for the South*, 1990. Cultural information specifically for the South; excellent sections on arranging and rose crafts will be of use to rosarians everywhere.

Young, Norman, *The Complete Rosarian*, 1971. A fascinating book from an original thinker and occasional debunker.

SOCIETIES AND ORGANIZATIONS

- The American Rose Society. The largest rose organization in the United States. Membership benefits include a colorful, magazine-format annual and a year's subscription (11 issues) to *The American Rose* magazine. Other publications, including *Rose Exhibitors Forum* (essential for anyone interested in exhibiting roses) are available at additional cost. The ARS can refer you to a consulting rosarian near you. Consulting rosarians are volunteers willing to answer your rose growing questions and, in many cases, visit your garden to diagnose problems. P.O. Box 30,000, Shreveport, LA 71130-0030, (318) 938-5402.
- Canadian Rose Society. Publishes a quarterly journal and a soft-bound annual that will be of special interest to rosarians in the North and Rocky Mountain regions. Write to c/o Anne Graber, 10 Fairfax Crescent, Scarborough, Ontario M1L 1Z8, Canada.
- Heritage Roses Group. An informal organization that publishes the outstanding quarterly *Heritage Roses Letter*. For membership information, send a stamped, addressed envelope to the regional coordinator nearest you:

Northeast: Lily Shohan, RD 1, Box 299, Clinton Corners, NY 12514.

Northcentral: Henry Najat, M.D., W 6365 Wald Road, Monroe, WI 53566.

Northwest: Judi Dexter, 23665 41st Avenue S., Kent, WA 98032.

Southwest (last names A–G): Betty L. Cooper, 925 King Drive, El Cerrito, CA 94530.

Southwest (last names H–O): Marlea Graham, 100 Bear Oaks Drive, Martinez, CA 94553.

Southwest (last names P–Z): Frances Grate, 472 Gibson Avenue, Pacific Grove, CA 93950.

Southcentral: Conrad Tips, 1007 Highland Avenue, Houston, TX 77009.

Southeast: Jan Wilson, RR2, Box 237A, Hillsville, VA 24343.

- The Heritage Rose Foundation. A more formal organization and also publishes a quarterly newsletter. For membership information, write to Charles A. Walker, Jr., 1512 Gorman Street, Raleigh, NC 27606.
- The Rose Hybridizers Association. An organization of amateur rose breeders and others who are interested in rose hybridizing. They publish a quarterly newsletter. For information, write to Larry D. Petersen, 3245 Wheaton Road, Horseheads, NY 14845.

American Rose Rambler

Edited by Peter Schneider, the *American Rose Rambler*, a bi-monthly newsletter, contains articles about exhibition, new varieties, importing, old garden roses, *Combined Rose List* updates, non-dogmatic cultural advice and news from the world of roses. It is especially noted for its book and catalogue reviews and has a reputation of being timely, accurate and fun. Subscriptions of $10.00 per year (6 issues) may be sent to Peter Schneider, P.O. Box 677, Mantua, OH 44255.

MAIL-ORDER ROSE NURSERIES IN NORTH AMERICA

The Antique Rose Emporium, Route 5, Box 143, Brenham, TX 77833, (409) 836-9051. Own-root, container-grown roses. Catalogue $5.00.

Arena's Rose Company, 536 West Cambridge Avenue, Phoenix, AZ 85003, (602) 266-2223. Old garden, English and exhibition roses.

The Roseraie at Bayfields, The Roseraie, Inc., P.O. Box R, Waldoboro, ME 04572, (207) 832-6330. Heritage and hardy roses. Printed catalogue available for first-class stamp; video catalogue $5.00.

Blossoms & Bloomers, East 11415 Krueger Lane, Spokane, WA 99207, (509) 922-1344. Hardy old roses on their own roots in biodegradable containers.

Bridges Roses, 2734 Toney Road, Lawndale, NC 28090, (704) 538-9412, fax (704) 538-1521. Miniature roses and own-root hybrid teas.

Butner's Old Mill Nursery, 806 South Belt Highway, St. Joseph, MO 64507, (816) 279-7434. Modern roses.

Carlton Rose Nurseries, Inc., P.O. Box 366, Carlton, OR 97111, (503) 852-7135, fax (503) 852-7511. Greenhouse roses, also available to home gardeners.

Carroll Gardens, 444 East Main Street, P.O. Box 310, Westminster, MD 21157, (301) 848-5422, fax (410) 857-4112. Retail source for Weeks roses. Catalogue $2.00.

Coiner Rose Nursery, 3000 B Street, P.O. Box 7217, LaVerne, CA 91750, (909) 593-1373, fax (909) 593-1235. Winchel exhibition hybrid teas.

Corn Hill Nursery, Ltd., R. R. 5, Petitcodiac, N. B. E0A 2H0, Canada, (506) 756-3635. Specialist in hardy roses; most roses own-root.

Country Bloomers Nursery, Route 2, Box 33-B, Udall, KS 67146, (316) 986-5518. Heritage and miniature roses in liners (2-inch pots).

Donovan's Roses, P.O. Box 37800, Shreveport, LA 71133-7800, (318) 861-6693. Modern roses.

Edmunds' Roses, 6235 S.W. Kahle Road, Wilsonville, OR 97070, (503) 682-1476, fax (503) 682-1275. Specialists in exhibition and European varieties.

Henry Field's Seed & Nursery Co., 415 North Burnett, Shenandoah, IA 51602, (605) 665-9391.

Flowers 'n' Friends Miniature Roses, 9590 100th Street S.E., Alto, MI 49302, (616) 891-1226.

Forestfarm, 990 Tetherow Road, Williams, OR 97544-9599, (503) 846-7269 (between 9 A.M. and 3 P.M. Pacific Time only). Species roses. Catalogue $3.00.

Garden Valley Nursery, P.O. Box 750953, Petaluma, CA 94975, (707) 795-5266.

Giles Ramblin' Roses, 2968 State Road 710, Okeechobee, FL 34974, (813) 763-6611. Roses budded on 'Fortuniana' understock (an understock particularly suited to rose growing in Florida).

Greenmantle Nursery, 3010 Ettersburg Road, Garberville, CA 95542, (707) 986-7504. Specialist in heritage roses; offer organically grown nursery stock. Rose list available for legal-sized stamped, addressed envelope.

Gurney's Seed & Nursery Co., 110 Capital Street, Yankton, SD 57079, (605) 665-1930, fax (605) 665-9718.

Heirloom Old Garden Roses, 24062 N.E. Riverside Drive, St. Paul, OR 97137, (503) 538-1576, fax (503) 538-5902. Vast selection of roses grown in deep 6-inch pots (miniatures in 4-inch pots). Catalogue $5.00.

Heritage Rosarium, 211 Haviland Mill Road, Brookeville, MD 20833, (301) 774-2806 (evenings and weekends). Catalogue list $1.00.

Heritage Rose Gardens, Tanglewood Farms, 16831 Mitchell Creek Drive, Fort Bragg, CA 95437, (707) 964-3748. Catalogue $1.50.

High Country Rosarium, 1717 Downing Street, Denver, CO 80218, (303) 832-4026 (telephone and fax). Old garden, shrub and species roses on their own roots.

Historical Roses, 1657 West Jackson Street, Painesville, OH 44077, (216) 357-7270 (4:00 P.M. to 9:00 P.M.). Old garden and Dr. Buck roses. List available for stamped, addressed envelope.

Hortico, Inc., 723 Robson Road, R.R. 1, Waterdown, Ontario L0R 2H1, Canada, (416) 689-6984, fax (416) 689-6566. In addition to a large selection of garden roses, also sells rose understocks for rosarians wishing to do their own propagating.

Howerton Rose Nursery, 1656 Weaversville Road, Allen Township, Northampton, PA 18067, (215) 262-5412.

Ingraham's Cottage Garden, 370 C Street, Box 126, Scotts Mills, OR 97375, (503) 873-8610. Antique and rare roses.

Inter-State Nurseries, P.O. Box 10, Louisiana, MO 63353, (314) 754-4525, (800) 325-4180.

Jackson & Perkins Co., One Rose Lane, Medford, OR 97501-0702, (800) 872-7673, fax (800) 242-0329.

J. W. Jung Seed Co., 335 South High Street, Randolph, WI 53957-0001, (414) 326-4100.

Justice Miniature Roses, 5947 S.W. Kahle Road, Wilsonville, OR 97070, (503) 682-2370.

Kimbrew-Walter Roses, Route 2, Box 172, Grand Saline, TX 75140, (903) 829-2968, fax (903) 829-2415.

V. Kraus Nurseries Ltd., P.O. Box 180, Carlisle, Ontario L0R 1H0, Canada, (416) 689-4022, fax (416) 689-8080.

Lowe's Own-Root Roses, 6 Sheffield Road, Nashua, NH 03062, (603) 888-2214 (please do not call after 8:00 P.M.; May 15 through October 15). Heritage roses grown to order. Catalogue $2.00.

Mendocino Heirloom Roses, P.O. Box 670, Mendocino, CA 95460 (nursery located at 720 Road N, Redwood Valley, CA). Own-root roses.

Michael's Miniatures, Inc., 9759 Elder Creek Road, Sacramento, CA 98529. Miniature roses and a limited selection of old garden roses and shrubs.

Michigan Miniature Roses, 45951 Hull Road, Belleville, MI 48111, (313) 699-6698.

Milaeger's Gardens, 4838 Douglas Avenue, Racine, WI 53402-2498, (414) 639-2371, fax (414) 639-1855. Modern roses.

The Mini-Rose Garden, P.O. Box 203, Cross Hill, SC 29332, (803) 998-4331.

Mini Roses of Texas, P.O. Box 267, Denton, TX 76202, (817) 566-3034.

Sequoia Nursery, Moore Miniature Roses, 2519 East Noble Avenue, Visalia, CA 93277, (209) 732-0190, 732-0309. Miniature, old and unusual roses.

Morden Nurseries, P.O. Box 1270, Morden, Manitoba R0G 1J0, Canada, (204) 822-3311. Hardy roses.

Nor'East Miniature Roses Inc., P.O. Box 307, Rowley, MA 01969, (508) 948-7964, fax (508) 948-5487.

Oregon Miniature Roses, Inc., 8285 S.W. 185th Avenue, Beaverton, OR 97007-5742, (503) 649-4482.

Carl Pallek & Son, Nurseries, Box 137, Virgil, Ontario L0S 1T0, Canada (near St Catharines), (416) 468-7262. Does not ship to the United States.

Pickering Nurseries, Inc., 670 Kingston Road, Pickering, Ontario L1V 1A6, Canada, (905) 839-2111, fax (905) 839-4807. Modern, antique and rare roses. Catalogue $3.00.

Pixie Treasures, 4121 Prospect Avenue, Yorba Linda, CA 92686, (714) 993-6780. Miniature roses.

The Rose Ranch, P.O. Box 10087, Salinas, CA 93912, (408) 758-6965. Own-root roses.

Roseberry Gardens, Box 933, Postal Station F, Thunder Bay, Ontario P7C 4X8, Canada. Canadian Explorer roses.

Rosehaven Nursery, 8617 Tobacco Lane S.E., Olympia, WA 98503, (206) 456-2340. Own-root roses in one-gallon pots.

Rosehill Farm, Gregg Neck Road, Galena, MD 21635, (410) 648-5538. Miniature roses.

Roses & Wine, 6260 Fernwood Drive, Shingle Springs, CA 95682, (916) 677-9722, fax (916) 676-4560. Rose list available for stamped, addressed envelope.

Roses of Yesterday & Today, 802 Brown's Valley Road, Watsonville, CA 95076, (408) 724-2755, fax (408) 724-1408. Catalogue $3.00.

Roses Unlimited, Route 1, Box 587, Laurens, SC 29360, (803) 682-9112. Own-root roses in one-gallon containers.

Royall River Roses at Forevergreen Farm, 70 New Gloucester Road, North Yarmouth, ME 04097, (207) 829-5830, fax (207) 829-6512. Old-fashioned and hardy roses.

Schumacher's Hill Country Gardens, 588 FM Hwy 1863, New Braunfels, TX 78132, (512) 620-5149.

Spring Valley Roses, N7637 - 330th Street, Spring Valley, WI 54767, (715) 778-4481. Old garden and winter-hardy roses.

Stanek's Garden Center, East 2929 27th Avenue, Spokane, WA 99223, (509) 535-2939.

Stark Bro's, Box 10, Louisiana, MO 63353-0010, (800) 325-4180, fax (314) 754-5290.

Tate Nursery, 10306 Fm Rd 2767, Tyler, TX 75708-9239, (903) 593-1020.

Taylor's Roses, P.O. Box 11272, Chickasaw, AL 36671-0272, (205) 456-7753. Taylor-raised miniatures and floribundas.

Tiny Petals Nursery, 489 Minot Avenue, Chula Vista, CA 91910, (619) 422-0385. Bennett miniatures.

Combined Rose List

Compiled and edited by Beverly Dobson and Peter Schneider, the *Combined Rose List* contains essential information about rose varieties and mail-order nursery sources in the United States, Canada and many overseas countries. It is the one international reference for rose sources: If a rose variety is offered in commerce, the *Combined Rose List* will tell you where. Fully cross-referenced information is provided for more than 8,500 roses and more than 200 nurseries. Updated annually. For current ordering information, write to Peter Schneider, Box 677, Mantua, OH 44255.

Trophy Roses Ltd, 1308 N. Kennicott, Arlington Heights, IL 60004, fax (708) 253-0738. Exhibition roses and *R. multiflora* understock.

Vintage Gardens, 3003 Pleasant Hill Road, Sebastopol, CA 95472, (707) 829-5342. Own-root roses.

Wayside Gardens, 1 Garden Lane, Hodges, SC 29695-0001, (800) 845-1124. English and other roses.

White Flower Farm, Litchfield, CT 06759-0050, (203) 496-9600, fax (203) 496-1418.

York Hill Farm, 18 Warren Street, Georgetown, MA 01833. Heritage roses. Catalogue $2.00.

Rose Lists

ROSES FOR HALF SHADE

These are the best roses to choose if you have limited sunlight. All will perform well given at least four hours of unfiltered sunlight per day, with morning sun preferable to afternoon.

Category	Rose
Hybrid teas	'Dainty Bess' 'Lady X' 'Limelight'
Floribundas	'Amberlight' 'Betty Prior' 'Escapade' 'Festival Fanfare' 'Jubilee Celebration' 'Little Darling' 'Playgirl'
Polyanthas	'Marie-Jeanne' 'The Fairy'
Miniatures	'Angel Darling' 'Anytime' 'June Laver' 'My Sunshine' 'Ruby Pendant' 'Simon Robinson' 'Stars 'n' Stripes'
Patio roses	'Conservation' 'Emily Louise' 'Laura Ashley' 'Minilights'
	'Sweet Chariot' 'Tear Drop'
Climbing miniatures	'Nozomi'
Climbers	'Altissimo' 'Chevy Chase' 'City of York' 'Clair Matin' 'New Dawn' 'Paul's Lemon Pillar' 'Phyllis Bide' 'Summer Wine' 'Veilchenblau'
Species and near-species	*R. palustris* 'St. John's Rose'
Old garden roses	'Celestial' 'Félicité Parmentier' 'Harison's Yellow' 'Königin von Dänemark' 'Maiden's Blush' 'Semi-Plena' 'Stanwell Perpetual'
Shrubs	'Lavender Dream' 'Morgenrot' 'Pearl Drift' 'Pink Meidiland' 'Rachel Bowes Lyon' 'Sally Holmes' 'Simplicity' 'Tall Story' 'Windrush'

Hybrid musks	'Clytemnestra'
	'Moonlight'
Rugosas	'Robusta'
	Rosa rugosa alba
	R. rugosa rubra
English roses	'Belle Story'
	'Lucetta'

LOW-MAINTENANCE ROSES

These are the toughest roses, demonstrating excellent disease resistance and winter hardiness. Planted in well-prepared soil and provided with ample water, they will thrive with a minimum of extra care. All are repeat-blooming, except those marked *NR* (nonremontant).

Category	Rose
Hybrid teas	'Beryl Bach'
	'Elina'
	'Evensong'
	'Folklore'
	'Freedom'
	'Ingrid Bergman'
	'Silver Jubilee'
Grandifloras	'Queen Elizabeth'
Floribundas	'Amber Queen'
	'Betty Prior'
	'Georgette/INTerorge'
	'Goldmarie'
	'Hannah Gordon'
	'Inner Wheel'
	'Showbiz'
	'Trumpeter'
Polyanthas	'The Fairy'
Miniatures	'Beauty Secret'
	'Debut'
	'Orange Sunblaze'
	'Robin Redbreast'

Patio roses	'Boy Crazy'
	'Hakuun'
	'Majorette'
	'Sweet Chariot'
Climbing miniatures	'Jeanne Lajoie'
	'Nozomi'
Climbers	'Chevy Chase' NR
	'City of York' NR
	'Compassion'
	'Freisinger Morgenröte'
Species and near-species	'Highdownensis'
Old garden roses	'Apothecary's Rose' NR
	'Baronne Prévost'
	'Celestial' NR
	'Common Moss' NR
	'Félicité Parmentier' NR
	'Frau Karl Druschki'
	'Harison's Yellow' NR
	'Maiden's Blush' NR
	'Rosa Mundi' NR
	'Semi-Plena' NR
	'Stanwell Perpetual'
Shrubs	'Angelica'
	'Bonica/MEIdomonac'
	'Carefree Wonder'
	'Esprit'
	'Lavender Dream'
	'Lillian Gibson'
	'Heidelberg'
	'Morgenrot'
	'Nevada'
	'Romanze/ TANezamor'
	'Pink Meidiland'
	'Sally Holmes'
	'Simplicity'
	'Windrush'
Hybrid musks	'Moonlight'
	'Robin Hood'

Rugosas	'Jens Munk'
	'Robusta'
	Rosa rugosa alba
	R. rugosa rubra
Dr. Buck's roses	'Carefree Beauty'
	'Distant Drums'
	'Dorcas'
	'Honeysweet'
English roses	'Mary Rose'
Groundcovers	'Ferdy'
	'Fleurette'
	'Rosy Carpet'

ROSES FOR EXHIBITION

These are some of the best roses to grow if you want to compete in the rose shows conducted by the American Rose Society and its affiliated local societies.

Category	Rose
Hybrid teas	'Asso di Cuori'
	'Bride's Dream'
	'Canadian White Star'
	'Dublin'
	'Elegant Beauty'
	'Elizabeth Taylor'
	'Folklore'
	'Joanne'
	'Narzisse'
	'Silverado'
	'Suffolk'
	'Touch of Class'
	'Trojan Victory'
	'Victor Borge'
Grandifloras	'Gold Medal'
	'Tournament of Roses'
Floribundas	'Anisley Dickson'
	'Grace Abounding'
	'Hannah Gordon'
	'Harkness Marigold/HARtoflax'
	'Hiroshima's Children'
	'Matilda'
	'Rosali '83'
	'Sexy Rexy'
	'Sun Flare'
Miniatures	'Chelsea Belle'
	'Fairhope'
	'Irresistible'
	'Jean Kenneally'
	'Linville'
	'Olympic Gold'
	'Pierrine'
	'Red Beauty'
	'Simon Robinson'
	'Snow Bride'
Patio roses	'Anna Ford'
	'Cider Cup'
Climbers	'America'
	'Compassion'
Old garden roses	'Elisa Boëlle'
	'Her Majesty'
	'Mme. Hardy'
	'Niphetos'
	'Roger Lambelin'
	'Souvenir de la Malmaison'
Shrubs	'Bonica/MEIdomonac'
	'Cardinal Hume'
	'Morgenrot'
	'Pearl Drift'
	'Sally Holmes'
Hybrid musks	'Penelope'
Rugosas	'Robusta'
	Rosa rugosa rubra
English roses	'Fair Bianca'
	'Fisherman's Friend'
	'Heritage'
	'William Shakespeare'

THE USDA PLANT HARDINESS MAP OF NORTH AMERICA

Average Annual Minimum Temperature

Temperature (°C)	Zone	Temperature (°F)
-45.6 and Below	1	Below -50
-45.8 to -45.5	2a	-45 to -50
-40.0 to -42.7	2b	-40 to -45
-37.3 to -40.0	3a	-35 to -40
-34.5 to -37.2	3b	-30 to -35
-31.7 to -34.4	4a	-25 to -30
-28.9 to -31.6	4b	-20 to -25
-26.2 to 28.8	5a	-15 to -20
-23.4 to -26.1	5b	-10 to -15
-20.6 to -23.3	6a	-5 to -10
-17.8 to -20.5	6b	0 to -5
-15.0 to -17.7	7a	5 to 0
-12.3 to -15.0	7b	10 to 5
-9.5 to -12.2	8a	15 to 10
-6.7 to -9.4	8b	20 to 15
-3.9 to -6.6	9a	25 to 20
-1.2 to -3.8	9b	30 to 25
1.6 to -1.1	10a	35 to 30
4.4 to 1.7	10b	40 to 35
4.5 and Above	11	40 and Above

This zone map provides a broad outline of various temperature zones in North America. However, every garden has its own microclimate.

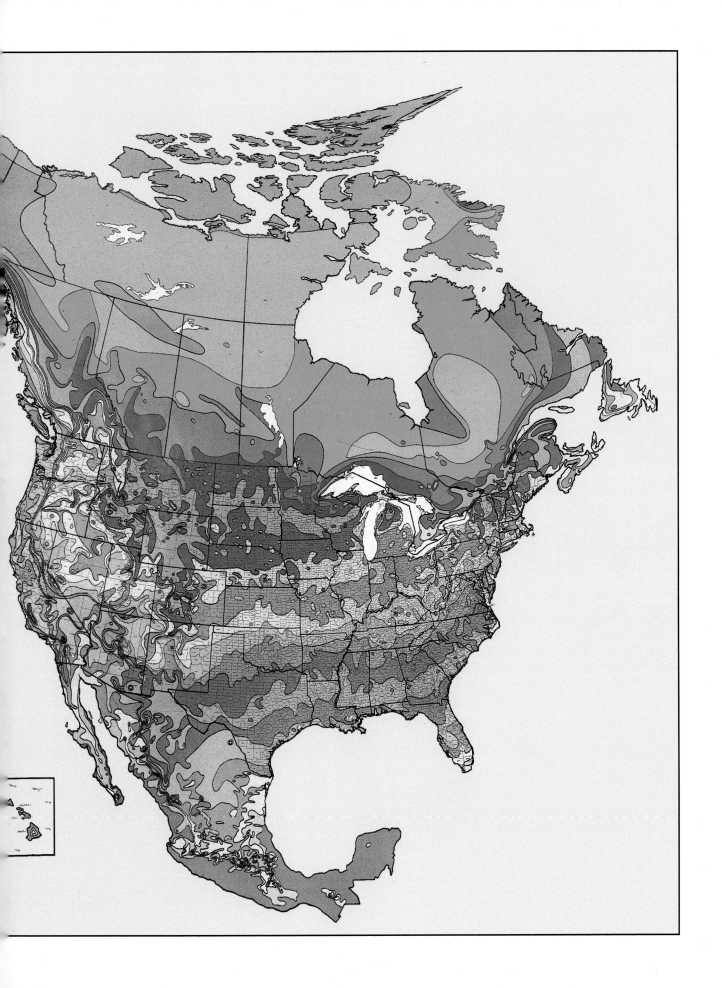

Index

Numbers in *italics* refer to illustrations.